Winning the Chain Restaurant Game

A RESTAURANTS & INSTITUTIONS BOOK

Winning the Chain Restaurant Game

Eight Key Strategies

CHARLES BERNSTEIN
RON PAUL

John Wiley & Sons, Inc.
New York/Chichester/Brisbane/
Toronto/Singapore

This publication is designed to provide accurate and
authoritative information in regard to the subject
matter covered. It is sold with the understanding that
the publisher is not engaged in rendering legal, accounting,
or other professional services. If legal advice or other
expert assistance is required, the services of a competent
professional person should be sought.

Library of Congress Cataloging-in-Publication Data:

Bernstein, Charles, 1934-
    Winning the chain restaurant game : 8 key strategies / Charles
Bernstein and Ronald N. Paul.
        p.   cm.
    Includes bibliographical references.
    ISBN 0-471-30545-6
    1. Chain restaurants.   2. Restaurant management.   I. Paul, Ronald
N. II. Title.
    TX945.B45   1994
    647.95′068—dc20   94-14858

Printed in the United States of America

10 9 8 7 6 5 4 3 2

*To Norma Bernstein and Georgeann Paul
for their understanding, support, and love*

Contents

oooooooo

Preface

What it takes to win in business has been explored in many management books. In this book we focus on the restaurant industry, with which we have both enjoyed long associations as close observers, and, more specifically, on chain restaurants. Thus, we began our own search for the critical links that must be forged and maintained if a chain is to grow successfully and prosper for the long run. We found that the principles that apply to winning restaurant chains also generally apply to all types of retail chains and, to some degree, to independents.

Restaurant chains deserve far more recognition than they have ever received as a force in the American economy. We set out to write this book in order to explore the attributes that have enabled the best chains to meet the industry's unique challenges, to capitalize on the advantages of multiunit operations, and to excel in customer service and performance. Examples of winning chains and highly successful executives abound in this book. We hope that they will provide inspiration to our readers. There is also much to be learned from some expensive failures.

The restaurant business offers great financial opportunities as well as the potential satisfaction to be gained in serving the public. Chain founders such as the late Ray Kroc of McDonald's, Burger King's James McLamore, Wendy's Dave Thomas, Steak and Ale's Norman Brinker, Outback's Chris Sullivan, California Pizza Kitchen's Larry Flax and Rick Rosenfield, and so many others have exerted extraordinary effort and have become rich well beyond their original dreams. Franchisees at a number of chains have also become millionaires, and small-to-medium-size chains are going public so fast that almost no one can keep score.

In the end, we have learned, the requisite for a healthy and growing chain is the ability to combine an independent's entrepreneurial spirit with a corporation's professional savvy. That accomplished, there remains the challenge of curbing the excessive turnover that plagues multiunit operations. All in all, the deck is stacked against any given restaurant concept making it as a chain.

Perhaps the secret ingredient is a true passion for the business. Sonic Corporation chairman Stephen Lynn declares, "My personal belief is that the success of a restaurant lies not in the location, the food, or the decor, but in the operator's feeling and confidence in the concept. If he or she truly believes in the potential of the concept, success is inevitable." All that it takes to win—the art, the craft, and the love for the business—is the subject of this book.

Charles Bernstein and Ron Paul
June 1, 1994

Acknowledgments

After writing a book as extensive as this, there are so many people to thank. First and foremost, we thank our families for being so patient and understanding during the many months of research, interviewing, and writing.

We talked with some 100 chain executives in an attempt to include as broad and diverse a spectrum of leaders and chains as possible. We tried to reflect their views accurately, but we also interpreted their comments and added our own opinions. We are especially appreciative of the many who gave freely of their time so that we could obtain their perspectives, and the others, hard-pressed by their schedules, who still managed to provide some help. All of these insights, as well as our own, can be read in these pages. If we missed someone who wanted to be in this book, we are truly sorry.

We thank all the people who helped us with this book—in particular, Georgeann Paul (who is very much related to Ron Paul), as well as Jackie Gray, Jan Sneesby, and Annette Hughes of Ron Paul's Technomic, Inc. staff, for their unstinting help in meticulously taking care of so many technical and mechanical details for this book; Claire Thompson of John Wiley & Sons, for her constant encouragement and perceptive guidance; Allison Ort Morvay of Wiley, who was so professional and dedicated in managing its editing and production; and Elizabeth Knighton, whose painstaking copyediting helped immensely.

We especially thank Max Pine, who shepherded Restaurant Associates through two exciting decades, for his steady advice and perspective on this book as well as his own thoughtful comments herein; Barry Klein, for his skillful help with the chapter on marketing; and the late Patt Patterson, a loyal friend who died tragically in a December 1993 auto accident, for his expert help with the sections on purchasing and distribution.

Finally, we thank each other. We are pleased that we meshed so well in undertaking and completing this book. Our respective talents complemented each other and made it possible to bring this book to final fruition.

Charles Bernstein
Ron Paul

Introduction

"Nobody can afford to rest on any laurels today. . . . This is all about having fun and trying new ideas all the time, tinkering with concepts."

—Richard Melman, president,
Lettuce Entertain You Enterprises, Inc., Chicago

Along Beltline Road in Addison, North Dallas, Texas, is one of the largest clusters of restaurants ever created. In 1994 the count had climbed to some 180, all crowded into a one-mile stretch, and was still rising. Just about every restaurant company under the sun, or at least most of the major ones that anyone has ever heard of, is in the fray. It is usual for restaurants to come and go. In this case, more come than go. Almost all the restaurants are chain units, many originating in the Dallas metro-plex area, where 50 restaurant chains are headquartered. This area epitomizes the emergence of chain restaurants as a dominant feature of the American restaurant scene.

We once thought that the restaurant industry was an entrepreneurial business in which individual establishments would prevail. But the ability to replicate a concept has resulted in major cost savings as well as large sales increases, and when an entrepreneurial instinct combines successfully with a chain's natural assets, the chain tends to win against the independent. This is today's economic reality.

Among the chain restaurants in the Addison restaurant megacomplex are Atchafalaya River Cafe, Bennigan's, Black-eyed Pea, Cantina Laredo, Copeland's, El Fenix, Hooters, I Can't Believe It's Yogurt, jojo's, Kobe Japanese Steakhouse, Le Peep, Magic Time Machine, On the Border, Sfuzzi, Steak and Ale, Taco Bueno, Tony

Roma's, Outback, and TGI Friday's. Furthermore, within the complex there are clusters of different chain restaurants owned by the same company: General Mills' Red Lobster, The Olive Garden, and China Coast restaurants; Brinker International's Chili's Grill & Bar, Romano's Macaroni Grill, and Grady's American Grill. Only a few independents pop up here. The chains dominate, and their seats are full more often than not, despite the apparent saturation.

So it goes in the United States—for better or for worse—with chain-dominated restaurant rows and clusters everywhere from Newport Beach, California, to the Maryland suburbs of Washington, D.C. The outskirts and suburbs are a mecca for chains of all types, although Addison, Texas, is the ultimate. For the shopping mall dining equivalent, one need only look at the gigantic Mall of America, which has arisen almost as a city of its own in Bloomington, Minnesota. Chain restaurants there comprise a cross section of the multiunit foodservice world, including A&W Hot Dogs, Alamo Grill, Albert's Family Restaurant, America's Original Sports Bar, Boogie's Diner, Bresler's Ice Cream & Yogurt, Burger King, California Cafe, Cinnabon, Fat Tuesday, Frank 'N Stein, Gators, Gloria Jean's Gourmet Coffees, Great American Cookie Co., Great Steak & Fry Co., Haagen-Dazs, Hibachi-San, Hooters, International Dairy Queen's Dairy Queen, Karmelkorn and Orange Julius units, Johnny Rockets, Little Tokyo, the New York Deli, Nordstrom's Cafe and Nordstrom's Espresso Bar, One Potato Two, The Original Cookie Co., Panda Express, Players, Ruby Tuesday, Sbarro, Steak Escape, Subway, Taco-Time, Tony Roma's, Tucci Benucch, and the Wolfgang Puck Pizzeria.

The 1994 *Chain Restaurant Operators Directory,* published by Chain Store Guide of Tampa, Florida, lists 3,277 U.S. chain restaurant companies of at least three units each, accounting for 235,491 company-owned and franchised units out of an estimated total of 406,000 U.S. restaurants. But the preponderance of units are in chains of more than 200 units, representing 200,720 locations or 85 percent of the total chain units.

See Table A for the top 25 U.S. chain organizations in 1993, according to Technomic, Inc. of Chicago. Technomic estimates

Table A
The Top 25 U.S. Chain Organizations

1993 Rank Chain	1993 U.S. System Sales ($000)	% Change	1993 U.S. System Units	% Change
1 McDonald's	$14,186,100	7.1%	9,283	3.6%
2 Burger King	5,460,000*	3.0%	5,996	5.1%
3 Pizza Hut	4,800,000*	11.6%	7,965	4.7%
4 Hardee's/ Roy Rogers	3,994,000	1.8%	3,997	0.9%
5 Taco Bell	3,717,000	17.1%	4,809	17.9%
6 Wendy's Old Fashioned Hamburgers	3,662,100	10.6%	3,791	5.1%
7 KFC	3,400,000	0.4%	5,128	0.8%
8 Dairy Queen	2,290,000*	4.1%	4,860	1.7%
9 Little Caesar's	2,230,000*	12.3%	4,687	7.3%
10 Domino's Pizza	2,200,000	−0.2%	4,750	−0.1%
11 Denny's	1,966,378	7.9%	1,452	4.4%
12 Subway Sandwiches	1,840,560	22.7%	7,813	13.9%
13 Red Lobster Inns	1,689,000	7.0%	601	4.9%
14 Arby's Restaurants	1,528,000	5.0%	2,515	1.5%
15 Shoney's	1,318,189	8.2%	915	7.0%
16 Big Boy	1,110,000	7.0%	852	−3.2%
17 Dunkin' Donuts	1,075,641	21.3%	2,342	16.6%
18 Olive Garden, The	1,011,000	12.5%	411	17.8%
19 Jack in the Box	989,000	−7.1%	1,164	0.9%
20 Long John Silver's	903,307	3.9%	1,411	−2.0%

Table A *(Continued)*

1993 Rank Chain	1993 U.S. System Sales ($000)	% Change	1993 U.S. System Units	% Change
21 T.G.I. Friday's	775,257	20.2%	233	18.3%
22 Chili's	743,323	19.0%	343	15.5%
23 Ponderosa	705,000*	0.6%	712	−4.7%
24 Sizzler	703,778	−12.7%	550	−10.4%
25 Sonic Drive-Ins	691,490	15.2%	1,274	7.0%

*TECHNOMIC estimate.
Source: Technomic, Inc., Chicago, IL.

that total U.S. commercial restaurant sales will rise from about $207 billion in 1993 to $220 billion in 1994. The chains' proportion of the pie will be about 65 percent, or some $140 billion, and continue to increase. Of that total, Technomic estimates that the 100 top-volume chains will increase from the activity shown in Table B to account for nearly $90 billion in U.S. sales (including McDonald's more than $15 billion). Of the top 100, quick-service chains alone, including McDonald's, account for more than 70 percent of the $90 billion in sales. These top 100 chains also operate more than 20,000 locations outside the U.S. that account for more than $20 billion in international sales. (See Tables C and D for the top 100 dollar and unit trends.) Table E, on pp. xxiii–xxvi, shows the Technomic top 25 chain organizations with their component companies.

The U.S. chain restaurant business has become not only economically but also culturally dominant around the world. Just as Hollywood sets the tone for the world's movie tastes, Oak Brook, Illinois (McDonald's headquarters) and the homes of other fast-food and casual-restaurant chains are the world's foodservice pacesetters. In creativity and variety of concepts, chains have come a long way

Table B
Summary of 1993 Activity by the Technomic 100

	1993	*1992*	*% Change*
U.S. System Sales ($000)	$88,729,564	$82,533,501	7.5%
U.S. System Units	109,715	103,837	5.7%
International Sales ($000)	$19,478,658	$18,025,558	8.1%
International Units	18,311	16,617	10.2%
Share of U.S. Restaurant Industry Sales	48.5%	47.6%	
Share of U.S. Restaurant Industry Units	30.9%	29.6%	
# Chains Controlled by TECHNOMIC 100	170	162	

Source: Technomic, Inc., Chicago, IL.

from the White Castles of the 1920s, the Krystals of the 1930s, the Howard Johnsons of the 1940s, the McDonald's, Burger Kings, Carl's Jrs., and Sonic America's Drive-In fast-feeders of the 1950s, and the Big Boy, Denny's, and Sambo's coffee shops of the 1960s.

The chaining of America is indeed a reality today in casual, fast-food, family restaurants/coffee shops, steakhouses, dinnerhouses, and even to some degree in fine-dining tablecloth restaurants. Why? Through economies of scale and leveraging their strengths, chains can achieve 10 percent to 15 percent profit margins, as compared with 5 percent or less for most independents. In today's hard-pressed economy, if you want to be a major player in the restaurant game, you've just about got to be able to do it as a chain or multiunit operation.

Of course, McDonald's Corporation continues to prevail based on its sheer size, but three corporations with similar expertise and commitment to foodservice operations may dominate much of the chain restaurant industry through the 1990s: Brinker International, Inc., General Mills, Inc. and PepsiCo, Inc.; each has its own arsenal of varied chains. Other major diversified restaurant groups to watch include America's Favorite Chicken Co. (Popeyes, Church's); Amer-

Table C
TECHNOMIC 100 U.S. Sales Trends
U.S. System Sales ($000)

Category	1993	1983	% Change
Total Top 100	$88,729,564	$41,854,548	112.0%
Total QSR (Quick-Service Restaurants)	$63,616,771	$28,803,641	120.9%
Hamburger	31,571,657	15,192,009	107.8%
Pizza	11,133,691	3,321,283	235.2%
Chicken	5,725,182	3,334,968	71.7%
Ice Cream/Yogurt	4,056,977	2,088,560	94.2%
Mexican	4,129,900	1,036,748	298.4%
Other Sandwich	3,906,178	2,044,725	91.0%
Seafood	1,447,864	783,220	84.9%
Donut	1,132,894	883,848	28.2%
All Other QSR	512,428	118,260	333.2%
Total MSR (Mid-Scale Restaurants)	$14,775,773	$8,609,253	71.6%
Family Style	9,480,527	4,948,079	91.6%
Steak	3,276,097	2,272,480	44.3%
Cafeteria/Buffet	1,658,132	1,182,744	40.0%
Mexican	305,817	154,000	98.6%
All Other MSR	55,200	51,950	6.3%
Total USR (Up-Scale Restaurants)	$10,337,020	$4,441,654	132.7%
Varied Menu	4,513,643	1,211,475	272.6%
Italian	1,327,308	121,000	996.9%
Steak	1,233,936	779,395	58.3%
Mexican	911,661	475,250	91.8%
Seafood	1,802,074	935,512	92.6%
All Other USR	548,398	919,022	−40.3%

Source: Technomic, Inc., Chicago, IL.

Table D
TECHNOMIC 100 U.S. Unit Trends
U.S. System Units

Category	1993	1983	% Change
Total Top 100	109,715	67,234	63.2%
Total QSR (Quick-Service Restaurants)	93,314	53,869	73.2%
Hamburger	29,054	17,633	64.8%
Pizza	20,721	8,821	134.9%
Chicken	8,631	7,791	10.8%
Ice Cream/Yogurt	10,923	8,537	27.9%
Mexican	5,623	2,530	122.3%
Other Sandwich	11,717	3,209	265.1%
Seafood	2,262	1,831	23.5%
Donut	2,573	2,925	−12.0%
All Other QSR	1,810	592	205.7%
Total MSR (Mid-Scale Restaurants)	11,658	10,532	10.7%
Family Style	7,826	6,423	21.8%
Steak	2,697	3,116	−13.4%
Cafeteria/Buffet	867	730	18.8%
Mexican	227	175	29.7%
All Other MSR	41	88	−53.4%
Total USR (Up-Scale Restaurants)	4,743	2,833	67.4%
Varied Menu	2,176	768	183.3%
Italian	602	132	356.0%
Steak	607	516	17.6%
Mexican	439	237	85.2%
Seafood	651	492	32.3%
All Other USR	268	688	−61.0%

Source: Technomic, Inc., Chicago, IL.

ican Restaurant Group (Stuart Anderson's, Spoon's); Carlson Companies, Inc. (TGI Friday's, Country Kitchen); Family Restaurants, Inc. (El Torito, Chi-Chi's, Carrows), Flagstar Companies, Inc. (Denny's, Quincy's, El Pollo); International Dairy Queen (Dairy Queen, Karmelkorn, Orange Julius); Metromedia Co. (Ponderosa, Bonanza, Steak and Ale, Bennigan's); Morrison Restaurants, Inc. (Ruby Tuesday, Mozzarrella's Cafe, Sweetpea's, Morrison's Fresh Cooking); Restaurant Associates Corporation (Acapulco, Charlie Brown's); Shoney's, Inc. (Lee's Famous Recipe, Captain D's, Shoney's); and Tennessee Restaurant Co. (Friendly, Perkins).

The restaurant business, now dominated by chains, has its own unique challenges, too. Based on almost $300 billion total U.S. annual foodservice sales and 9 million employees, the business is highly labor intensive with just $33,000 average annual sales per employee. This figure is notable in contrast to the far higher productivity of retailing and banking, which have, respectively, $125,000 and $94,000 average annual sales per employee, according to McGraw-Hill's Data Resources, Inc.

Restaurants are subject to the ups and downs of the economic cycle similar to other retail business. Chain restaurant year-to-year customer comparable gains or losses provide an excellent barometer of the state of the economy.

Furthermore, as part of an individualistic industry that finds it hard to take one united stand, restaurant chains share a position with independents as the government's favorite whipping boy when it comes to finding ways to raise more taxes and revenues. Even with all the industry's volume, and as the third leading employer in the United States, neither chains nor independents have been able to achieve the clout they merit in Washington, D.C., or in state legislatures, where it may be even more critical. Measures chipping away at the restaurant industry's economic base are enacted repeatedly.

Despite their prominence, chains do not have the most positive or prestigious public image. Typically, a July 1993 article in *The Quill,* the Society of Professional Journalists magazine, commented that "Each year the beginning journalists of America are told they have better shots at flipping burgers at McDonald's than defending the public's First Amendment rights. Each year the quality and quantity of [journalism] jobs has further diminished." This impression, that chain foodservice careers are the pits, or a benevolent form of servitude, is fairly widespread. The low sales average per restaurant employee dramatizes the crucial importance of quality recruiting, training, and motivation to encourage maximum employee performance in this people-dependent business. Chains have a lot of work to do in providing stronger training and encouraging an attitude of true hospitality in employees, as well as involving employees in the decision-making processes. Certainly, the 70-hour workweeks at some chain restaurants must be abolished if the industry expects to improve its image.

Leading by example, chain executives need to demonstrate that foodservice is not a form of slavery but, rather, that serving the public is something to be proud of and that career opportunities in the chain restaurant industry have excellent potential. Moreover, those chains showing flexibility by encouraging individualized menus for different regions and localities are already gaining extra momentum.

We strongly feel that the chain restaurant business requires diversity at its executive levels and urgently needs to engage the talents of women and minority group members to a much greater degree. Their small numbers constitute a glaring inadequacy in a business where 75 percent of restaurant employees are female or minority members.

Service to the customer is today's overriding business consideration, and chains must adjust their thinking to that objective and to the concept of thinking outside of the box. In a 1993 *EDK Forecast* consumer attitudes survey of 500 women, 79 percent cited service as a crucial factor in choosing a restaurant, whereas only 41 percent named price.

With significant capital required for each restaurant location (a lot more per square foot than for retail locations), site selection is especially critical too.

Other key characteristics and challenges of the restaurant industry, and of chains in particular, are the following:

- Intense competition; an easy-entry (easy-exit) business
- A high volume of customer traffic but a relatively low average per-person ticket (ranging from $2 to $20 for most chains)
- Seven-day-a-week operations with long hours
- "Unforgiving" customers who generally don't accept mistakes
- A need to spend money to remodel restaurants and keep them up to date
- A need for executives to visit each restaurant location periodically to understand what is really happening on the front lines and to communicate personally with employees
- A cluttered marketing environment
- Intense public scrutiny regarding sanitation, health, and nutritional matters

Because customers tend to identify an entire chain with their own experience in one or two units, a restaurant chain can be as strong as its strongest link but also as weak as its weakest link. This was amply demonstrated when two burger-related food-poisoning fatalities occurred at a Seattle Jack in the Box in early 1993 and the chain's volume plummeted in greater Seattle and dropped off almost everywhere else for several months. Some customers had a hard time differentiating between one unit and the entire 1,200-unit chain itself. This sometimes is also the reaction when a shooting or other violent incident occurs in one unit of a chain.

Winning in the chain restaurant game is never easy. A strong chain requires the eight strategic links that we identify in each of the first eight chapters. These eight principles are illustrated in Chapter 9 on McDonald's. A final chapter draws the dividing line between those chains that succeed and those that fail.

Table E
The Technomic Top 25 Chain Restaurant Companies

1993 Rank Company Name	1993 U.S. Systemwide Sales ($000)	% Sales Change vs. 1992	1993 U.S. Systemwide Units	% Units Change vs. 1992
1 McDonald's Corp.	$14,186,100	7.1%	9,283	3.6%
McDonald's	14,186,100	7.1%	9,283	3.6%
2 PepsiCo Inc.	12,342,609	12.1%	18,406	8.6%
Pizza Hut	4,800,000*	11.6%	7,965	4.7%
Taco Bell	3,717,000	17.1%	4,809	17.9%
KFC	3,400,000	0.4%	5,128	0.8%
Hot 'n Now	123,000*	64.0%	246	80.9%
California Pizza Kitchen	105,000*	36.4%	44	51.7%
Chevys Mexican Restaurants	90,609	7.8%	41	13.9%
D'Angelo Sandwich Shops	89,000*	16.7%	167	22.8%
East Side Mario's	18,000*	N/A	6	N/A
3 Grand Metropolitan, PLC	5,535,000	3.0%	6,241	4.9%
Burger King	5,460,000*	3.0%	5,996	5.1%
Haagen-Dazs	75,000	1.4%	245	0.4%
4 Imasco, Ltd.	3,994,000	1.8%	3,997	0.9%
Hardee's/Roy Rogers	3,994,000	1.8%	3,997	0.9%
5 Wendy's International, Inc.	3,662,100	10.6%	3,791	5.1%
Wendy's Old Fashioned Hamburgers	3,662,100	10.6%	3,791	5.1%
6 Flagstar Companies, Inc.	$ 3,107,401	7.6%	2,435	4.4%
Denny's	1,966,378	7.9%	1,452	4.4%
Hardee's (Flagstar)	681,742	12.4%	564	6.8%
Quincy's Family Steakhouse	279,000	−3.8%	213	−1.8%
El Pollo Loco	180,281	6.5%	206	4.6%
7 General Mills, Inc.	2,707,500	9.1%	1,021	10.5%
Red Lobster Inns	1,689,000	7.0%	601	4.9%
Olive Garden, The	1,011,000	12.5%	411	17.8%
China Coast	7,500*	172.7%	9*	350.0%

Table E *(Continued)*

1993 Rank Company Name	1993 U.S. Systemwide Sales ($000)	% Sales Change vs. 1992	1993 U.S. Systemwide Units	% Units Change vs. 1992
8 International Dairy Queen, Inc.	2,378,000	3.7%	5,305	0.7%
Dairy Queen	2,290,000*	4.1%	4,860	1.7%
Orange Julius of America	75,000*	−5.1%	360*	−7.5%
KarmelKorn	13,000*	−13.3%	85	−15.0%
9 Little Caesar's Enterprises, Inc.	2,230,000	12.3%	4,687	7.3%
Little Caesar's	2,230,000*	12.3%	4,687	7.3%
10 Domino's Pizza, Inc.	2,200,000	−0.2%	4,750	−0.1%
Domino's Pizza	2,200,000	−0.2%	4,750	−0.1%
11 Shoney's Inc.	$ 1,972,614	7.7%	1,849	3.3%
Shoney's	1,318,189	8.2%	915	7.0%
Captain D's	452,457	6.0%	645	0.0%
Lee's Famous Recipe	151,817	8.0%	266	−1.8%
Pargo's	26,768	18.5%	12	33.3%
Fifth Quarter	23,383	1.4%	11	10.0%
12 Doctor's Associates, Inc.	1,868,560	22.0%	7,883	13.6%
Subway Sandwiches	1,840,560	22.7%	7,813	13.9%
Cajun Joe's	28,000*	−9.7%	70	−12.5%
13 Allied−Lyons, PLC	1,687,998	8.0%	4,892	7.1%
Dunkin' Donuts	1,075,641	21.3%	2,342	16.6%
Baskin−Robbins	542,104	0.8%	2,284	2.9%
Mister Donut	57,253	−54.5%	231	−22.2%
Caffe Classico	13,000*	8.3%	35	−14.6%
14 Metromedia Co.	1,670,000	1.8%	1,346	−2.8%
Ponderosa	705,000*	0.6%	712	−4.7%
Bennigan's	460,000*	3.6%	223	0.0%
Bonanza	280,000*	1.8%	255	−1.2%
Steak and Ale	225,000*	1.8%	156	−0.6%
15 Triarc Companies, Inc.	$ 1,535,000	N/A	2,527	N/A
Arby's Restaurants	1,528,000	5.0%	2,515	1.5%
Daddy-O's Express	7,000	−6.7%	12	−7.7%
16 Foodmaker, Inc.	1,412,500	−5.1%	1,380	1.2%
Jack in the Box	989,000	−7.1%	1,164	0.9%
Chi-Chi's	423,500*	0.0%	216	2.9%

Table E *(Continued)*

1993 Rank Company Name	1993 U.S. Systemwide Sales ($000)	% Sales Change vs. 1992	1993 U.S. Systemwide Units	% Units Change vs. 1992
17 Tennessee Restaurant Co.	1,148,058	6.6%	1,176	−0.1%
Perkins Family Restau-rants	578,058	8.2%	419	2.9%
Friendly Ice Cream	570,000	5.0%	757	−1.7%
18 Elias Brothers Restau-rants, Inc.	1,117,200	7.0%	860	−3.2%
Big Boy	1,110,000	7.0%	852*	−3.2%
Top Hat	7,200*	1.4%	8	0.0%
19 America's Favorite Chicken Co.	1,004,066	2.0%	1,720	−3.3%
Popeyes	563,900	1.6%	766	0.4%
Churchs	440,166	2.5%	954	−6.1%
20 Carlson Companies Inc.	990,218	16.5%	468	8.1%
T.G.I. Friday's	775,257	20.2%	233	18.3%
Country Kitchen	189,961	5.3%	224	−0.4%
Dalts	25,000*	0.8%	11	0.0%
21 Brinker International, Inc.	$ 903,485	26.4%	404	22.1%
Chili's	743,323	19.0%	343	15.5%
Romano's Macaroni Grill	77,308	107.7%	28	86.7%
Grady's American Grill	76,625	45.1%	29	52.6%
Spageddies Italian Food	6,229	N/A	4	N/A
22 Long John Silver's Res-taurants, Inc.	903,307	3.9%	1,411	−2.0%
Long John Silver's	903,307	3.9%	1,411	−2.0%
23 Restaurant Enterprises Group	890,900	−4.9%	532	−10.0%
Family Restaurant Div. (REGI)	489,500	11.1%	359	1.7%
El Torito	306,400	−12.4%	132	−20.0%
Far West Concepts (REG)	95,000	−35.0%	41	−43.8%

Table E. *(Continued)*

1993 Rank Company Name	1993 U.S. Systemwide Sales ($000)	% Sales Change vs. 1992	1993 U.S. Systemwide Units	% Units Change vs. 1992
24 Morrison Restaurants Inc.	733,958	11.5%	426	10.1%
Ruby Tuesday	338,400	28.2%	206	25.6%
Morrison's	290,790	−0.8%	151	−4.4%
L&N Seafood	68,910	−6.6%	37	−11.9%
Silver Spoon	33,605	27.1%	22	15.8%
Fresh Cooking	2,084	252.6%	9	125.0%
Mozzarella's	169	N/A	1	N/A
25 Sizzler International, Inc.	703,778	−12.7%	550	−10.4%
Sizzler	703,778	−12.7%	550	−10.4%

*TECHNOMIC estimate.

N/A Not applicable.

Source: Technomic, Inc., Chicago, IL.

The Leadership Touch

An extroverted leader who communicates a vision,
values, and a bottom-up organizational philosophy.

"The ability to change is the only competitive advantage."
—*John Martin, chairman,*
Taco Bell, Irvine, California

HIGHLIGHTS

- The CEO makes the difference
- Change is a necessity
- Be an innovator
- Different paths to success
- Complete focus
- Learn from failure
- Inspire the troops
- Think win-win
- Firmness and understanding
- Set the tone and culture

Leadership styles vary, and there are different approaches to reaching the same objective. But the leading chief executives don't manage people. They lead and help. Dictatorial management is out of style—although there are some exceptions—and team building is what counts. The most successful CEOs tend not to get wrapped up in corporate bureaucracy, but instead find ways to make decisive choices and get the job done. Their emphasis is on results and sharing rather than long hours and taking credit for every achievement.

A Heidrick & Struggles executive search firm survey of restaurant chain CEOs found that most emphasize growth and change. Among the responses from CEOs on the greatest challenges they face are "getting people to recognize that change is a way of life"; "creating change in a rigid culture"; "the turnaround and repositioning of an old franchise system"; "restructuring for future profitability and growth"; "growing market share in a highly competitive environment"; "positioning the company to be a player after the 90s."

People are creatures of habit and often will fight against change. It is a CEO's job to encourage change in a constructive manner—not to rip everything apart nor to allow success to lead to complacency.

The survey also showed that 61 percent of the CEOs were grooming a successor to replace themselves (or perhaps letting two or three executives fight it out for the top spot). Most significantly, half thought that increased competition would force restaurant chains to recruit top executives from outside the industry—something that the industry traditionally has been reluctant to do, but a necessary step in giving the industry greater objectivity and perspective. Restaurant chain top executives are sometimes recycled almost as frequently as major league baseball managers, often with the same sporadic results.

Of respondents to the Heidrick & Struggles survey, 30 percent of the chief executives characterized the ideal CEO as primarily people oriented, 23 percent as visionary, 19 percent as a motivator, and 19 percent as a leader. Listed as the three best restaurant CEOs in the United States were Brinker International's Norman Brinker, 88 percent, the number one choice by a wide margin; General Mills' Joe Lee, 30 percent; and Taco Bell's John Martin, 23 percent. (The totals were well over 100 percent because of multiple responses. Chances are that the results also reflect images based on maximum press and publicity exposure, but these are three solid choices who illustrate prime leadership principles.)

WINNING STYLES

Brinker, founder of Steak and Ale (S & A) in the mid-1960s and chief executive of Dallas-based Brinker International, Inc. (formerly Chili's, Inc.) since the early 1980s, exercises firm leadership with a deliberate style. He engages in fact-finding about a problem's full background and only then proceeds to seek solutions. "I always study the real problem and how to solve it before talking to anyone about a situation," he says. He focuses on a specific single set of clear goals. He has an acute sense of timing and an uncanny way of knowing exactly where the consumer is going. He knows when to push and expand and when to slow down.

When he returned to work as Brinker International CEO in April 1993, four months after suffering a near-fatal head injury in a polo accident, the then 61-year-old Brinker acknowledged that he had worked 20-hour days (probably because he loved the constant challenge) but that he no longer chose to do so. Thereupon he set up a schedule of eight-hour workdays but subsequently was sometimes spotted putting in 12 hours or more in the office and in his restaurants, mostly because he enjoyed it so much. He realized that to be effective, he needed to delegate and that there was a limit to his own capacity. He still worked intensively while undergoing a continued rehabilitation program.

In general, we find that the executive with wider interests who knows how to take a vacation or a break is more effective in the long run than a workaholic, dedicated as he may be. Vacations were always precious to Brinker. His wife, Nancy, would meticulously plan for them to go with friends to Europe for three weeks each summer. Nothing could interfere with this. Even after Brinker's injury, they took their usual three-week July trip. If the nation's number one restaurant chain executive can do it, so can others.

Ron McDougall, Brinker International president and chief operating officer, is the classic highly disciplined marketing and numbers expert. He is a team builder. McDougall, who temporarily succeeded Brinker after Brinker's injury, is a serious, hardworking, and dedicated executive with a fairly casual approach. He gets the job done, and the two executives complement each other. Each succeeds because of the other. In fact, Brinker was McDougall's mentor in the 1970s when McDougall was rising at S & A Restaurants.

To McDougall, leadership means diverse goals and open communication with the entire management team. "A restaurant manager must be on the front lines like a free safety in football," he says. "The manager has got to make sure the tables are getting bused and every other detail is being taken care of. That all starts at the top with the president." McDougall liked to take managers' chairs away from their offices so they would be out on the floor, greeting and talking with customers and interacting with employees, rather than doing paperwork in the office.

Keeping the leadership together in the restaurant is crucial too. McDougall is a firm believer in restaurant managers being owning partners and in having the same team run the restaurant for several years. Too many chains make the mistake of constantly shuffling managers around "so they can change and grow," overlooking the stability factor so important to a restaurant, which, to be successful, must project a constant image in the neighborhood.

Joe Lee, General Mills Restaurants president for many years and now parent General Mills, Inc. vice chairman, feels that the road to winning leadership lies in "selecting good people, sharing your vision with them, getting them to understand it, and respecting employees." When he began running Red Lobster under General Mills in the early 1970s, he sensed that a dependable source of seafood supply was desperately needed. It was the key to Red Lobster's future, to building a chain in the highly individualized seafood business where only independents supposedly could thrive. There were more seafood brokers and peddlers than gas stations in those days.

Lee, who to this day is seriously allergic to shellfish, made an arrangement with Anastasio Somoza in Nicaragua for the seafood supply. This enabled Red Lobster to introduce red snapper, grouper, and spiny lobster throughout its chain. But when Somoza's government was overthrown in the mid-1970s, the supply collapsed and Lee forged new alliances in Central America, which included guaranteed shrimp supplies.

"I originally was a burger flipper," says Lee. "That's no dead-end job, and I can prove it. We've got to do a better job to boost the industry's image. A true leader can spot these opportunities, and we need a cadre of leaders who feel that way." He is convinced that restaurant leaders can succeed in other businesses too. "We are exposed to more leadership demands in the restaurant business," he asserts.

"Every successful restaurateur or chain executive has had at least one failure," he observes. "You've got to keep trying new things to finally succeed." Lee had not just one failure but many, with various small restaurant chains that General Mills tried or acquired. Each time, he learned something that would help him toward success in other ventures, so that in time General Mills Restaurants led the way with three moderately priced chains—Red Lobster, The Olive Garden, and its new China Coast.

Are the principles the same for running restaurants as in corporate and manufacturing enterprises? Not really. The restaurant business is a more personal, entrepreneurial one. Lee's greatest challenge was moving from Orlando and the restaurants division offices to General Mills' corporate headquarters in Minneapolis. "I had the basic people-oriented skills," he says. "But to move to the financial side and the legal side required a new sophistication. I had to learn how the research and manufacturing plants operate, how to run a Cheerios plant rather than Red Lobster restaurants." The marketing side was similar for Lee at General Mills corporate headquarters. But although restaurants in effect meant a factory in every store, one big General Mills manufacturing plant was a whole business in itself.

A passion for excellence was crucial to Lee in his transition. "I needed to learn about the plants, the research center, the advertising," says Lee, who has the unstinting intellectual curiosity so vital to success in any aspect of foodservice. He had the flexibility to cut General Mills' manufacturing costs by 2 percent, or a full $80 million, in his first two years at headquarters.

Ron Magruder, who was groomed by Lee, emerged as a great leader too, becoming president of General Mills' The Olive Garden and emphasizing a special brand of "hospitaliano Italiano" for customers. He believes in "empowering our restaurant employees to fix things as well as screw them up." An innovative leader, Magruder hired a train in 1990 for a leisurely trip from Chicago to San Antonio to Los Angeles. The object was not to see the scenery, but rather for Magruder and his staff to get away and create new thinking and fresh ideas. It is not a coincidence that The Olive Garden is by far the dominant midscale Italian restaurant chain and a real leader in the entire casual restaurants market.

Magruder feels that the key to leadership is flexibility. "Ten restaurants are easy to manage," he says, "but managing 400 is quite hard and you have to be flexible to do it." When The Olive Garden started and had just 10 restaurants in the mid-1980s, he could visit them all each week. But the more the chain grew, the more he had to change his style and delegate authority.

John Martin's biggest achievement—and one that paved the way for everything else—was the turnaround he achieved at PepsiCo, Inc.'s Taco Bell between 1983 and 1985. When he arrived as president, Taco Bell's real sales growth that year had dipped to a pathetic minus 10 percent. "To turn that around, I had to be a benevolent dictator," he recalls, "but by 1985 it was accomplished." Then he could start thinking about empowering his people and perhaps emphasizing his role of benevolent ruler rather than that of dictator.

We can learn several lessons from the Taco Bell of the early 1980s. Before Martin arrived, it was just an average chain. As the driving force and inspiration for constant change, Martin completely turned it around. He showed that the chief executive can make all the difference through his leadership qualities. Such leadership is transmitted through the ranks. Prior to Martin's arrival, Taco Bell was going nowhere in particular, not so much because its concept had any fundamental flaws, but rather because of a lack of inspirational leadership and vision. Taco Bell grew into such a dominant Mexican fast-food power that by 1993, its $4 billion sales were capturing almost 75 percent of the entire Mexican fast-food market.

Martin, who emphasizes "less structure, more individuality, and more fun," started his career in 1967 as an assistant manager at the Newport Beach, California-based Wienerschnitzel hot dog chain. He gravitated to Canteen Corporation and ARA Services but "couldn't stand" contract feeding (which often involves managing a company's or factory's foodservice) and its captive audience. "A corporation can hinder you terribly in this business," he concedes. In any case, he fervently believes in "hands-on, grass-roots management."

Martin was a Burger King executive briefly and then became Indianapolis-based Burger Chef operations director in 1977. After 18 months he was named president. When Hardee's acquired Burger Chef from General Foods, Martin actually served as Hardee's president for six months while Jack Laughery was Hardee's chairman. PepsiCo brought him in as Taco Bell president in 1983 at a time when Taco Bell had just 1,493 units and $500 million in annual sales. More than a few people thought Taco Bell was the Mexican phone company. In the next 10 years under Martin, it soared to 4,800 restaurants or units and $4 billion in sales. Its $250 million net income for 1993 was equal to the combined revenues of the 10 preceding years. He became chairman in mid-1994.

Martin outlines his winning recipe: "Happy customers equal happy employees and vice versa. Restaurants are often too rigid. We try to create an environment where the managers and employees in effect own the business." He loves to get into his Levi's and go to all kinds of restaurants, including Taco Bells. He feels that the office is the enemy—if one sits in it too much—and the field is the friend. "Restaurants have their own personalities," he says. "I only get a feeling for the flow by going there." He loves to sit down and casually talk to crew people and managers. (His executive committee members go into Taco Bells constantly, which makes the executives happy in being able to give constructive advice but can also drive restaurant managers and employees crazy.)

Martin has sharply reduced Taco Bell's kitchen space from a much-wasted 70 percent to 25 percent and is eyeing a virtually kitchenless restaurant, dependent on automated equipment. He envisions putting everything into sales space and jumping the average unit sales potential from $400 an hour to an astounding $1,500 an hour. He has a penchant for steadily raising productivity and sales while finding more efficient, less costly methods of operation. Martin travels with an entourage, not to massage his ego but to make each trip more productive. Six executives report to him, and these or others go on some of his airplane trips. His credo is "Change, change, change . . . value, value, value."

Martin recalls that when he became Burger Chef president in 1979, the company probably had the worst sites in the history of real estate. All kinds of sites had been sold to undercapitalized franchisees. Parent General Foods had given real estate agents the latitude and incentive to buy as many sites as possible and thereby achieve maximum commissions. Apparently no one had specified that these should be high-traffic, high-quality sites. Furthermore, the real estate agents knew very little about the restaurant business, in stark contrast to Burger Chef's ousted field people who had done a superb job of site selection in earlier years. Martin introduced the bacon cheeseburger and kids' meals, and sales soared—but from a base that was too low in the first place. Burger Chef sales had declined too far, and Martin's magic could not save the day.

However, it did work at Taco Bell, where research was done mostly through direct contact with customers. "The ability to change is the only competitive advantage," Martin says. By the end of the 1990s, he projects Taco Bell as "a paperless restaurant with robots to help take away the drudgery so that employees can concentrate on the important, challenging tasks—particularly contact with customers." In Martin's scenario, robots "will enable employees to reach out and grow." Already, the chain's new Taco-Matic machine can make 900 tacos an hour, each one "perfect." "We're eliminating the processes and the drudgery," Martin declares, "and striving to make everyone efficient in an on-line network."

He also believes in spending as much time as possible in the field. The Taco Bell chief executive estimates that he spends 80 percent of his time traveling and visits as many as 800 Taco Bell units annually. He is always one step ahead of anyone else, willing to try new things and perhaps given to hyperbole as a result of his ultraenthusiasm for new projects.

Martin is breaking down the walls that separate people and creating a genuine synergy. Many Taco Bells operate without a full-time manager. "A team runs it, and it's a team environment," he says. "The restaurant team huddles and then performs." Industry skeptics doubt that a fast-food chain can succeed without official managers. But Martin points out that Taco Bell was too oriented to top-down management. "If you give people the right environment, they'll stand behind you," he says. By 1993 each Taco Bell market manager was responsible for 30 to 35 units instead of the former five units. The idea was to give the unit "team" more responsibility and flexibility in running the restaurant with less outside interference.

He believes that executives and employees should think differently and innovatively. "My chief financial officer has a much broader outlook by being responsible for development and purchasing in addition to finance," he notes. His innovative approach to human resources is also illustrated by the fact that after he hired Stuart Anderson's Restaurants' talented marketing vice president, Julia Stewart, in 1992, he switched her from marketing to operations as Taco Bell's northern California and Northwest zone chief. (In an industry notable for its lack of women in top executive chain jobs, Stewart is hoping to keep moving upward. Ruth Fertel, founder and chairman-CEO of the 45-unit, $110 million volume New Orleans-based Ruth's Chris Steak House chain, is one of the industry's most successful female executives. Others include Jackie Trujillo, vice chairman of the Los Altos, California-based leading KFC franchisee Harman Management; Julie Brice, chairman of Dallas-based Brice Foods; and Ella Brennan, a leader of the family-run New Orleans-based Commander's Palace, Inc.)

Among Martin's significant leadership moves have been his resisting the temptation to raise menu prices, heading the trend toward fast-food value-priced meals, putting Taco Bell products on supermarket shelves to gain more exposure, and moving Taco Bell into carts and kiosks at every conceivable location.

Corporations often are too bureaucratic and don't have the entrepreneurial flexibility to succeed in the restaurant business. "A company just helps you run faster in place," Martin asserts. "For so many years we have looked only within the industry for our executives. We've got to expose ourselves to other points of view." His leadership philosophy is summarized by his frank advice to parent PepsiCo to tout its restaurant chains and not worry about Coca-

Cola's assertions that Pepsi favors its own chains. "Let's just go out there and beat the hell out of the competition on the chain side," Martin insists.

Herman Cain, the most visible African American foodservice leader, is a shining example of a leader who became a top chain executive the tough way. A mathematician for the Department of the Navy who had studied science at Purdue University, he gravitated to the Coca-Cola Company and then to Pillsbury as a management information systems expert. In 1982 he accepted the challenge of going to the front lines of Pillsbury's Burger King, and in three years turned around the Philadelphia area, which had been the chain's weakest performance region. Next, he took on the challenge of changing the course of its Omaha-based Godfather's Pizza and succeeded there as president in what some Pillsbury officials called "the turnaround of the quarter century." Following this, he led a 1988 management buy out of Godfather's, has kept it moving ahead, and also is 1994–95 president of the National Restaurant Association (NRA).

"Directed coaching toward specific goals, concentrated focus, and developing inspired fellowship are the main ingredients of leadership success," Cain says. "You can inspire people by removing barriers, such as a lack of self-confidence, that keep them from motivating themselves." When he arrived at Godfather's in 1986, he found that the employees did not believe in themselves but did believe in the product. "They felt the business could be turned around," he recalls, "and I was passionate about the idea that we could do it. So we did." He provided directed coaching by giving his troops a road map and directions on how to reach the desired goals. Some units were closed, others opened, the menu and pricing structure greatly simplified, and the marketing streamlined.

Cain keeps his mind squarely on "focus, focus, and more focus" at all times. "A deficiency of leadership causes failure far more than a bad product or bad idea," he asserts.

Can leadership be divided in a cooperative effort? Cain says no, that "people need one boss" and that matrix management with multiple bosses makes no sense. He believes in leading and managing by instinct. "A restaurant manager must be on the move all the time and anticipate challenges. But a regional manager should have responsibilities for only one concept, not other concepts that would divert him."

Dave Thomas, founder and senior chairman of the nearly $4 billion volume Columbus, Ohio-based Wendy's, has a number of key principles for successful leadership: Make a lot out of a little; be smart in the utilization of time, and don't waste it; work hard, and don't feel sorry for yourself; don't cut corners or you'll sacrifice quality; have fun doing whatever you do, and enjoy your work as much as you can; be strict, but let people know you care about them; tackle problems head-on, and don't run away from challenges; and pray (maybe the most important one).

Thomas, an orphan who later won the Horatio Alger award, started work in a service station at the age of 10. He subsequently delivered newspapers and bagged and delivered groceries. He lied about his age to get a job at a Walgreen's soda fountain when he was 12 years old. His first experiences with a restaurant occurred when his grandmother took him to her "white tablecloth" restaurant, and he quickly gained an appreciation for quality and maximum focused efforts in a restaurant. His first restaurant job was at the Regas restaurant in Knoxville, Tennessee.

Thomas learned some of his quality management ideas from KFC founder Harland Sanders in the mid-1950s when he became a KFC franchisee: Always maintain high-quality standards, and never let the quality of any product slip; be a stickler for cleanliness; criticize employees but still leave them feeling good; and, in a turnaround situation, get rid of any deadwood in management, as a poor restaurant manager can kill the business.

For years, a pattern has been evident: top executives winning the biggest national awards in the restaurant industry and then seeing their chains fall from their plateaus. This is a result of complacency—a deadly sin in the restaurant industry. Yet many of the award winners just keep plowing ahead, never resting on past successes.

The greatest challenge facing Richard Melman, president of Chicago-based, multifaceted Lettuce Entertain You Enterprises, Inc., is not letting the acclaim and the awards he receives go to his head. With two or three smash-hit restaurant debuts each year in Chicago, Melman tries to steer a steady course. "Nobody can afford to rest on their laurels today," he affirms. "This is not brain surgery or curing a disease. This is all about having fun and trying new ideas all the time, tinkering with concepts." He takes pride in never being in the office but always in or en route between any of his 35 different restaurants.

Melman's success rate is high and his failure rate relatively low. Yet he has learned something from each failure. His biggest flop in the 1980s was Lawrence of Oregano. Its location was not a good one for lunch, but Melman kept trying and found that when he closed for lunch, the total dinner volume equaled the combined previous lunch and dinner volume. Finally, he closed the restaurant for good. His one weakness—and perhaps one could call it a strength of emotional attachment—was that he took too long to realize that certain restaurants just wouldn't make it. He changed the name of the Great Gritzbe's Flying Food Show to the Not So Great Gritzbe's, but it was still a loss. Fritz That's It expired when the lease ended. Melman sold Ed Debevic's, his own innovative 1950s diner chain idea, when he was outvoted by partners.

Melman leads by inspiring his troops and treating his managers as equal partners. He understands the importance of maintaining balance and perspective, putting great emphasis on his family and finding time to spend with them even when working 15-hour days and nights. Perhaps the most sacred thing for him is his Sunday morning softball game, which can rarely be interrupted for any business event, no matter how important.

Even critics who claim his restaurant styles are too funky still admire Melman's magic touch and unprecedented diversified array of winners such as Ambria, Bub City, Hat Dance, Foodlife, Maggiano's, The Pump Room, Scoozi, Shaw's Crab House, Tucci Benucch, Tucci Milan, and Un Grand Cafe. Showing a distinct partiality to Italian restaurants, he is starting to replicate some of his best Chicago places in Seattle, Phoenix, and other cities. Whether his success will continue is a question we have been asking for two decades, and the answer has been yes virtually every time.

Melman has a unique instinct and feel for what the public wants and thrives particularly in the casual restaurant field. The prime reason is that he is a reflection of a typical customer in his own casual dress and level-headed approach. Still, he is very definitely considered a "jock" with unparalleled flair on the Chicago scene. When he is in town—usually in one of his restaurants—there is a crowd of business people and friends waiting to see him. He is unflappable in trying to talk to each for at least a few minutes and in giving each his full attention.

Robert Rosenberg, chairman-CEO of Dunkin' Donuts and Baskin-Robbins U.S.A., learned about hubris after reading David Halberstam's *The Best and the Brightest* regarding U.S. overconfidence in the Vietnam War. Rosenberg then realized the mistakes he had made in the 1960s when he took everything for granted at Dunkin' and did not see the need for change. Ever since, he has used a 10-year model to test objectively various models for strategic planning. He has learned that it is important to "be prepared to give up what you create" and to "always run a little scared."

By the early 1970s, Rosenberg—who started at Dunkin' as president in 1963 under his father, founder-chairman William Rosenberg—had created four separate groups to project into the future and work on four distinct strategic changes. "Leaders need victories for their troops," he says. "It was important to create a mood or interpretation for the future and to communicate that to our entire management team. We then were able to create a winning environment and to think of ourselves as winners."

Vincent Orza, founder-president of Oklahoma City-based Eateries, Inc. (Garfield's Restaurants & Pubs) knows how to overcome challenges. When he started the chain in 1984, he quickly ran out of cash and went without pay for seven months. The same thing happened three years later, and he survived again. By 1994 the chain had grown to 35 restaurants and was profitable.

Orza's pride and joy is "teaching and instilling a sense of pride and professionalism in the unit-level managers, getting them to think like customers to enhance customer satisfaction." From the start, he sought mavericks, young people who had their own minds and did not necessarily agree with him all the time. He is one of the few chain executives who take their restaurant managers to major executive conferences and get them to interact with industry leaders. "There's no better way for them to grow in confidence and stature," he says. "I try to instill a belief that everything is possible if you try, while at the same time letting them know that failure is OK and a natural consequence of necessary risk taking."

Orza is setting a leadership example on the political scene too, while far too many chain executives are ready to criticize government legislation but are not willing to run for office. He was the highest vote getter in the 1990 Oklahoma Republican gubernatorial primary but lost in a runoff. He was ready to try again in 1994 but did not enter the election campaign, deciding to devote his full energies to his restaurants.

Fred DeLuca has had a meteoric rise in the restaurant industry. In 1965, at the age of 17, he opened a Subway Sandwich take-out shop in downtown Bridgeport, Connecticut, with the help of partner Peter Buck and a $1,000 check. They specialized in sub sandwiches. Initially, all DeLuca wanted was to make enough money to pay his tuition at the University of Bridgeport, where he was a psychology major. The first unit quickly began to lose money, but they opened two more and started to move into the black. DeLuca and Buck had a dream of possibly opening 30 units in the next decade. They surpassed their goals. By 1978, they had opened 100 units, 200 by 1982, 5,000 by 1990, and some 8,000 (two years ahead of their plan) in the United States and 13 other countries by late 1993. DeLuca has done it through franchising to the tune of 1,000 new units annually thus far in the 1990s. He is now president and chief executive, and Buck is semiretired.

DeLuca's free and easy leadership style works for Subway. He never seems to be pressured or stressed as so many other executives are, but just takes things as they come. The employees reflect his style and the relaxed pace he sets. About once a month he rents a movie theater and invites his entire headquarters staff and guests to previews of the latest movies. On the spur of the moment, he sometimes throws parties for the staff at a local pub "just so everyone can have fun." The relaxed atmosphere he prefers is reflected in the different types of posters many of the employees have in their work spaces and by the variety of music they play in their offices while working—with DeLuca's blessings.

For Tom DeNomme, managing partner of Apple Partners, an Applebee's International, Inc., St. Louis and Portland, Oregon, franchisee, details are the essence of leadership. "We're hounds for details," he says. "We have a methodical approach to site selection and don't like any surprises." For instance, he spent more than $500,000 and looked at 34 locations before finding the initial four Applebee's sites in Oregon. He also markets Applebee's in community public schools with the slogan "A is for Applebee's." Students receiving an A in any class are rewarded with a free dessert at Applebee's, and this program has been adopted by the entire chain. "We live by the due diligence we do, and we die by the due diligence we don't," declares DeNomme, who is averaging $3 million per unit in annual sales in his restaurants, as compared with the chain's $2.1 million average.

Incidentally, Applebee's strength as a chain is reflected in its name: Applebee's Neighborhood Grill & Bar. The trend in restaurants today is to project a chain unit as a neighborhood place, and that is doubly effective if the concept is already incorporated in the name.

THE SUCCESSION DILEMMA

It is extremely difficult for a founder-entrepreneur to drop out of a leadership position that he has held for years. It is hard to admit that it is time to step aside and open the way for new management. The entrepreneur often feels he is the indispensable leader and that nobody else can do the job like he can. In some cases that assessment is overwhelmingly correct.

A dramatic example of this dilemma was the Anaheim, California-based Carl Karcher Enterprises' (CKE) late 1993 ouster of 76-year-old Carl Karcher as board chairman. He had founded CKE's Carl's Jr. fast-food empire in 1941 with a $311 loan for a Los Angeles hot dog stand. The chain was built into a power through a series of ups and downs over the next half century. After his brother, president Don Karcher, died in 1992, Karcher brought in former KFC International president Don Doyle as president-CEO and gave him the authority to run the chain. Inevitably, the two clashed over policies, and the CKE board finally voted 5 to 1, with Karcher's son the only dissenter, to remove Karcher as chairman. This action was a devastating blow to his ego and, unfortunately, was carried out in a humiliating fashion—although there is never an easy way to do this. Afterward, Karcher seemed to regain some status when he was named CKE's chairman-emeritus and two of his banker supporters were appointed to the board. But things will never be the same.

The twin lessons of this situation are that perhaps Carl Karcher should have stepped down on his own (an unlikely possibility for an entrepreneur who achieved so much by exercising his own entrepreneurial style) and that a board should somehow let a great leader depart with his ego intact.

Don Callendar, who founded the California-based Marie Callendar's Pie Shops in the 1960s and built them into a leading restaurant chain, resigned in anguish in 1990 two years after he had sold the chain to Ramada Inns. "They ruined my company, and I can't stand to see this happen anymore," was his reaction. But his departure was inevitable.

Robert Farrell, who built up Farrell's Ice Cream Parlors through the early 1970s and then sold the chain to the Marriott Corporation, had a similar reaction and inevitably resigned. He was always convinced that Marriott did not understand his concept and had ruined it. Both he and Callendar were probably right. Too often the entrepreneur is the only one with the real feel for, and belief in, the concept, and the successors tinker with it to the point of losing the focus. The challenge of new management thus is to remain true to the origins while professionalizing—not an easy task and a real dilemma in many cases.

Frank Carney, who cofounded Pizza Hut in the late 1950s with his brother Dan and sold it to PepsiCo two decades later as by far the number one pizza chain, has kept silent about the reasons for his subsequent departure. He too apparently had no patience with the corporate leadership. Ego clashes are inevitable in such situations.

VARIED STYLES

It takes different leadership styles to succeed, depending on the particular situations. Ray Danner thrived as chairman-CEO of Shoney's, Inc. for many years with an autocratic style but finally stepped aside completely in the early 1990s as a more liberal administration took over. The company was not necessarily more successful under its new-image leaders than it had been under Danner's tough, meticulous direction. He had a Marine Corps approach but was a winning leader in his time. "People who are successful gravitate to a particular organization and a particular leadership style," observes one human resources executive.

Jerry Richardson, chief executive of the Spartanburg, South Carolina-based Flagstar Companies, with $4 billion annual revenues, composed of Denny's, El Pollo Loco, Quincy's Family Steakhouses, and a 550-unit Hardee's franchise, is another example of a hard-nosed leader who gets the job done and also gains the respect of his people. He can be tough as nails, but beneath what some see as a hard exterior are warmth, sensitivity, empathy, and modesty. Richardson is uncomfortable in the limelight and believes in a maximum of teamwork—a lesson he first learned as a gutsy rookie wide receiver for Johnny Unitas's pinpoint passes on the Baltimore Colts 1959 world championship football team.

Then there is the shared and participative leadership style. Charles Cocotas, president of Little Rock, Arkansas-based TCBY Enterprises, Inc. from 1992 to early 1994 and former president of Boston Chicken, Inc., is a prime example. He believes in the power of collective management, that "two brains are better than one," and that "a good idea can come from anyone."

"It is extremely important that the staff of an organization has a vested interest in the company's financial and strategic plan," Cocotas says. "If they are brought into the process at the development stage it becomes their program, their goals, and their objectives in which they have a vested interest, responsibility, and accountability for results and success." He also believes in the strategy of finding a way to "catch them doing something right" and focusing on achievements and positives while seeing problems as opportunities. However, he also strongly believes in these cliches: "Winning isn't everything . . . it is the only thing"; "Winners don't quit . . . and quitters don't win"; and "Tough times never last, but tough people do."

Honesty and credibility mean everything in leadership no matter what the style, Cocotas emphasizes. "You don't gain respect by telling people what they want to hear but rather what the truth is and what reality is. Problems must be addressed, confronted, and resolved with compassion, logic, and the understanding that the solution may not be perfect for either party." Above all, in any franchise system, equitable compromise is absolutely critical. Franchisors and franchisees often have different interests, but they must find ways of working for the common good of both sides— actually, there is just one side, that of the chain.

Courage and integrity are the cornerstones of any type of leadership. "Courage is by far the most important ingredient for an executive today," declares Ted Balestreri, of Monterey, California, chairman of the DiRoNA (Distinguished Restaurants of North America) awards, former president of the NRA, and president of Restaurants Central. "There are too many wimps in this business who try to agree with everything. You've got to have the courage to do it the right way and stand up for what you believe. I would rather disagree with people and thus keep their respect than kowtow to them. Unfortunately, people want to blend in with others all the time. They don't have the courage to stand up and disagree at a board meeting, an association meeting, or a company meeting. Too many people are willing to compromise whenever possible. Be yourself, don't be a yes-person, and when you want to take a firm stand, don't procrastinate."

To Stephen Elmont, 1993–94 NRA president and owner of Boston's Mirabelle restaurant, the greatest leadership challenge is "telling the truth, whether it involves an employee who did something wrong or a management strategy that backfired. We have to develop a deep trust with our employees over time, a dialogue of common ground." As president of Creative Gourmets in the 1970s and 1980s, Elmont rewarded employees who had tried certain projects and failed "as long as they told the truth to one another and to me." He also engaged a corporate psychiatrist to help employees with their problems.

Another successful leader is Samuel (Sandy) Beall, president-CEO of Mobile, Alabama-based Morrison Restaurants, Inc. This is one of the oldest foodservice companies in the United States, having been founded as Morrison's Cafeterias in 1920 and publicly traded since the late 1920s. He spends almost all of his time in the field reinforcing his values and fervently believes in the *Principles of Success* booklet that he has authored for his staff. He brings the management team together for quarterly "partner" meetings that also include the area directors.

A strong leader sets forth a definite statement of ethics and values in the enterprise's mission description (or elsewhere). Such statements should be customer-oriented and indicate that managers in the restaurants are to be given authority to make immediate decisions on customer complaints themselves without having to consult executive-level staff.

Bill Fisher, veteran NRA executive vice president and staff chief, perhaps with tongue in cheek but with keen perspective, in 1993 described the "perfect executive" as one with the following attributes: curiosity of a cat, tenacity of a bulldog, pride of a peacock, humility of an understudy, eagerness of a student, wisdom of a professor, hope of an optimist, courage of a champion, skin of a rhinoceros, sensitivity of a teenager, work ethic of a beaver, organizational ability of a spider, persuasiveness of a car salesman, inspiration of a coach, resiliency of a rubber ball, stability of the Rock of Gibraltar, motivation of a treasure hunter, communication ability of a crusader, goal orientation of a hockey player, heart of a lion, intellect of a Socrates, and spirit of a winner.

The point is that it takes many great qualities to make a winning leader, but there is no such thing as a perfect leader. In the very act of trying to innovate, the leader is bound to fail at something. It takes an assortment of special characteristics to succeed, and the formula varies from chain to chain and CEO to CEO.

The best managers really don't manage. They sponsor or facilitate. Generally, team building seems to win the day, simply bypassing the corporate structure to do whatever needs to be done. There must be a willingness to change the organization's structure as the market shifts, to share information rather than keeping it secret, and to focus on results—not on long hours.

An ideal leader sets the entire culture of a chain, primarily through communication and motivation. He or she should be rational—yet show passion at crucial times—provide objectivity, and avoid bias in decision making. A leader must take risks to succeed. There is no sure thing in the restaurant chain business.

"You have only two choices, to be either a spectator or a player," observes Oklahoma City-based Sonic Corporation chairman-CEO Stephen Lynn. "If you're a player, you're going to have to get out on the playing field, take some risks, get hurt, experience some losses."

This is what happened to General Mills in the 1970s when it tried such concepts as Betty Crocker Tree House, GuadalaHarry's, York Steak Houses, and The Good Earth, among others, and basically failed with them. Meanwhile, it had also tried Red Lobster and The Olive Garden and enjoyed spectacular success. It may be on the road to the same success with China Coast.

Winning leaders also are people oriented. "You have to care about people," says Lynn. "It does not take more time to be nice. Management is much like parenting—sometimes the most loving thing we can do is build boundaries or say no. But we can still care. You have to be tough and tender at the same time." A leader also needs to be effective as a listener, communicator, salesperson, optimist, and student. "Life should be a continuous education," Lynn observes.

A leader must have some nonnegotiable standards and ethics, strong beliefs that cannot be compromised. A leader must also be accountable for his or her own actions. "The idea that leaders are accountable to nobody is dangerous because the mind has an infinite capacity for self-rationalization," Lynn declares.

One of the major problems is that people tell leaders what they think those leaders want to hear, he suggests. "But we need people around us who hold us accountable. "We need people who are ruthlessly honest with us when we're not performing." Chain restaurant leaders sometimes have an inner circle of a few executives—trusted advisers—who are encouraged to be completely honest with the chief executive. But it doesn't always happen that way, unless the advisers have complete security and no fear.

Lynn goes a step further by meeting each week with three Oklahoma City business people who share his faith and values. "Our goal is to bring out issues and concerns and mutually use one another as one more level of accountability." Perhaps the most important thing a leader needs is balance in his or her life. Lynn expresses it beautifully: "Find a mate with whom you can share your successes and failures. Keep focused on the simple. Play by the rules regardless of what everyone else does. Laugh at yourself once in a while and, above all, have fun."

Lynn has the courage of his convictions, as evidenced by his own rebounds from adversity. As 1993–94 president of the International Franchise Association (IFA), he had the courage to reverse years of blatant favoritism toward franchisors and balance the scales through an IFA Franchisee Advisory Council and gradual admission of franchisees to IFA membership, just as he had the courage to stand up for the franchisees of his own Sonic company in the 1980s, after years of their being neglected.

Joseph Micatrotto, president of South Pasadena, California-based Panda Management Company, parent of Panda Express, the Chinese fast-food chain, and former president of Chi-Chi's Mexican restaurants, is convinced that chain leaders "must be educators and developers at all levels. They must find a way to stress strategic thinking, continuous learning, and the need for thorough, ongoing training and development." But today's leaders "must learn to roll up their sleeves and listen to all levels of their corporations to truly find out the pulse of the business. Decision making was never more important in regard to speed and involving more parties directly."

Also crucial, says Micatrotto, "is the need to teach all how to embrace, encourage, and manage change." A true leader has to do all of these things "while also protecting the integrity of the bottom line."

Lou Neeb, president of Dallas-based Spaghetti Warehouse, Inc., from 1991 to 1993, believes in "leading by example from a clearly articulated vision of where the organization is going and what is in it for the individual." He feels that the toughest challenge for a CEO is to move into an organization with a different style and culture. "Either you change your own style or you change the culture," he says. It seems as if Neeb, a former Washington-based government official, did a little of each in his stints as Steak and Ale president, Burger King president, W. R. Grace's fast-food president, a Pizzeria Uno franchisee, and Spaghetti Warehouse president. Today his aim is to deliver predictable results for stockholders. "But don't just try to please Wall Street," he says.

Working 12- to 15-hour days has typically been a common practice for many top executives. Today it may be more important to remain fresh and alert and to delegate key tasks rather than driving oneself endlessly. It also is essential for a CEO to take vacations of at least two or three weeks at a time in order to get completely away from the relentless pressure.

Craig Nickoloff, president of Irvine, California-based Claim Jumper Restaurants since 1977, has ceaselessly dedicated himself to the restaurant business since the age of 12 when he was washing dishes at his local restaurant. "You have to really sacrifice your personal life to do this business right," he says. "You've got to have the passion." Finally, in the early 1990s, with a wife and three young teenagers, he reoriented his priorities a bit, delegated more of the work as the chain grew to 10 restaurants doing $50 million worth of business, spent weekends at home whenever possible, and tried to limit his travels to one-day trips. He even took an occasional vacation with his family, which he found vital to recharge the batteries and retain the passion.

When two of Nickoloff's key executives resigned in 1992, he had to reorganize the company. He took on more duties and continued to spend four days a week in the field at the restaurants. Then he brought in a chief financial officer to do a heavy portion of the headquarters administrative work, as well as a human resources director and new regional and district managers empowered to run their ends of the business. "Now I can sometimes take off two weeks and let my people enjoy running the restaurants," he says.

In today's highly complex and rapidly changing restaurant environment, a successful leader must be a visionary. "You have to see and understand the mid- and long-range effects of any decision, as well as short-term effects," says Alan Stoner, former longtime operations senior vice president of the Corpus Christi, Texas-based Whataburger, Inc. fast-food chain. "A true and effective leader has to have the ability to communicate his vision for the chain, and his plans for the future should incorporate a concise understanding of the pros and cons of his vision."

David Overton of The Cheesecake Factory chain, based in Calabasas, California, has a vision of service and generosity as being crucial to leadership. "I want to be everything I can be—creative and always trying new things. We're getting to the point of being a race car that's driving faster than we've ever driven before."

Chicago- and Florida-based Nick Nickolas, who started in the business at the age of 15 in an Oakland, California, restaurant and over the years has launched Nick's Fishmarket and numerous other restaurants, leads by example. He tended bar and showed his bartenders and restaurant general managers each aspect of the business, and they in turn taught their employees.

Nickolas also believes that leadership is based in part on gut feelings and "being willing to roll the dice and take risks to succeed." He recalls convincing his partner, Jeff Harman, to open Nick's Fishmarket restaurant with him in Hawaii in 1968 with no assurance that the restaurant would last even a year. It did, but as is perhaps typical in the restaurant business, Nickolas has persevered over the years and has had a total of more than 40 restaurants (including openings and closings) through the early 1990s, with about six in operation now. This kind of perseverance may be what it takes to succeed as a leader.

David Wachtel, president of Nashville-based Western Sizzlin' and former president of the Nashville-based O'Charley's chain, characterizes his leadership style by saying, "Join me, and your chances for success in your career will be enhanced. I will work you hard and long and pay you well. If you're really good, you will probably obtain wealth. That's my winning leadership style, and over the years our company has demonstrated that approach."

A real leader tends to be an activist, rather than a passivist. A passivist-type CEO could be successful, but it's more efficient to be an activist. The activist deals with problems before they become serious, and gets early input. This leader's casual meetings often succeed in bringing together people who can help solve problems at an early stage.

The true leader keeps management levels to a minimum. Companies too often fall into the trap of adding management levels as they grow. They should try to cut the fat at the executive level, not among on-line performers such as sales managers or division vice presidents. But to avoid morale problems in eliminating a position, it is usually better to wait until a senior manager leaves the company or retires. A winning leader also places a high priority on manager development, emphasizing management training and not waiting too long to promote people.

Mavericks and risk takers are needed at the top, not conformists. These independent thinkers don't have to fit into a corporate mold. They are the creative idea people, valuable in making the final decisions. As one chief executive notes, "If you leave decisions up to a committee, it will work to find the one fault with an idea, not the nine other things that are right about it."

Top executives must stay in close touch with customers themselves. They can't rely on subordinates to provide accurate customer views, because the feedback is then filtered before the executive hears it directly. Norman Brinker and Ron Magruder are excellent examples of executives who frequently chat with and question customers. James Maynard, chairman-CEO of the Raleigh, North Carolina-based Investors Management Corporation, parent of Golden Corral and Ragazzi's Italian Restaurants, insists on treating all customers as if they were guests in his home.

Craig Miller, president of Boston-based Uno Restaurant Corporation, operator of Pizzeria Uno, says, "The leader must set a tone and attitude. Most all employees want to take guidance. They look for stability and an air of confidence and can always sense weakness. The employees deserve respect, benefits, and a good workplace. In return, they have an obligation to perform. They want to feel your focus is on the customer, and then theirs will be. In the ideal company, your philosophy matches employee expectations."

Miller's view is that an ideal top executive has spent time in the industry and has learned it from the ground up. He started in the restaurant business by washing dishes when he was 13 years old and growing up in Florida. He worked under Joe Lee at General Mills Restaurants from 1973 until 1984, when he joined Uno as president. "General Mills had a successful inbred management," he says.

Miller sees the president's role as laying out short-term and long-term objectives. "Our clear focus now is a handful of restaurants that need improvement. And the franchise system needs direction. We spend hours with the marketing managers talking about each restaurant. We also need to broaden our menu while still focusing more on the deep-dish pizza, which is our unique proposition." Pizzeria Uno had strayed from that base and had thereby lost customers.

"We're looking at locations everywhere," said Miller, who had just driven 800 miles in two days, looking at sites in Plattsburgh, New York, in Vermont, and elsewhere. Indeed, he says, the president has to be out in the field personally seeing to everything. He can't just sit in an office and expect to do the whole job. Casual meetings with employees may be more important than all the executive and board meetings held by chains and companies. "If employees feel you are listening to them, they will gladly work for you," Miller affirms. Uno's turnover is almost zero.

When everyone is saying, "you can't do it," true leadership plows ahead. Ronn Teitelbaum was a successful apparel merchant as owner of Eric Ross & Co., Los Angeles, when he decided in 1985 to launch a business he loved. Like a lot of people in those days, he was enamored with restaurants. So he sold the business and launched an old malt-shop concept of the 1940s. All his friends told him: "Don't do it, Ronn. You're crazy to even think of it. The restaurant business is too hard and has the highest failure rate of anything. You'll just be another cult-burger stand."

Teitelbaum flipped the dice anyway. He opened a 20-seat malt-shop burger place called Johnny Rockets, realized $1 million in sales the first year, and had 48 units by 1994. He has developed an ambitious national expansion plan, which might or might not jell during this decade, depending on financing, consumer trends, and whether the chain is acquired, as so many inevitably are. Still, this gut-feeling leadership style, "just doing it no matter what anyone tells you" and despite any surveys to the contrary, is one to be admired. We're particularly impressed that Teitelbaum now tells his employees, "Have fun, then make money," rather than invoking his former apparel business slogan, "Make money, then have fun." Having fun is the entrepreneurial approach, which almost inevitably leads to the money, rather than vice versa.

The question is often raised: Can a restaurant chain leader come from outside the industry? Why not? There's no law against it, although some people think there is. Outsiders can bring an objectivity and a stronger long-range outlook to the business and can adjust to the necessary personal approach. Teitelbaum is one example. Other examples are Larry Flax and Rick Rosenfield, two Beverly Hills-based federal lawyers who launched California Pizza Kitchen in 1985 and put it under PepsiCo's wing in 1992. Their empathy for the defendants they were prosecuting in the early 1980s led them to the philosophy of ROCK: *r*espect, *o*pportunity, *c*ommunication, and *k*indness. "We live by those precepts," they agree. "We focus on mutual respect and inbred kindness. We give our employees special training in all the types of behavior needed to help customers. We constantly remind them to be kind to customers and to show empathy."

Former Blockbuster Video executives are making a major impact on the industry. Two of the most prominent are Taylor Devine, former Blockbuster international vice president, who has led Herndon, Virginia-based Takeout Taxi to a top position in the foodservice delivery business, and Scott Beck who, with his team of former Blockbuster executives, has led the Naperville, Illinois-based Boston Chicken, Inc. rotisserie chicken chain on a remarkable turnaround surge.

Indeed, leadership can come from outside the foodservice industry—in California or anywhere else. The reverse is also true, as evidenced by former Howard Johnson's Restaurants and Ponderosa president Thomas Russo's success as chief executive of Hanson Industries' Framingham, Massachusetts-based, nine-company housewares group, and former Arby's and Shoney's president Leonard Roberts becoming president of Dallas-based Radio Shack in mid-1993. Russo rejoined the restaurant industry in early 1994 as president of Ft. Lauderdale, Florida-based Miami Subs. Winning concepts seem to be based more on entrepreneurial instinct and tinkering than on extensive surveys. And the winners focus on managing factors that create the numbers, not vice versa. Any company that constantly focuses on the numbers and makes decisions based on profit-and-loss (P and L) statements is missing the boat. "Problems and opportunities occur inside the restaurant, not on the P and L," says Patrick Morris, former Tony Roma's marketing senior vice president. "When your constant focus is on the numbers, the fundamental aspects of the restaurant business tend to be neglected."

Profit-and-loss accountability should be assigned two or three levels below the chief executive "so that a manager who handles it has direct control of the factors that influence profit and loss," Morris declares. "The manager needs the full support of the financial staff. I have always emphasized the inherent dangers of financially driven leadership where executives set financial goals for profit percentages instead of first focusing on key operational goals to improve the operation to attract more customers and keep the seats as full as possible—the prime objective of any restaurant operation. That prime objective is not market share or high profitability, but rather the entrepreneurial approach. If this is done properly and the seats become fuller more often, market share and profitability will inevitably shine."

A financially oriented restaurant chain executive can succeed, but only if there also is an operations executive with entrepreneurial instincts. All too often, the financially oriented executive tries to go it alone and is rarely successful. A notable exception is Warren Simmons, who founded San Francisco-based Chevys Mexican restaurants in the late 1980s and relied on former Victoria Station and veteran industry operations executive Fred Parkin to keep the enterprise going. "I was the key person for Warren then, the guy who knew how to do it," he says. Parkin remains operations vice president, but the chain is moving ahead with Mike Hislop as president and PepsiCo's Taco Bell having acquired it. In effect, Parkin did keep it going and helped to build it to the point where Chevys was attractive to PepsiCo as a potential leading Mexican restaurant chain.

A typical pattern of leadership—an entrepreneur starting a chain and then engaging professional management at a later time—is part of the necessary cycle. Robert Hawk, who founded Dallas-based Spaghetti Warehouse in 1972, finally named Lou Neeb president in mid-1991 and two years later turned over the chairmanship to Neeb as well. But Hawk then decided he really did not want to yield control and ousted Neeb.

There's a saying that people are promoted again and again until they get well beyond their point of maximum efficiency. Overpromoting ruins people's potential, yet it happens constantly. A noteworthy example is provided by some chain restaurant managers who feel pressured to move up far beyond their capacity, when in fact they are invaluable as managers. Another is the superoperations vice president or marketing vice president who is promoted to become executive vice president and finally president, at which point that individual is doomed to fail. Overpromotion occurs frequently, but restaurant chains apparently are willing to chance it, figuring that the worst that can happen is they'll be looking for another new president. They fail to grasp the very different qualities needed in the various steps on the ladder.

Richard Frank, chairman of Irving, Texas-based ShowBiz Pizza Time, Inc., has a clear list of leadership objectives. He starts with quality people and establishes clear goals and statements of what he expects from them. "Then I try to back off and let the people make their own decisions. I'm there to support them. I want a relationship with two-way accountability—that I'm accountable to them and vice versa. But they must know my expectations, and it is up to me to make this crystal clear. I really want to not get in their way and let them do the job."

Viewing the organization as an upside-down pyramid, with the unit manager at the top and the chief executive at the bottom, is crucial. "Major paradigm shifts are occurring," observed longtime Whataburger president Jim Peterson in early 1993. (After 20 years at the helm, he was replaced at the end of 1993 by Thomas Dobson, son of owner Grace Dobson.) "We need a different kind of leadership in the industry," Peterson asserted. "We need to take people to new levels of management, autonomy, and empowerment . . . new forms of food sanitation and cleanliness, new food preparations. Leaders today need a lot more vision and flexibility. In the past you could possibly get away with holding the same ground, but now we need a climate to reward innovation. We need ways to communicate our direction directly to the customer. What's needed is leadership with a vision, the ability to communicate one's agenda and promote self-confidence all the way along the line. The best ideas come through all the ranks, not just from the executive suite."

Richard Rivera, former Dallas-based, TGI Friday's president (who jumped to the Atlanta-based Longhorn Steaks chain in late 1993), also is convinced that leaders have to enable people to perform, to make quick decisions. "It's like a basketball game," he observes. "People respond in drills, but they must learn to react during the actual game. Fundamentals are always crucial and must be ingrained so that they are automatic when it really counts."

Kenneth Reimer, who was president of Dallas-based Romacorp, Inc., parent of Tony Roma's, for 10 years until the chain was acquired by Pittsburg, Kansas-based National Pizza Company in mid-1993, calls the consumer "virtually the emperor." He also feels that "you must work hard to understand the motivation of your employees. You really can't take anything for granted, and you have to be able to relate to them in terms they understand."

Being one of the troops is a frequently used management style too. "I am no better than anyone else," affirms Howard Berkowitz, president of the San Francisco-based Oh-La-La gourmet coffee chain. "We are all on a team to better our families, our companies, and ourselves."

John Y. Brown, president of Ft. Lauderdale, Florida-based Roasters Ltd., parent of Kenny Rogers Roasters rotisserie chicken chain, recalls the leadership exercised by KFC from 1964 to 1971 after he and Jack Massey bought it from Colonel Harland Sanders. "I saw the dream, and it worked," says Brown, whose main experience until then was selling *Encyclopaedia Britannica.* "I was a 29-year-old law school graduate, and with the tremendous help from (industry veteran) Jack Massey we were far ahead of McDonald's and had 3,500 units by 1970. We were the chain leader, the first to go international, the second to go public."

He terms their 1971 sale of KFC to Heublein "the biggest mistake I ever made" but concedes that he had worn himself out by then. No significant products ever came out of KFC after that, he asserts. In essence, he suggests, the chain rested on its laurels. If that is so, PepsiCo certainly is pushing it to shape up in the far more competitive 1990s. Yet the innovative instincts of Colonel Sanders, Brown, and Massey have not been regained.

Brown, a supersalesman and promoter who subsequently was chairman of Lums, governor of Kentucky, inventor of Ollie's Trolley mobile units, and involved with a number of other enterprises, is hoping to expand the more than 150-unit Kenny Rogers chain to 500 by 1999 and to launch a new Road House Grille steakhouse concept.

Leadership is everything. In the late 1970s and early 1980s, William Spoor was a great chief executive for Pillsbury, and the corporation and the chains thrived (also partially because of Norman Brinker at the chain level). When Jack Stafford succeeded Spoor as chief executive, he faced serious obstacles but did not bring in a chief operating officer to oversee the daily details. Pillsbury declined from that point.

Something similar happened at PepsiCo, where in the 1970s Donald Kendall was a great chief executive and PepsiCo thrived as a corporation. It was hard for any CEO to measure up to him after that, and PepsiCo encountered its share of difficulties in the 1980s in trying to integrate all its restaurant chains and in other efforts. However, as we move into the mid-1990s, KFC is trying to rebound, PepsiCo's Taco Bell and Pizza Hut are doing well, and the PepsiCo restaurant empire also includes Chevys Mexican restaurants, California Pizza Kitchen, Hot 'n Now double drive-throughs, D'Angelo Sandwich Shops, and East Side Mario's Italian restaurants.

One leader can make the difference throughout an enterprise in determining success or failure. Burger King just hasn't been able to find the right person to lead it—at least neither Pillsbury nor Grand Metropolitan have found that person in at least the last 10 years. In the late 1980s, between Pillsbury's bureaucracy and Burger King's stubbornness, the two scarcely even talked to each other; Pillsbury either wouldn't or couldn't provide the necessary funds for the changes needed at Burger King and for the rapid growth required to gain its market share.

Each chain must have a clear definition of what the market really is. So many chains fail because they expand too fast and outflank their managerial or financial capacities, or both.

Robert Kriegel, author of the book, *If It Ain't Broke, Break It,* feels that balance is essential for an executive and that most executives push themselves too much and thereby lose efficiency. "Pushing yourself too hard only leads to out-of-balance stress, which hurts communication and quality," he warns. "You start making mistakes, and then your confidence and trust break down. It's a whole cycle."

He is convinced that "a passionate 90 percent effort produces 110 percent results, but a panicked 110 percent effort openly creates more mistakes along with less quality and less innovation." Thus, less is more in the frantic executive game.

Kriegel strongly suggests finding ways to ignore the constant "it can't be done" and "don't change a winning team" advice so often given. "The passion to chase dreams and take risks" is in effect a fire that needs fuel, not a "negative fire hose." He urges executives to "recognize the fire hose, dodge the spray, and always fight for change and against complacency."

A number of observations on the balancing acts of chief executives appeared in a 1993 *Restaurant Hospitality* article by David Farkas:

- Barry Krantz, president of Irvine, California-based Family Restaurants, Inc.: "I can juggle better than most people. Sometimes eight things at once. So when I'm faced with 20 things at work, I just have to figure out which 12 to let drop. I never look back."

- Fred Hipp, president of Kansas City, Missouri-based Gilbert/ Robinson: "If you put a premium on balancing home life, you become more productive. This means you're not taking any work home. Instead, you're paying attention to your family. The guilt goes away, and in its place is a sense of well-being."

- Les Kimbrough, regional operations director of Louisville, Kentucky-based Chi-Chi's: "Five years ago (in 1988) I worked seven days a week. I came in on off days. I was newly promoted, and figured I had to do more than what might be considered normal. I was always putting in systems and developing training programs for my staff. The goals I set for myself were higher than those the company set for me."

Still, balance and delegation don't always win. As Charles Lynch, chairman of Bojangles', LaSalsa, and Greyhound Bus Lines, among others, expresses it well: "Nordstrom's department stores eats, sleeps, and breathes the customer 24 hours a day. You can never waver from this type of total commitment in any business."

With the accelerated pace of change, a winning leadership style must include the ability to make quick decisions based on the immediate facts at hand. Windows of opportunity will be narrower and shorter in duration, so procrastination will be a fatal mistake. Chain leaders will have to make decisions even with limited amounts of information. They may have to live by the slogan, "Fire, aim, ready," rather than the traditional reversal. They will also have to organize a staff that can manage through delegation. The day when a restaurant chain leader can have the final say on every decision in this increasingly complex business is over.

In the 1960s, when the chain restaurant business was evolving, there was plenty of time for entrepreneurs to grow into professional management. For example, Frank Carney's Pizza Hut and Glenn Bell's Taco Bell had two decades to develop before being acquired by PepsiCo. But today the evolution from first-stage entrepreneurship to professional management might take just a few years. The chains that have evolved through those phases to a sophisticated management system can grow at a faster pace and dominate their segments if they handle their growth properly. General Mills and Brinker International are excellent illustrations.

The style of the leader also dictates the degree of overconfidence that may eventually develop in a successful chain. Complacency and the often resultant bureaucracy are deadly. This pattern essentially caused the failure of Sambo's and Victoria Station after each had risen high in the full-service restaurant world of the late 1970s. The respective symbols of upcoming collapse were Sambo's glistening, overbuilt new headquarters offices in Santa Barbara, California, and Victoria Station's state-of-the-art San Francisco headquarters basketball court, which too many executives used too often during business hours. Seeds of potential failure can indeed be found in success.

Obviously, the chain leader must have a vision of what he or she wants the business to be, and must clearly communicate that vision. Max Pine, president of New York-based Restaurant Associates Corporation (RA) from 1976 to 1993, recalls that after he first took command he somehow did not clearly communicate to the individual restaurants the fact that RA's Charlie Brown restaurants in New Jersey were a steak and salad chain. "I assumed they all knew that, but it was a false assumption. They kept adding trendy items to the menu to reduce food costs until I finally made it totally clear that they needed to be dedicated to a concentrated approach on Charlie Brown's as a steak and salad chain with steady quality and not with all kinds of trendy items. Sales and food costs subsequently improved."

True leadership means empowering people to do the very best they can. Leadership and success in the chain restaurant business hinge partly on Pine's three Ps: *people* (having quality, well-motivated employees), *p*roduct (in terms of concept, execution, and food quality), and *p*rofits (making maximum profits, not losses). Of course, nothing is so overwhelmingly simple or he and other executives would not have had to endure up-and-down cycles over the years. However, Pine's concepts do provide some general guidelines.

According to Pine's theory, a restaurant needs all three Ps working in unison to succeed. "If just one of them is not keyed in properly, that may lead to failure," he says. "If you look at any chain that failed or is failing, you will inevitably find that one, two, or even all three of these links are faulty." More often, it is just one link that has been overlooked—at great eventual cost to the chain.

For example, opening a phenomenally creative restaurant is not enough to ensure success. In the early days of Restaurant Associates, in the late 1950s and early 1960s, president Joseph Baum—arguably the nation's greatest creator of innovative restaurants—had sensational products (restaurants such as the Newarker, Forum of the Twelve Caesars, La Fonda del Sol, and the Four Seasons) and sensational people. But there were heavy costs involved, the restaurants did not generate a decent return on investment, and only the Four Seasons has survived. (Another example might be an entrepreneur having a wonderful restaurant concept with a low investment cost, primed for large profits, but still not achieving high enough sales.)

In essence, there is a delicate balance among the three Ps. One needs to make priorities on which to concentrate. The third P, profits, is usually a product of the first two, people and product.

"You must understand what you're doing with the concepts and products you develop," adds Pine. "Don't wander off the path. You can use customers to give you clues on how to proceed, but you must have a direct feel for it yourself."

Promoted to RA president in 1976, Pine's tenure was one of the longest in a chain industry with a high rate of turnover. He joined RA in 1968 in the marketing department and was appointed chief financial officer in 1972, although he had no accounting or financial background and RA's public accounting firm advised against it. Apparently, RA wanted to bring a fresh perspective to the financial side of the business and needed to fill a job that had just been vacated. "I took it as a challenge, did a lot of reading, and educated myself on the financial side," Pine recalls. Martin Brody, RA chairman, helped him learn the principles.

Brody moved Pine up to president in 1976 when the business faltered. Pine's challenge was to turn it around, to reduce a bloated overhead, and improve quality. He took the risk of upgrading the food and the restaurants during a severe New York City recession. RA spent the money, and it seemed to pay off.

In 1984 Pine faced the challenge of whether to acquire California-based Acapulco Mexican restaurants. Acapulco, having taken a scattershot approach to expansion, opened in Ohio, Kansas, and Nebraska and was losing money. "Everyone warned me to stay away from Acapulco, but I took the chance and it turned out to be our most important deal ever," he asserts. He apparently went for Acapulco because RA—with all its individual restaurants in greater New York, such as Mamma Leone's and Brasserie, and its Charlie Brown's steakhouse chain in New Jersey—needed a larger regional chain to bolster its sales and profits. Pine pulled Acapulco away from its scattered Midwest locations so that it would focus on California—a more than big enough market. He also steered it toward a more authentic Mexican cuisine.

By 1987 Acapulco was accounting for one-third of RA's $180 million in annual sales, and at least half its cash flow. This was the prime reason that Kyotaru Ltd. of Japan acquired RA in 1990, after RA had gone into heavy debt in a leveraged buy-out by RA's executives. Kyotaru eventually demanded better bottom-line results than RA could give and its capital to solve Kyotaru's own Japanese problems.

Through it all, RA managed to keep an effective corps of executives at the top for years: Nick Valenti, chief operating officer; Richard Cattani, restaurants group president; Frank Guidara, theme restaurants and Charlie Brown's president; and Phillip Ratner, Acapulco president. It takes a stable team like that to make things work for a chain. Even stronger examples are Brinker's executive team, McDonald's executive team, and the team that James Near assembled at Wendy's.

There is a dilemma in seeking the type of creative people that a chain needs because of the natural restlessness of such people, who want to keep moving up or else move out. In any case, they need freedom and opportunities to try and to fail, and they need to be given real challenges that test their mettle.

Among the qualities necessary to be a strong chain leader are the abilities to provide visible, hands-on direction, to get the entire organization to focus on the same goals, to make constant change an expectation rather than a trauma for the organization, to decentralize the operations team so that there is more authority in each area, to have fewer but more talented management players, to establish clear and effective lines of communication throughout the company, and to build mutual trust within the system.

Still, the ideal executive is someone you can almost never get on the phone. He is rarely in the office but always out in the field, seeing the action first-hand and drawing his own conclusions. Above anything else, he is a dedicated entrepreneur.

ㅇㅇㅇㅇㅇㅇㅇ **Link Two** ㅇㅇㅇㅇㅇㅇㅇ

Motivating to Win

A culture that provides both motivational and monetary rewards.

"What we're going to do from now on is hire or promote a manager who loves Boise, Idaho, and wants to stay there."
—*Ron Magruder, president,*
The Olive Garden, Orlando, Florida

HIGHLIGHTS

- Teamwork
- Games at headquarters
- Unit managers crucial
- Pride and bonus incentives
- A stake in the action
- Mentors drive the business
- "Mentees" grow into mentors
- Brinker's Boys

"YES, WE CAN"

Effective motivation requires a culture that everyone knows, feels comfortable with, and wants to implement. It requires a full commitment to teamwork that encourages employees to work together for success.

Norman Brinker is perhaps the all-time motivator. It is no coincidence that his Brinker International chains invariably seem to succeed. He motivates his employees to provide top service through

37

fostering an informal atmosphere characterized by casual dress and friendliness among employees. Brinker believes in visiting as many of his (and other) restaurants as often as he can and loves to talk, not only with the managers, but also with the waiters, bartenders, and cooks—and especially the customers. That is how he gets direct feedback.

He encourages a spirit of friendly competition, even setting aside a "game day" once a year when the headquarters office is turned into a miniature golf course and the scene of other sports activities that build morale and camaraderie among the employees. To foster teamwork, Brinker also introduces all his restaurant managers to a challenge course. The managers cooperate with each other in climbing walls, walking on a high wire, and leaping from high poles.

Ron McDougall, who has endured the course himself, views it as "a learning experience showing that a team—not an individual—operates a restaurant." The managers indeed learn teamwork and perseverance on the course, assuming they complete it. Cynics might be inclined to call it an old-time macho exercise, but it achieves the objectives.

Another type of teamwork program is that of Hamburger Hamlet's Team Commitment to Total Quality (TCTQ). "This focuses on building a team, from the dishwasher to the manager, to make guests feel that they are number one," says Tom McFall, who was chairman-CEO from 1988 to April 1994. Employees wear "Hamburger Hamlet TCTQ" buttons, and when guests inquire what these are, the answer is supposed to be, "We are working as a team to ensure the best dining experience for you."

Among the features of the varied program are the headquarters executives taking turns working at hourly positions in the restaurants; constant evaluations by teams of three employees sent to other Hamburger Hamlets to see how they can be improved; a series of employee sales contests; periodic discussions at each restaurant on sanitation, safety, and other aspects of the industry; and a campaign focusing on "we caught you doing something right."

Atlanta-based Ritz-Carlton Hotels sets some of the finest examples for training employees to be 100 percent customer oriented.

The company philosophy is explained by training manager Rebecca Powell, who emphasizes to new employees: "You serve, but you are not servants. You are ladies and gentlemen serving ladies and gentlemen."

Ritz-Carlton executives point out that the business of this luxury hotel chain is not really selling rooms and food, but rather service and cleanliness to the top 5 percent of corporate and leisure travelers. If guests are to see the Ritz as a necessity, one executive says, "no detail is too small, no request too large." The strategy is to boost employees' confidence, to assure them that they are crucial members of an elite team that strives to keep improving. This type of employee attitude is why more than one Ritz customer has said, "They can never do enough to please you here."

Wanting to go the extra mile is the key to motivation of employee and customer alike. When one couple's son became ill at the Naples, Florida, Ritz-Carlton, hotel staffers brought him hot tea with honey through the night. When the boy's father had to fly home for a business emergency and his return flight was delayed, a hotel driver waited in the lobby for hours during the night until he finally got word on when the plane was arriving.

Horst Schulze, Ritz-Carlton chief operating officer, personally conducts the orientation session at each new hotel when it opens. He is committed to the Ritz's own brand of Total Quality Management. It is no wonder that the Ritz-Carlton in 1992 became the first hotel company ever to win the Malcolm Baldridge National Quality award for excellent management.

Another type of morale booster is an employee incentive program geared to specific criteria in satisfying customers. Eateries leader Vincent Orza has fashioned a program based on employees' commitment to customer satisfaction. Its success has resulted in a surge of repeat business—the lifeblood of the restaurant industry in an age when the only true customer loyalty is to the next hot new concept around the corner.

To Joe Lee of General Mills, the answer was training, training, and more training. "First you've got to select the best people," he says, "but then you must set up an intensive training program for them, give them the tools to grow, send them to school, do whatever is necessary. Don't let them stumble around in tough situations because they were never shown what to do."

"Breakfast with Joe" was always one of Lee's favorite times at Red Lobster, and he made the young recruits feel very much at home, talking with them, listening to their ideas, and encouraging them.

A number of chains honor employees with awards and fetes. Louisville-based Chi-Chi's annually honors its best employees with special recognition. Its 1992 top employees of the year were especially versatile, chosen from among 20,000 employees at the more than 200 company-owned restaurants: Annette Nowicki, an employee events coordinator at the Newport News, Virginia, restaurant who achieved strong sales growth there for two consecutive years and sponsored charity events; Bob Sikorski, who triples as a server, bartender, and corporate trainer at Clarence, New York, recognized for leadership, motivation, and dedication; Molly Coudron, hostess and guest service representative, honored for her special attention to guests in Cedar Falls, Iowa; and Keith Binion, who doubles as a line cook and trainer, for his extra efforts at Dublin, Ohio. All went the extra mile and were role models for the other employees, who saw that it could be done.

The awards, which vary each year, consisted of a trip for two to one of several places, plus $1,000 cash, for each winner. In addition, the four were feted at Louisville headquarters with a special tour of the city and dinner with president-CEO Joseph Micatrotto and other Chi-Chi's executives, and each was presented with a trophy and a color television—not a bad morale builder at all.

Vincent Orza calls unit general managers "the lifeblood of this business." He is one of the few who encourage and reward their best general managers, helping them to grow in stature by taking them to key industry conferences where they meet industry executives. Most chain executives believe that "only we biggies" should attend these conferences, but Orza astutely reverses the pyramid. Each year, he recognizes the top general managers in a different way. In 1992 he rewarded 24 of his leading general managers with a trip to Rome "to see food and service like the Romans do it."

Leonard Roberts, Radio Shack president and former chairman-CEO of Shoney's, Inc., deplores the general industry working conditions for restaurant managers. Based on an industry survey he unveiled at the 1993 annual International Foodservice Manufacturers Association Chain Operators Exchange Conference, he says that 20 percent of the unit managers were working 60 hours or more and that managers' average annual salaries were only $27,900 (plus an average of a $6,200 bonus for males and $3,500 for females—a discriminatory trend that apparently affects much of the industry).

Furthermore, the extensive survey showed, unit managers often don't have enough time for any social life, for their families, or for educational opportunities. Unit managers and their employees were portrayed as often being under more stress than is healthy. With 60- and 70-hour workweeks in some cases, and with pay scales often starting below $10 an hour for employees, the chain restaurant industry is still not the attractive career that it could and should be for young people. Although the image has gotten better, it still needs improvement. Annual employee turnover continues to be well over 100 percent for many chains.

"Managers don't have enough time for social life or for their families," Roberts observes, "and they want educational opportunities too. If we are to survive in this industry, we must do better. We have ample opportunities to create better work environments and to help managers cope with stress." He calls foodservice "obviously not an attractive career choice." Yet it can and should be an appealing career.

Furthermore, along with the long hours and lack of balance in life style that characterize the foodservice field, the divorce rate is one of the highest of any U.S. industry. In fact, in the mid-1970s the divorce rate among more than 1,000 Sambo's Restaurants' managers in the United States was well over 50 percent, Sambo's executives acknowledged. This indicates that incentive compensation plans don't solve everything. We don't have any specific figures on restaurant manager divorce rates in the 1990s, but we suspect they are still well above the national average.

INCENTIVES

In the chain restaurant business, the unit manager is the absolute key person, the very top of the pyramid. Any chain that can invert the normal corporate pyramid and put the unit manager (and hence the customer) in the number one position, and the president or chairman at the bottom, is way ahead of the game. By truly empowering the unit manager, a chain can only win. After all, the unit manager is the one closest to the action. The true action is not in the office but out on the "selling" floor where the customers are, and the unit manager is the one person who knows how to make them happy.

Yet somehow the pyramid is rarely reversed like this, and the unit manager tends to end up at or near the bottom. In such cases, so all too often does the customer. Chains that claim they empower the unit manager sometimes have a not-so-subtle method of undermining their own message. Simply by calling that person "manager," the company downgrades him or her. Without question, the title must be *general manager, general partner,* or *proprietor* to reflect the full authority that the manager must have as, in effect, the restaurant's chief executive.

But even when recognized as the general manager, a person often does not measure up to the challenge. Instead, he or she finds an endless array of paperwork to perform in the office and becomes a hidden manager or supervisor, more often heard than seen. Somehow the general manager's job must be to get out onto the floor, supervising the servers, cashiers, and kitchen staff—and receiving direct feedback from the customers—rather than trying to solve every technical and paperwork problem that arises.

Something is wrong with these patterns. Most often the problem is that the unit general managers see themselves as employees, because that is how the headquarters executives or the regional directors view them. This model has to be reversed by making the general manager, in effect, an owner.

Why does the Tampa, Florida-based Outback Steakhouse chain seem to outperform its competition around the country? Possibly it has something to do with the price-value image this chain has established, but more likely it is directly related to the big sign in each Outback restaurant proclaiming the name of the general manager as "Proprietor."

Can you imagine how proud that general manager feels about the restaurant—a chain restaurant that shows individuality in its own way? And can you imagine the extra effort he or she will make to shine and to encourage employees to excel? Such self-esteem can often make a difference.

Actually, Outback Steakhouse, Inc. chairman-CEO Chris Sullivan establishes the authority of the unit manager, not only by calling him or her managing partner and proprietor, but by making the manager an owner in a financial sense. Each proprietor must buy 10 percent of the restaurant for $25,000 (possibly with a bank loan). Bonuses are based on 10 percent of the monthly operations cash flow, with the proprietor getting half and his assistants the other half. The proprietor can also invest in stock options. Joint-venture partners buy 10 percent of the restaurant for $15,000 under the same arrangements. This gives the managing partners and joint-venture partners equity and helps to pay for the initial opening costs of the restaurant as well.

Total annual salaries plus the incentive income of these managing partners range from $75,000 to $130,000 annually. After a managing partner's initial five-year contract expires at a restaurant, Outback determines the restaurant's appreciation during that five-year period and returns the initial $25,000 investment plus as much as $100,000, based on the restaurant's increased sales and value. Is it any wonder that Outback is well ahead of most of the pack? It all starts with this incentive compensation program, instilling a feeling of ownership.

"We want our general managers to have an ownership in the restaurants, to create stability and a feeling that this is their restaurant," says Sullivan. "It encourages entrepreneurship and builds real continuity." In the chain's first five years, from 1988 to 1993, Outback lost only five general managers, and annual employee turnover in its restaurants was cut to 50 percent—far below the industry average. Furthermore, Outback serves only dinner so that managers and employees have a large part of their days free and the focus is entirely on the high-profit part of the business.

Outback manages to achieve a $3 million average per unit volume doing just this and achieves a 25 percent pretax profit. Outback's philosophy applies to the entire chain restaurant industry: Convert managers to owners by giving managers a stake in the business. Incentives and stock options are critical for long-term success.

John Farquharson, chairman of the gigantic ARA Global Food Services, puts it this way: "I try to stay as close as I can to the front-line manager, the person who executes my vision, the one who finds out what's really going on, the unit general manager."

Obviously, a good compensation package alone is not enough. Praise and recognition are also needed, and it is imperative in most cases to keep that same managing partner, as the restaurant's chief executive, in the same place for as many years as he or she is happy there, not to transfer managers constantly in a seemingly endless shuffle, as so many chains do, from one restaurant to another. The general manager knows more about the customers and the nuances of the market area, and chains falter when they incur heavy turnover this way. Of course, if the general manager is regarded as the chief executive, then there is no need to keep trying to move that person up the pyramid or to transfer him or her to a restaurant that is about to open so the person can perform the same magic there.

Sambo's Restaurants, Inc., which by the mid-1970s had become the number one volume full-service restaurant chain, collapsed by the early 1980s because it lost virtually every one of its 1,117 general managers in 1977–78, within a year after scaling back a previously successful unit managers "fraction-of-the-action" plan. The Securities and Exchange Commission directed Sambo's to change its accounting procedures and not to count the 20-percent manager purchases of individual restaurants as part of company profits. However, Sambo's instead took the "opportunity" to gain back a lot of the equity from managers and, in effect, destroyed the chain. If ever there was a dramatic example of the crucial importance of well-motivated owner-managers, this was it.

Certainly, egotism, the growth of a complex executive bureaucracy, and the demise of the 10-cent bottomless cup of coffee contributed to the downfall. But the overwhelming fact is that without a continuity of general managers, a chain cannot win. It might suffer from turnover at the top headquarters level (or on occasion might prosper because of it), but a chain's very survival is in doubt if it can't establish reasonable continuity at the unit level.

The Olive Garden's Ron Magruder has decided that constant shuffling of general managers is counterproductive. "What we're going to do from now on," he declares, "is hire or promote a manager who loves Boise, Idaho, and wants to stay there. He will do the annual business plan for that restaurant and every other bit of strategic thinking for it for 5 years, 10, maybe even 15 or more, and our entire chain will be better for this type of continuity." No more 2 or 3 years and out to another restaurant for a change of scenery, he affirms.

"We still pay quarterly bonuses to our restaurant general managers," Magruder says, "but we don't move them around constantly." Where necessary, he is determined to hire general managers locally or to move them up from within the local community. Besides, a chain generally tends to work better when it is operated locally.

Steven Leipsner, former chairman and chief executive of Dallas-based S & A Restaurant Corporation (Steak and Ale and Bennigan's), is convinced that bonus incentive plans for general managers are essential. "This industry has a horrendous mortality rate in marriages," he notes. "Managers have to keep grinding it out in restaurants, and they dread the long hours. Life-style is crucial today, and most young general managers are not so hyped up on stock plans. They want to work on bonus incentives."

Leipsner believes in a balanced approach, with five-day workweeks and maximum 10-hour days. Whether he or anyone else can actually achieve this dream under economically tight conditions is a realistic question. Yet he is dedicated to having the managers operate together as a community, allowing them to achieve tenure in a particular restaurant, and paying them the extra dollars, thus giving them a stake in the business so that they too will want to grow with the company.

He was determined to establish a pay base that "allows managers to have a decent quality of life, not reliant on a bonus for essentials." Bonuses would be based on the cash flow that the manager generates from the restaurant "with appropriate penalties if they try to shortchange the business," as apparently happened under the administration of Leipsner's predecessor. He also wanted a compensation plan more internally equitable and externally competitive, a new performance appraisal system, and bonuses based on employees' specific attainment of goals.

Leipsner finally established what he regarded as a more balanced incentive program at S & A in mid-1993, a few months before he was ousted by parent Metromedia Co. He tied 75 percent of projected annual compensation for each restaurant general manager to a base salary and 25 percent to a profit-oriented bonus incentive. The previous ratio of 40 percent salary and 60 percent incentive was "unfair to managers, who deserve the security of some type of guaranteed income," he asserts.

Pete Harman's Los Altos, California-based Harman Management Corporation, KFC's largest franchisee, was probably the first to start an incentive compensation program for managers and to push the ownership concept. The plan has evolved since the company started in 1953, and now each of the 250 units is a separate corporation, with the general manager owning 20 percent and a partner eligible for 10 percent ownership.

Harman is a strong supporter of the family ethic, and when husband-and-wife teams were eligible for 40 percent of the ownership and 40 percent of the pretax profits, families made well over $100,000 a year in salary and percentage shares. Generally, the percentage totals were reached gradually, as individual general managers and married couples saved their money and accrued greater percentages over the years. With the professionalization of the business, husband-and-wife teams are less common, and the plan has evolved to one whereby general managers receive a one-third year-end bonus, based on operating profits minus $25,000. For example, at a unit averaging $100,000 in annual operating profits, the general manager would receive an annual bonus of one-third of $75,000 and could convert some or all of that into stock options.

After the collapse of Sambo's in the early 1980s, Golden Corral family steakhouses, based in Raleigh, North Carolina, hired a number of its managers and executives. James Maynard, Golden Corral chairman-CEO, was impressed with Sambo's former "fraction-of-the-action" plan and adapted it to the needs of his own chain.

By 1993, the Golden Corral program evolved to a point where, at the 5,000-square-foot restaurants, which still constitute the bulk of the chain's operations, general managers receive a $28,000 annual base salary. The managers pay $5,000 for 5 percent ownership shares and can buy four separate increments over the years up to a maximum of 20 percent. They receive a share of the monthly controllable operating profits equivalent to their ownership percentage. In 1993 those who had reached a 20-percent level were averaging a $1,000- a- month bonus on their operating profit line, plus another $16,000 to $18,000 annually on operating income—an average of $57,000 annually in total compensation.

At the newer Golden Corral metro restaurants of up to 11,000 square feet, the managers have greater opportunities. They can own up to 20 percent and receive 1 percent of sales in excess of $1 million annually (at restaurants averaging nearly $2 million sales) plus about 10 percent of operating profit. In 1993, these managers were averaging $84,000 annual compensation.

Originally, Golden Corral adopted some of Sambo's crazy-quilt pattern, by which managers would own equity in other restaurants of the same chain as well as their own, leading to a maximum effort for various restaurants by those managers and not a complete focus on their own restaurant. When Golden Corral started the program in the early 1980s, managers had a lower base salary and could get as much as 30 percent equity in their own restaurants, as well as 40 percent in various other restaurants. The problem with this type of equity is that it shifts the equity balance away from the company. Thus, Golden Corral established a 20 percent limit, and the equity could be only in a manager's own restaurant.

In the mid-1980s, Boston-based Au Bon Pain Company studied

both the Harman Management and Golden Corral incentive compensation systems and came up with their own version. Ron Shaich, president, and Len Schlesinger, a Harvard Business School professor who was brought in for a few years as executive vice president, devised a plan whereby each unit manager receives a $25,000 base salary and a potential $7,500 maximum monthly bonus, half of which is held in reserve until the contract expires. "They're the owners of the restaurants," says Shaich, "and like company owners they just can't walk away very easily."

The managers have the challenges of solving their own problems at the restaurant, setting their own wage scales, hiring and firing, and making deals with suppliers. This system has fueled Au Bon Pain's rapid growth.

Robert Giaimo's Silver Spring, Maryland-based Silver Diner Development, Inc., parent of Silver Diners, launched a plan in mid-1993 to have its managers share in the profits, and its general managers become true managing partners who would share in the fledgling diner chain's profits and equity as it grows. Under a profit distribution plan, 30 percent of a restaurant's pretax profits in excess of budget are distributed as a bonus to the unit's general managers and associate managers (three or four at each of the chain's four restaurants) on a monthly, quarterly, and annual basis. The ownership plan enables a general manager to convert his or her year-end bonus (which could be as high as $25,000 to $30,000) to company stock options at a major discount. The entire plan would enable the general manager "to accumulate wealth on a tax-free basis," says Giaimo. Thus, a $25,000 bonus could multiply greatly without incurring any tax liability—until the options are converted to stock.

"This plan focuses the management team on the performance of their restaurant while enabling them to participate in the upside growth of the company," Giaimo says. It allows managers to become owners and to empower their associate teams with a sense of participation in the unit and the company in "furthering our mission of being the best we can be." He hopes to fuel growth by going public, which in turn would make the stock options more valuable.

Louisville-based Rally's, Inc., a chain of double drive-throughs, launched a plan in early 1993 whereby each general manager could own up to 20 percent of his or her restaurant and would also receive a 20 percent share of the profits. Unit managers can become general partners by buying 5 percent or 10 percent shares in their units, after two years of employment and if they have obtained "consistently high scores" on monthly performance evaluations. They can buy 5 percent more after four years with the company and a final 5 percent after five years, when they become fully vested in this bonus incentive program.

These programs are geared to a five-year cycle so that a manager can be retained at one restaurant and excel there for at least five years—a far cry from the former shuttle-service operation whereby managers were constantly moved from one unit to another. If a manager leaves the system, the chain generally buys back the shares so that a manager who is employed by another competing chain could not retain partial ownership of any unit in the first chain.

Sonic Corporation's Stephen Lynn calls the industry "empowerment" slogan a buzzword and emphasizes, "We're committed to quality, to making things better for our employees and franchisees. Inclusion is what we are seeking."

Lynn fervently believes in the ultimate empowerment, in making all employees owners. Managers and employees can buy stock in the company or obtain stock options. A unit manager can purchase a 20 percent to 25 percent ownership in his or her restaurant, and a 20 percent to 24 percent stake goes to the associate managers, always leaving Sonic with at least 51 percent ownership. Lynn got the idea from his larger franchisees. Monthly manager compensation averages $1,500 in salary and a $1,500 share of a unit's operating profits. Sonic's annual manager turnover today is less than 10 percent, as compared with an industry average of more than 100 percent.

Robert Colombo, president of Dallas-based Sfuzzi, Inc., has developed a program whereby each general manager receives a quarterly incentive bonus based on five criteria: beating the sales budget, surpassing the operating income budget, leadership, accountability, and training/management development, as evaluated by Sfuzzi executives.

Each criterion or point is worth 1 percent of base salary per quarter. Thus, 20 points, or 20 percent of annual salary, would be the maximum each year. Annual salaries range from $40,000 to $55,000. The best general managers receive a $55,000 base salary, a $10,000 bonus, and $3,000 in stock options.

Quantum Restaurant Group, Inc., led by Allen J. Bernstein, also has a point system geared separately to its Mick's, Peasant, Morton's, and Bertolini concepts. Service, value, food, incremental sales, operating profits, and cash flow to the bottom line are all in the formula. Restaurant general managers receive a combined bonus percentage and stock option percentage that are part of approximate annual compensation packages ranging from $50,000 at Mick's restaurants to $80,000 at Morton's steakhouses (Morton's of Chicago, Inc.).

Each chain program has its own nuances. Waterbury, Vermont-based Ben & Jerry's ice cream chain, a prime motivator, has had a full pension and profit-sharing program since 1978. Employees are gradually vested until reaching a full 100 percent level after seven years and then become eligible for further incentives tied to the company's profits.

Bill Bouffard, president of Dallas-based Bay Street Restaurants, has an incentive program for general managers based on reaching or exceeding the planned financial goals and on the quality of operations, judged against a checklist. Annual general manager compensations range from $35,000 to $80,000, with the incentive plan accounting for as much as half the total.

John Creed, chairman-CEO of Chart House Enterprises, Inc., based in Solana Beach, California, rewards his restaurant general managers with bonuses based on a percentage of pretax profits. He has steered away from any system geared to a direct share of profits "because the financial costs and structures of restaurants vary so much from one area of the country to another."

Incentive compensation programs of any type need periodic updating. Creed seemed to have an adequate incentive system as based, since 1972, on a percentage of pretax profits for his executives. But in 1992 he realized that it needed to be invigorated. "Like our federal income tax system, it had become obsolete," he concedes. "We started to add doodads and gewgaws, twists and turns, to accommodate different circumstances. I finally came to the realization that the system was broken, couldn't be repaired, and so I needed to buy a new one.

In 1993, Creed simplified the system to one tied entirely to net after-tax profits. "No excuses on this one," he says. "If the company makes a lot of money, shareholder equity rises and the management team is rewarded." He calls the 1993 model "simpler, more realistic" and on point with shareholders. "We get paid when you do," he now is fond of telling them."

Creed's restaurant general managers still receive incentive compensation based on a percentage of pretax profits. He has not included general manager investments or direct sharing of profits—the systems used by Harman Management, Golden Corral, and Outback, among others—"because the financial costs and structures of restaurants vary so much from one area of the country to another."

A unique plan was developed by Joel Stern, managing partner of Stern Stewart Management Services, New York. He calls his Economic Value Added (for stockholders) formula the best possible incentive for the restaurant industry—or for any industry. EVA, a fairly complex program, is determined, as explained by Stern, by "multiplying net assets by the difference in the rate of return on assets and the required or designated rate of return."

Atlanta-based Longhorn Steaks, Inc. adopted Stern's EVA plan in early 1993 to reward restaurant general managers and other executives for the actual economic value added for shareholders. A general manager quarterly receives 40 percent of a specified percentage of a restaurant's EVA, plus an added percentage if the EVA continues to rise. The restaurant's associate managers share the other 60 percent. Two-thirds of the money credited is set aside each year during a five-year vesting period, after which the managers receive all the money due them and can continue in the EVA plan with all monies paid them each year. Other Longhorn executives participate in the plan within their own context.

Although EVA sounds like a trend-setting idea, it may be too complex for most restaurant chains to use in providing incentives.

Managers and others appear simply to accept the figures as given
them and are perfectly happy if they get a decent return for enhanc-
ing the stock's value. However, this incentive is not necessarily
directly connected with a chain's operating performance and its
preparation for future growth. Yet many in the restaurant business
today maintain that a restaurant chain's main purpose is to enhance
the value of the stock—an oversimplification of a chain's role. Morrison Restaurants, Inc. has launched an EVA-oriented plan, but
only for its own investment purposes.

An incentive system tied to profits can have drawbacks. In striving to achieve higher profit margins, a general manager might
make too many staff cuts or compromise on quality. Presumably,
most managers and executives have too much pride to allow this to
happen. Sales, however, should be part of the formula.

The consequences of an incentive compensation plan tied entirely to profits were drastic for Metromedia's S & A Restaurants in
1992 when Metromedia ousted S & A's four top executives, claiming that they were compromising quality and the company's future
sales growth by focusing only on bottom-line profits. Other factors
may have been at work here for the four executives, who were part
of a 10-percent ownership group and were nearing the end of a
three-year incentive contract plan based entirely on profits. This
situation may show the possible dangers of such a plan. Steven
Leipsner was then named president in September 1992, and lasted
there for just under a year.

Richard Rivera, president of Longhorn Steaks, Inc. and former
president of TGI Friday's, has been developing an ownership structure for his managers. "A lot of restaurant managers want to stay in
the same restaurant today," he says. "They want a stable life, and
we have to adapt to this change and give them the freedom and the
money so they can stay in the same restaurant with their invaluable
market knowledge. The last thing they want is any corporate nit-
picking."

Trying to reach a delicate balance in emphasis between sales and
profits, TGI Friday's switched its unit general manager bonus ratio
to an approximate 50-50 split between sales and profits respec-

tively. The ratio had been 30-70 and then 70-30, but neither seemed equitable.

Ownership percentage plans have their own pitfalls. One danger is that a chain can yield too much equity to restaurant general managers over a period of years. On the other hand, if a chain is using the manager's percentage investments to finance restaurant openings, that can be self-defeating. Finally, all too often managers get into debt over their heads in taking out bank loans to buy their restaurant percentages. Yet even with all these pitfalls, it is still a virtual necessity for chains to develop reasonable ownership plans for general managers so that the restaurant becomes "my business" instead of "theirs."

MENTORS: THE "BRINKER EFFECT"

Most top restaurant chain executives had mentors whom they looked up to and admired, and from whom they learned many of the principles that made them successful. These executives in turn have "mentees" who look up to them.

It is no surprise that a number of chain presidents are known to insiders as "Brinker's Boys," people who trained under Norman Brinker and grew to become CEOs at other chains. The list is endless, showing that one person does make a tremendous difference. Some consider it a weakness that Brinker could not find a top spot in his own chains through the years for some of the most talented people, but he glories in their growth and accomplishments elsewhere. And at Brinker International, he has at least two former key executives from Steak and Ale—Ron McDougall and Lane Cardwell, executive vice president for strategic development.

Brinker's leadership has spawned at least 25 top executives from his 1960–70s days as founder-leader of Steak and Ale restaurants, a veritable who's who of the restaurant industry: George Biel, Atlanta-based Houston's Restaurants, Inc. founder-president; Longhorn Steaks, Inc. president and former TGI Friday's president Richard Rivera; former Spaghetti Warehouse president Lou Neeb;

El Chico Restaurants, Inc. president Michael Jenkins; ShowBiz Pizza president Richard Frank; Outback chairman and president Chris Sullivan and Robert Basham, respectively; Kyle Craig, a Boston Chicken executive and former KFC-USA president; Hal Smith, a highly successful Oklahoma franchisee of Outback after serving as Louisville-based Chi-Chi's president; Joe Micatrotto, Panda Express president and former Chi-Chi's president; and Mike Connor, an S & A graduate who was a partner in Grady's American Grill (acquired by Brinker International) and then launched his own Chop House chain in Knoxville, Tennessee.

Brinker has molded winning teams and winning spirits by getting people to believe in themselves and developing their maximum capabilities. If all his executives were on the same team, they would form an all-time, all-star company, although their desires to be number one might not permit them to mesh so well. It would be like having Joe DiMaggio, Willie Mays, and Duke Snider in the same outfield.

Ron McDougall gained invaluable marketing experience at Procter & Gamble and then became Steak and Ale marketing director under Brinker in 1974. McDougall was instrumental in creating the Bennigan's concept and is himself a mentor to many at Brinker International.

Richard Rivera, now president of Longhorn Steaks, Inc., became S & A Restaurants executive vice president in 1980 after working several years under Brinker. Rivera then became president of El Chico, Del Taco, and Applebee's International, Inc. He joined TGI Friday's under president Mike Jenkins in early 1987 as operations executive vice president and moved up to president a year later when Jenkins was apparently ousted.

"Norman Brinker has a knack for finding people who succeed," says Lane Cardwell, Brinker International strategic development executive vice president. "He is the industry's best in delegating and teaching." Brinker is always thinking ahead of his time. He is never satisfied with a concept, always making subtle changes, always asking himself as a consumer whether he likes it, and personally asking customers their opinions at his restaurants. Brinker is also modest. "There are a lot of very talented and imaginative people for whom I have the highest regard and respect in this industry," he says. "I simply do my best to tag along."

Brinker is indefatigable and indomitable. After he was critically injured when trampled by a horse in a polo match collision in January 1993, doctors despaired of his condition. He not only survived severe brain damage, but bounced back miraculously and was in the office working again—although not his former 15-hour days—in just four months. He continued with an intensive rehabilitation program. Unparalleled willpower and stamina saved Brinker, who turned 63 in 1994—a very young 63 at that, as he contemplates the next challenges.

In a sense he is a mentor to Philip Romano, who earlier created the Fuddruckers chain, and then more recently created Romano's Macaroni Grill and Spageddies. Romano turned them over to Brinker to launch as chains while he worked on other concepts. Brinker himself learns from Romano's ultracreativeness, and the two complement each other. They both enjoy themselves immensely in this business—while making a good deal of money.

Joe Lee, likewise, has developed quite a number of top executives from his 1970–80s leadership of Red Lobster and General Mills Restaurants, many of whom remain as General Mills executives: Ron Magruder; Red Lobster president Jeff O'Hara; and Blaine Sweatt, who created and fashioned The Olive Garden and China Coast. Moreover, Uno Corporation president Craig Miller, Taco Bell senior vice president Tim Ryan, and Pizza Hut International president Randy Barnes worked under Lee in the 1970s. Joe Baum's leadership spawned well over 100 leaders of various operations from his 1950–60s days as RA's (Restaurant Associates) most creative figure and as president.

Yet these leaders had mentors too. Norman Brinker's was Robert Peterson, founder of Jack in the Box. "Bob Peterson helped me in more ways than anyone can imagine when I was young and green and just starting at Jack in the Box in San Diego," Brinker recalls. "Everyone needs a mentor to look up to and to grow." Brinker loved the restaurant business from his days at Jack in the Box when he was in his twenties. Joe Lee's mentor was Bill Darden, the founder of Red Lobster. And Jerrico–Long John Silver's founder, Warren Rosenthal, was a mentor to Ernest Renaud, who miraculously turned around Popeyes and Church's in the early 1990s; Howard Berkowitz, Oh-La-La gourmet coffee chain president; and Ted Papit, president of Dallas-based Black-eyed Pea Restaurants. Renaud in turn was a mentor to Berkowitz and to so many others. Peers may have helped some individuals on the tough climb up the executive ladder, but they needed encouragement from mentors more than anything else.

Companies and individuals also launch careers and other restaurants as well. Among RA's many alumni are George Lang, the famous restaurateur and consultant who now has two major restaurants in his native Budapest; Tom Margittai and Paul Kovi of New York City's Four Seasons restaurant, who made a startling success of it after spinning away from RA; Drew Nieporent of Montrachet and the Tribeca Grill; Michael O'Neal, a New York City restaurateur; Dan Andrus, president of H. Dundee steakhouses; and Patrick Terrail, who founded Ma Maison restaurant in Los Angeles.

ARA Services spawned a number of leaders, including Joe La-Bonte, who became president of Twentieth Century Fox and Reebok; Manfred Doblinger, president of Canteen of Canada; and John Dee, president of Service America.

Larry Flax and Rick Rosenfield gained much by studying the methods of Norman Brinker and McDonald's chain founder Ray Kroc. "We got our inspiration from the examples they set," recall Flax and Rosenfield. Kroc was mentor, in person and via reputation, to a whole generation of McDonald's executives and to the entire fast-food industry.

But Harry Lewis, chairman of Hollywood-oriented Hamburger Hamlet in the 1960s and 1970s, was Flax's and Rosenfield's real hero. "In those days Harry and Marilyn Lewis were doing innovative, wonderful things in the restaurants," Flax and Rosenfield say. (They later started to lose the luster and finally sold the chain to Tom McFall and Paul Brockman in 1988.)

John Y. Brown recalls that when he and Jack Massey purchased KFC from Colonel Harland Sanders in 1964, Brown was a 29-year-old greenhorn, lacking both confidence and savvy. Massey shepherded him through that stage, and Brown is now hoping to increase the Kenny Rogers Roasters chain to 500 units. Brown, in turn, was a mentor to Bruce Lunsford and gave him confidence when he needed it. Lunsford went on to become Kentucky's secretary of commerce and then chief executive of a large corporation.

"I grew up in an era when everyone thought I couldn't win," Brown says. "But I showed them." When he suddenly decided to run for governor of Kentucky, his friends told him that he was crazy and would have no chance. "Out of 200 people I talked to, all 200 said I would be a sure loser." Brown won the primary and the general election in stunning upsets. But as his political career was sidetracked because of a heart attack, he returned to the restaurant business, where, with his boundless enthusiasm, he continues unrivaled as a promoter.

Ray Danner and Alex Schoenbaum, Shoney's, Inc.'s driving forces starting in the 1960s, generated a number of top executives, including National Pizza Company president Mitchell Boyd and O'Charley's, Inc. founder David Wachtel. As part of their hardening experiences, both Boyd and Wachtel were ousted as Shoney's president before succeeding on their own. Others spawned by Shoney's are Shoney's CEO Taylor Henry, TPI Enterprises, Inc. (Shoney's largest franchisee) president Gary Sharp, and O'Charley's chief financial officer Gregory Burns.

Robert Rosenberg, Dunkin' Donuts chairman, was a mentor to Sidney Feltenstein, Dunkin' Donuts' marketing chief for many years and then Burger King marketing chief from 1991 to 1993, and to Charles Cocotas, former president of TCBY, among others.

Sonic's Stephen Lynn translates the Brinker Effect in terms of Sonic's franchisees. He calls it his and Sonic's responsibility to nurture the next generation of franchisee entrepreneurs. "In addition to sons, daughters, and other young family members of our franchisees," he says, "a great proportion of the more than 30,000 people working at Sonic are still under 19. Those employees are not only the key to our current success, but they also are the leaders of tomorrow. It is imperative that we prepare these young people for the challenges they will face in the years to come."

A number of Sonic's franchisees emphasize leadership development and ownership programs. They act as mentors to new Sonic franchisees and as consultants for Sonic franchisees breaking into new Sonic markets.

Many of the Sonic families have brought family members into the business with them. There are son-and-daughter, brother-and-sister, and husband-and-wife teams, making the operation literally a family business. Lynn and many other chain leaders see the role of mentoring as keeping employees growing upward within the company, rather than grooming them to become executives of other companies. However, some chains feel it is not fair to block a talented executive from advancing and that if there is no higher position for that person within the company, then it is inevitable that he or she will leave for a better offer.

Donald N. Smith rose to chief operations officer and senior executive vice president of McDonald's Corporation in 1976 at age 36, then was wooed to Burger King as president and, after PepsiCo restaurants and Diversifoods, has been Perkins Family Restaurants CEO since 1985 and Friendly's Restaurants CEO since 1988. Smith was a mentor for many through the years: McDonald's USA president Edward Rensi and McDonald's Corporation chief executive Michael Quinlan, who both worked under Smith when he was the hottest rising executive in the McDonald's chain; John Martin, whom Smith brought to PepsiCo and positioned to move into the Taco Bell presidency; Ron Petty, Denny's chief operating officer, whom Smith brought into Burger King as a development executive in the late 1970s; Jeffrey Campbell, Pepsi-Cola's national marketing senior vice president, moved by Smith from Burger King marketing onto a special fast-track program as a Northeast regional vice president, and positioned by Smith for his eventual move to the Burger King presidency; Norman Hill, a Flagstar human resources director whom Smith brought to Burger King and later to Perkins; Zane Leshner, a former Taco Bell operations chief, promoted by Smith from Burger King legal counsel to international president and then franchising vice president; Charles Boppell, former president of Hudson's Grill of America, Inc., whom Smith moved from Pizza Hut to the Taco Bell presidency in 1980; Arthur Gunther, Miami Subs marketing executive vice president, moved by Smith to Pizza Hut president; and Mike Guido, whom Smith promoted from Burger King operations director to research and development vice president, where Guido excelled with a new engineering and quality assurance program.

Almost inevitably, chains are quick to say, "Sorry, we don't have any openings or any budget for you, so we can't do anything." Often, this amounts to losing a real opportunity. Smith was one of the few who dared to hire promising talent even when there was no opening, then waited for a spot to develop that would permit the maximum use of the person's ability. Once Smith had the person aboard, he encouraged him and positioned him to grow into or move into a key top position. Although some of the executives mentioned earlier would say they made it themselves and would not give Smith full credit, he clearly was helpful in their emerging from the pack.

Smith's mentor was Fred Turner, who in 1965 was a McDonald's operations vice president and was impressed with the 25-year-old Smith when the two met by chance at a neighbor's house in a small Minnesota town. Smith quickly was on his way to a McDonald's assistant manager's job in California—thanks to Turner's and his own enthusiasm and belief in McDonald's potential. Turner, whose mentor was founder Ray Kroc from almost the very beginning in the mid-1950s, would go on to become McDonald's chief executive.

When it comes to motivation, nothing succeeds like grooming others to grow and move upward—if the CEO has the desire, confidence, and ability to do this.

The Customer Is King or Queen

An absolute dedication to doing everything for the customer's benefit and not for the short-term benefit of executives or stockholders.

"Don't worry about what the customer's question is. The answer always is yes."

—*Bill Post, president,*
Levy Restaurants, Chicago

HIGHLIGHTS

- "Larry chairs" win customers
- Legendary storying around
- Unstinting dedication to customer
- Turning embarrassments to riches
- Servers create the image
- Extra touches
- Price-value always
- Passion and emotion
- Learn from retailers
- Treat customers like your family
- Think customers, not finances

Great customer service beyond the call of duty is the number one requirement for keeping a restaurant chain on top. It is based on

61

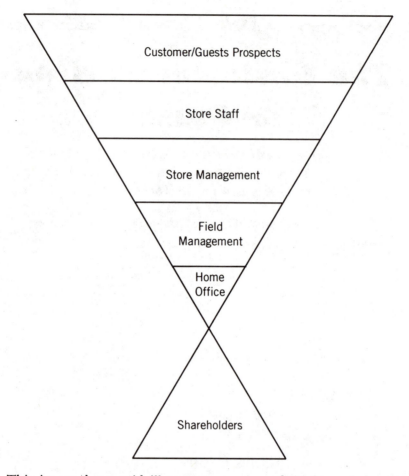

Customer/Guests Prospects

Store Staff

Store Management

Field Management

Home Office

Shareholders

This inverted pyramid illustrates one way of thinking about the philosophy of winning chains.

the concept of a bottom-up pyramid in which the customer is at the top, and the manager and employees are there to serve the customer, not merely to satisfy themselves. Just doing what is expected is not enough; the restaurant must provide something unusual or unexpected in the way of service that will stay in the customer's mind in contrast to what the competition offers.

CHAIN-STYLE HOSPITALIANO

The chain restaurant industry has its own goodwill ambassadors who keep the pyramid inverted, with the customer at the top. Ron Magruder, president of The Olive Garden Italian restaurants chain, emphasizes a "Hospitaliano" service culture and legendary service.

One day a heavyset man named Larry phoned Magruder, who also happens to be heavy. Larry told Ron how he had waited almost 90 minutes just to get a seat at an Olive Garden restaurant—only to discover that there wasn't a single chair or booth where he could sit comfortably. All the chairs had arms, and the booths simply weren't big enough.

Magruder responded by having his staff contact The Olive Garden's chair manufacturer and ask it to redesign some 1,000 chairs without arms so that anyone could fit in them. Within seven weeks, three such chairs, dubbed "Larry chairs," were in each of The Olive Garden's restaurants, and the heaviest people now had a choice. Then Magruder confidently had one of his executives contact Larry to invite him back to the restaurant with his family as guests. Imagine Magruder's surprise when Larry proudly related that because of the incident he had lost 50 pounds in the interim and now could fit into The Olive Garden's regular chairs.

Larry and his family did come to the restaurant, and they became regular customers. Because such heroics that go beyond the call of duty are repeated in various ways, it is no wonder that The Olive Garden has been able to keep its seats a lot fuller than most other chains. The value of the incident is what Magruder likes to call "storying around," whereby legends are created and heavily publicized to all employees. "They know we're going to go the extra mile for any customer no matter what the situation, that we really care." This is leading by direct example, and it works. Employees then try to outdo the boss in heroic deeds they can perform for the customer.

The true legend of the Larry chairs is often retold among The Olive Garden restaurant employees, who see this as a symbol of their chain's dedication to pleasing the customer no matter what it takes. We personally know this for a fact, because whenever we ask Olive Garden restaurant employees who Larry was and why there are chairs without arms, they tell us the whole story in specific detail. It is also important to note that The Olive Garden's regular chairs, which have arms, are extremely wide, on rollers, and comfortable.

Another legend created by Magruder precipitated his maxim, "Thou shalt not run out of birthday cakes." The Olive Garden typically serves some one million birthday cakes annually. When Magruder discovered one day that a restaurant had somehow run out of birthday cakes and was planning to serve cheesecake slices for birthdays that evening, he took drastic action. He ordered a plane to fly 400 miles to pick up the necessary birthday cakes immediately, and he made sure that word of these exploits quickly got around the entire chain.

Magruder does not hesitate to invent new rules spontaneously to solve a customer problem. On one occasion he was in a restaurant when an order was placed for a fruit salad. "Fruit salad is not on our menu, so we can't do it," the chef said. "Fine, let's make one ourselves," Magruder decided. He and the chef simply mixed together some fruit that was in stock and served the fruit salad. Voila! A new Olive Garden item was created. Rather than bothering with any corporate decision on what to charge for the fruit salad, Magruder asked the manager to decide, and thus a price of $4.50 suddenly emerged.

Other examples of Magruder precepts include: "Never tell customers that we don't take reservations, but find ways to get them seated anyway"; "Be fully prepared with umbrellas to give customers when it suddenly rains or snows." In late 1993, Magruder launched a new program whereby cassette tapes for every part of the menu are always available at each of the chain's restaurants for customers with vision problems or who just prefer to hear the menu at their own pace rather than read it.

He fervently believes in Burger King's slogan, "Have it your way," for the customer. Unfortunately, Burger King and too many other chains don't implement that slogan nearly enough.

Chicago-based Levy Restaurants has its own program with a mission statement entirely dedicated to "winning one customer at a time." As president Bill Post describes it to employees: "Don't worry about what the customer's question is. The answer always is yes. What is the question? The customer is always right! Be sure to give customers free food samples at your own discretion."

Levy Legends means taking the initiative, having pride in one's work, being creative in the job, and, above all, being an inspiration to the team through dedication and loyalty. The basic winning strategies taught in Levy Restaurants include smiling whenever possible, remembering the customer's preferences for next time, specifically inviting the customer back, knowing and using the customer's name, and doing a little extra for the customer. Annual Levy Legend awards are given to employees who excel in these principles. Post personally knows the immense value of making the customer king or queen. One day a cashier at McDonald's Chicago Rock'n Roll unit recognized Post's son, who was celebrating his fifth birthday. He had gone to a Chicago Cubs game at Wrigley Field, and hence had come to McDonald's. By chance, the cashier overheard that it was the child's birthday. Taking the initiative, the cashier got a group of employees to sing "Happy Birthday" and made sure that the boy and his friends got free sundaes. This attitude reflects Levy Restaurants' philosophy of "giving your job, your employees, and your customers a sense of passion and love."

To make the system work, Levy Restaurants uses the reverse-pyramid structure, designating its guests as bosses, followed by the service people, restaurant management, headquarters executives, and, finally, the chairman.

John Farquharson, ARA Global Food Services chairman, has his own heroic story to tell of how, on the opening day of a major athletic event, ARA, which excels in foodservice management and noncommercial operations, was to serve dinner to 1,000 persons, including the President of the United States. But the owner of the team, who had personally picked the menu, suddenly decided he did not want one of the dishes served cold and requested that it be presented hot, just five minutes before dinner was to be served. ARA's manager on the scene made sure that the item was pulled and put in chafing dishes to be served hot. Somehow, he got it ready in time—with at least a minute to spare.

Another challenge arose when the visiting prime minister of an allied country was going to be guest of honor at a dinner for more than 1,000 persons. The dinner's host had chosen veal chops as the entree, and ARA had ordered more than 1,000 and was ready to cook them when the host suddenly decided he preferred salmon. This was just two hours before the entree was to be served—it seemed like an impossible task. Yet the manager pulled it off, somehow finding enough salmon steaks, serving them on time, and receiving rave reviews from the assembled dignitaries.

On another major occasion, ARA had to perform emergency deadline services for 10 times as many people as expected. At an annual stockholders meeting for 10,000, a sit-down dinner was served under a tent and the entree was being made with a cucumber sauce. Upon serving the salad, the ARA manager for the event was suddenly told that one of the guests of honor was violently allergic to cucumbers and how pleased they were that no cucumbers were in the salad. Without missing a beat, the manager and his crew raced to a local market and managed to buy enough zucchini to use in the sauce for the entree. The allergic guest of honor was so grateful for the manager's thoughtfulness that he is now one of ARA's leading clients.

Such feats are all in a day's (or night's) work for John Farquharson and his staff. But any contract feeder or chain has to be able to do a turnabout at a moment's notice and make it look effortless, much like a graceful outfielder making a sensational catch look easy. In reality, it isn't easy. It takes unstinting dedication to giving the customer what he or she wants, not what we like or what we think the customer should like. It is well worth the effort and is the only real way to achieve a distinct advantage and beat the competition.

How about this one? Princess Stephanie of Monaco craves the pastries and coffee of the San Francisco-based Oh-La-La gourmet coffee chain—so much that she "simply can't live without them." They beat any of the tasty treats available in her own kingdom. Thus Oh-La-La president Howard Berkowitz delights in over-nighting a constant flow of pastry and coffee supplies for Princess Stephanie. The benefits of this kind of heroic service are twofold for any chain: (1) pleasing the customer and gaining the business, and (2) being able to weave these true tales into legends that sell employees and other customers alike on a chain's absolute commitment to the consumer.

Former TGI Friday's president Richard Rivera loved to spread stories and legends about his chain as well. One of his favorite tales, which he often related to trainees, is about a woman who called a TGI's in San Diego and said she wanted to bring her boss and nine other employees for lunch to observe "Boss's Day." (This was an interesting twist from the usual "Secretary's Day.") And what could be done special for the boss? The story goes that the restaurant employees spread a big red carpet, tied up a bunch of balloons, passed champagne around the table, and hosted a fete that thrilled the boss, his secretary, and their associates. Rivera still takes pride in relating this story and, perhaps, embellishes it a little with each telling.

JUST SAY YES

Pleasing the customer means always saying yes, no matter how crazy a request may seem—within reasonable limits, of course. "Our restaurants never say no to any customer request no matter what," declares Lee Cohn, president of Phoenix-based Big 4 Restaurants, which has grown to some 10 restaurants as a direct result of this policy.

Tampa-based Outback maintains complete flexibility toward the customer and works hard to "always say yes for whatever they want," chairman Chris Sullivan asserts. "The customer wants to be accommodated and doesn't care about our problems in doing it." He cited an example of an Outback manager running a mile to a liquor store to get a bottle of champagne for a couple celebrating their 55th anniversary. Besides keeping managers and employees in good physical shape, this type of running on behalf of customers shows how much a chain cares.

Excellent service also may mean going into uncharted territories. Sullivan recalls being asked to cater a 400-person black-tie dinner at Tampa in the spring of 1992 and accepting the challenge with some trepidation. "Outback had never catered anything except cookouts," he says, "but we tried this and pulled it off successfully, opening up new horizons for us." Just a week later, Outback catered a fund-raising dinner for Ted Turner and Jane Fonda at the Atlanta Zoo and found that its steaks and service again could please upper-crust customers.

Eateries' Vincent Orza relates some dramatic examples of the exceptional customer service he emphasizes. One of Garfield's managers noticed that a regular customer had not ordered any dinner although the three other people in her party had ordered. He asked her why she was not eating, and she responded that she just was not in the mood for anything. Finally, after a little prodding by the manager, she admitted that she wanted only an A & W chili dog. The manager promptly sprang into action, asked another manager to cover his shift, and ran to a nearby food court to buy a chili dog. He raced back and surprised the customer by routinely presenting it at the same time the other meals were served.

In a real winning stroke, Garfield's closed one of its restaurants to the public on February 14, 1991, during the Gulf War and invited the families of overseas soldiers to spend Valentine's evening as Garfield's dinner guests. Some 400 persons attended, and the event was therapeutic for both the guests and the staff. "We wanted to let Garfield's be the families' Valentine while their Valentines were away," recalls Orza. Those customers who may have been disappointed that they could not go to Garfield's that particular evening understood the importance of the event and viewed it as a plus for Garfield's.

Orza has codified his customer-oriented philosophy with these 10 commandments for his chain:

1. The guest comes first.

2. The guest is always right.

3. Anticipate the guest's needs.

4. Whatever the guest wants, the answer is yes.

5. Every table is your table when the guest wants something.

6. Employees should look at the restaurant through the guest's eyes.

7. Take a risk—playing it safe means you'll always be second best.

8. Employees should treat the restaurant as if they are the owners.

9. Seek perfection in customer service, and always strive to be better.

10. Be proud of whatever you do, and try to do it right the first time.

OVERCOMING ADVERSITY

What happens when a customer simply has a bad experience? This was the challenge facing a Spaghetti Warehouse restaurant in Dallas when a family celebrating a special occasion had an atrocious evening there. The general manager and his staff proceeded to more than recoup the damage by creating a really special new night for the family to celebrate in style, including a stretch limousine and free dinners. That family, at first totally disillusioned with the restaurant, became its regular customers.

Little Rock, Arkansas-based TCBY turned around an embarrassing situation when a unit manager's mother died the night before a scheduled birthday party at that unit. When a mother, her birthday daughter, and 12 young friends showed up, there was absolutely nothing ready for the party. The mother, having to leave with all the disappointed children, complained bitterly to the manager and the headquarters office. The manager phoned all 12 children, put together a special cake and party decorations, hired a clown, and showed up at the customer's home later that day with a delivered birthday party that made everyone happy.

Everything that could go wrong did go wrong for a Seattle Godfather's Pizza customer one evening. The pizza that he ordered for himself and his three children was unsatisfactory, and the service was abominable. Herman Cain, president of the chain, heard about it and arranged a special dinner for that family at the very same Godfather's Pizza unit. The family would be guests of the president. Cain hosted the white-tablecloth dinner, and the district manager was the waiter. This time the pizza was superb, the service was perfect, and Cain was an extra-gracious host. The father who was so embittered from his previous Godfather's Pizza experience was so pleased that he wrote Cain a thank you letter.

Cain did not take any action against the manager who had been on duty the night of the catastrophic first episode or against the district manager who was responsible. Instead, he showed the district manager how to train the managers and assistant managers in better customer service. The story became a positive legend for the entire Godfather's Pizza chain.

Customers don't easily forget these extra courtesies. David Wachtel, former president of Nashville-based Shoney's Restaurants, delights in recalling a 1959 incident in which a family ordered two luscious takeout strawberry pies from a Shoney's restaurant where Wachtel was working. On the way home to a dinner party, the family had an accident and the pies were ruined. When they called the store to see if the pies could be replaced, owner Ray Danner had Wachtel personally deliver two strawberry pies to their house. Naturally, these customers and their guests became regular Shoney's customers. Perhaps not surprisingly they became Wachtel's loyal customers three decades later when he acquired O'Charley's, and they later invested in O'Charley's when it went public.

Sometimes too much of a good thing can be a challenge. Tom McFall, former chairman of Hamburger Hamlet Restaurants, fondly remembers opening day at Crystal City, Virginia, across from Washington, D.C., when 600 people were already lined up outside as the 250-seat restaurant initially opened its doors at 12:01 P.M. The restaurant quickly ran out of burgers, although the customers did not run out of patience and waited to be served. The manager jumped into his station wagon, zipped around the corner to a supermarket, managed to purchase 250 pounds of hamburger meat, and survived the ordeal, with most of the customers wanting to return again.

PERSONAL CONTACT

An ideal way to project a restaurant's dedication is through the server, the one person who has the most direct contact with customers—or certainly should. The server in many chain restaurants is emerging as a personality in his or her own right, occasionally to the annoyance of the customer but mostly as a plus that adds to the customer's enjoyment of the experience.

Len Schlesinger, the Harvard professor who is a service guru and once was an Au Bon Pain executive, sees immense value in "waiters or waitresses whose relationship with customers absolutely transcends the restaurants in which they serve." Customers have told Schlesinger the only reason they go to a particular restaurant is to talk with the waiter or waitress. He figures that the kind of customer loyalty and repeat business built by this rapport translates into $5,000 in extra weekly profits for a particular restaurant.

"We hear more about our servers and their interesting personalities than anything else we hear from today's sophisticated consumers," observe California Pizza Kitchen (CPK) partners Larry Flax and Rick Rosenfield. "The server becomes part of the table scene. Our food quality is a given, but the interaction of the server with customers is the point of difference."

The success of such interaction hinges on hiring servers with some sort of "people skills" in the first place and then training them to implement these skills in relating to the customer. CPK gives a two-week classroom training program that includes lectures and discussions to stress the importance of server interaction and to give employees the confidence to carry it out effectively.

In their 1991 book, *Service That Sells,* PENCOM president Jim Sullivan and Premier Ventures president Phil Roberts urge restaurant employees to learn, remember, and use guests' names and to treat other employees as internal customers. They warn against some of the mortal sins we encounter too often in restaurants such as idle servers holding a discussion, failure to acknowledge waiting guests, pouring coffee from a stained coffee pot, and answering the phone with a too-simple "hold, please."

The model we admire is one promulgated by Dennis Berkowitz, the irrepressible president of San Francisco-based Max's Restaurants. His credo for all his restaurants is based on Max's (his late father) laws and includes these classics: "This restaurant is run for the enjoyment and pleasure of our customers, not the convenience of the staff or the owners"; "You must get your mustard and ketchup before your burger, sandwich, or fries"; "If your fries are soggy or aren't crisp the way you like them, send them back and the kitchen should get the message"; "We bring pastrami and ice cream sauces from New York City. Eat here, and save the airfare"; "This is a bad place for a diet but also a good place for a diet"; "Substitutions are fine, and don't be bashful about asking"; "If you are a single diner and are greeted with the expression, 'Just one?' dinner is on us."

CONSISTENCY

Some chain executives don't think in terms of dramatic customer-service experiences but rather of consistent excellence. "Instead of encouraging and rewarding those one-in-a-million experiences," says Sonic Corporation chairman Stephen Lynn, "our goal is to maintain a constant level of superior service, to deliver cutting-edge service with each and every transaction. That's our marketable point of difference and our competitive edge over the rest of the quick-service restaurant segment." Sonic owner-managers are empowered to make decisions on the spot and to pass on this philosophy to car-hops and crews, encouraging them to use their own judgment in solving problems.

Irvine, California-based Claim Jumper Restaurants, reflecting a theme of the Gold Rush era, offers a consistent extra by weighing each child who arrives there to eat and charging only a nickel per pound when the child orders from the Little Jumpers children's menu. Actually, there is an understood $3.95 maximum no matter how much the child weighs.

This gimmick not only provides the family with a perception of price-value, but also adds to the child's enjoyment of the experience. Most of the children love getting weighed at Claim Jumper, and the families get a kick out of it too. No wonder president Craig Nickoloff is chalking up $5 million average annual unit sales for the chain.

INDEPENDENT INITIATIVE

Chains can learn from the price-value orientation of Frannie's lunchroom in Yates Center, Kansas. With a $1 price for a full meal, it is the leading attraction in the town, which has just 1,900 people and is 100 miles east of Wichita. An average of 200 customers flock daily to the lunch, which includes one hot entree with a salad and corn on the cob, or a sandwich platter. Running a tight menu and wasting no ingredients, Frannie Ward keeps food and labor costs low. Although she won't get rich, she operates at a reasonable profit margin and shows what price-value and a simple homespun menu can do in drawing traffic from a small area. Chains could not afford to have such a low price, but they certainly can afford to think of the customer's needs first when picking menu items and pricing them. The sales line and the bottom line can only benefit from this type of thinking.

Chains can also learn from independents that do unique and surprising things to put a glow in their customers' eyes. Special gimmicks create customer excitement and high volumes; for instance, a New York City restaurant features a strolling musician on Valentine's Day; a Newton, Kansas, Mexican cafe builds a half-ton burrito that stretches as long as five football fields; and a franchised Church's chicken unit in Center Point, Texas, offers a drive-through windshield washing service.

These ideas spread a restaurant's fame. Chains have a critical need to project an individual image and overcome the notion that they are standard and boring. Again, legends can be created and spread, with tremendous results.

One day in the late 1950s, at a small cowboy restaurant called the Pinnacle Peak Patio near Scottsdale, Arizona, some men dropped in all dressed in business attire. To make his point extra-clear, the owner—who wanted to keep everything casual—ordered them to take off their ties. When they refused, the owner took a chapter from the Old West tradition, cut off their ties with a butcher knife, and stapled the ties to the ceiling. That legend has grown bigger each year and is a major reason that the restaurant's 1,600 seats are often packed. The owner still cuts off the tie of anyone daring to enter wearing one, which some do just to test the rule, to the point where some 1 million clipped ties of every variety hang from the ceiling and walls today. It is arguably the largest collection of ties in the world.

Today this is just part of the restaurant's entertainment, and business cards are attached to many of these ties. But Pinnacle Peak has other innovations. When a customer asks for a well-done steak, he or she is first given a leathery boot on a plate. Still, Pinnacle Peak's unique niche is its reputation throughout Arizona and beyond as "that place where they cut off your tie." Perhaps Pinnacle Peak could be a successful chain, or at least a minichain! No one would be bored.

The unexpected often carries the day. At La Nicoise, a French tablecloth restaurant in Georgetown, Washington, D.C., waiters and waitresses race from table to table and provide the fastest service in town. Later in the evening, they offer their own songs and skits for the customers' entertainment. Many restaurants are show biz, and chains can be too. Singing servers are featured at a number of restaurants, and opera singers sometimes perform, so the food isn't always the main attraction. At Molly Murphy's House of Fine Repute in Oklahoma City, Mickey Mouse, Superman, and other uniformed servers thrill their customers. Unfortunately, sometimes the play becomes the thing and the restaurant and the food suffer in these gimmicky situations. This is probably why they stand out as independents but don't offer a broad enough appeal to be chain-able.

Certainly, chains of all types can prosper from the type of exceptional service that one often finds at independents. Isadore Sharp, chief executive of the Toronto-based Four Seasons luxury hotel chain, believes in spending money to give business travelers extra amenities that go beyond a free overnight shoeshine or an upgrade to a suite. Sharp, who far more often is found traveling to his hotels around the world than in the office, has propelled the Four Seasons to the number one position in hotel luxury chains—just a slice ahead of the Ritz-Carlton, although the Ritz can claim number one status at some of its properties, especially when it, too, offers meaningful extra amenities.

Harvard's Len Schlesinger likes to tell of an 84-year-old security guard at Harrah's hotel-casino in Reno, Nevada, who always carries a supply of extra money in his pocket to help people who have lost their money get to their next destination. He inspires other employees at the casino to show understanding for the customers, mostly all of whom need it at one time or another. "You can't calculate the economic value someone like this has to an organization," Schlesinger declares.

PASSION NEEDED

Mike Hurst, owner of the 15th Street Fisheries, Ft. Lauderdale, Florida, and former National Restaurant Association (NRA) president, believes in hiring only people who have emotion and passion for the restaurant business and the customer. He learned his most valuable lesson when he was 12 years old, washing glasses in a restaurant. He simply could not keep an adequate pace and worked two hours past his scheduled shift. He apologized to his boss and also asked how many customers had been in the restaurant. "Almost 200 more than I expected," the boss replied. "We're all winners on this one."

Ever since that day, Hurst has always asked any complaining employees at his restaurant: "How many customers did we have here tonight? Did we break the record?" He knows that getting the customers in the seats and keeping the seats full constitute a restaurant's prime mission—a lesson that some chains still haven't learned as they worry about every type of financial factor and profit margin before focusing on how many repeat and new customers are being attracted to each restaurant.

Hurst offers some other valuable lessons for chain operators—namely, that food is fun and that the customer will try tasty, unusual items if they are presented with pizazz. But he constantly reminds his staff that "the gift of friendship is even more important than good food or wonderful decor" and that the greatest compliment he can receive is when customers ask him, "Where did you get all the nice people who work here?"

Often the boss has to be a demanding customer in establishing and maintaining the highest customer service standards at restaurants. "I've always viewed myself as the most critical customer who could possibly visit one of our restaurants," declares Ray Danner, senior chairman and a founder of Shoney's, Inc. "Our success is determined strictly by how much we benefit and satisfy our customers with innovation and personal service."

RETAIL PACESETTERS

Retailing provides some excellent examples of the positive results of doing everything for the benefit of the customer. Seattle-based Nordstrom, Inc. department stores empowers its employees around the country to use their best judgment at all times—without fear of any penalties. This philosophy is implemented through the concept of the inverted pyramid which, in department store parlance, puts the customer first as the leader, the store sales staff of employees next, then the department manager, and, finally, the buyers and sales-support people. If we take this model to its logical conclusion, Nordstrom's corporate chief executive is at the bottom of the pyramid—at least in theory.

Among the things that Nordstrom's employees smilingly and voluntarily do for customers without being asked are carrying merchandise outside to the car, reserving merchandise ordered without requiring deposits, calling customers to alert them whenever any merchandise goes on sale, doing most apparel alterations free, and writing personal thank you notes when customers, especially new customers, purchase any items. This is why the merchandise is extra special to many customers, even if it may be a bit more expensive than that of competitors. The price-value is in the careful personal attention and recognition of the customer as an individual. No wonder, more often than not, customers feel that Nordstrom's is worth the price—something they don't necessarily feel about other department stores whose merchandise may be as appealing but whose attitude tends to be less caring. The store salespeople dress very well because they have pride in themselves, in Nordstrom's, and in serving the customer.

These values are all built into Nordstrom's culture, which starts with a personal-touch service staff in each store whose entire job is to work with customers in putting together special wardrobe and makeup requests, aiding disabled customers, and helping employees to carry out the full customer service mission. "The customer is everyone's boss," asserts Linda Jarnig, personal-touch manager of Nordstrom's Oak Brook, Illinois, store outside Chicago. "Everything my personal-touch staff does is designed to help the customer. Much of this is done by special appointment so that we have the time to work with each customer's special needs."

Does all this sound like a pipe dream? Admittedly, there inevitably are glitches in the system, where service is nothing special or is even notably noncaring and unsatisfactory. But that is the exception rather than the rule. More often, Nordstrom's service is exemplified by two specific instances provided by Jarnig:

One evening in 1992 at about 8:30 P.M., just a half-hour before closing time, Nordstrom's Oak Brook store got a phone call from a desperate businesswoman whose luggage had not shown up on her flight to O'Hare Airport. She was dressed casually, she said, had no other clothes or anything else with her, and had a crucial meeting scheduled early the next morning. She had checked into the Drake Hotel on Chicago's North Michigan Avenue and had tried to find a store that could outfit her. But everything was closed by then. Having heard of Nordstrom's reputation, she called their only Chicago area store, in suburban Oak Brook. The alert Nordstrom receptionist taking her call immediately referred it to the personal-service department, which promptly swung into action. Within a half hour, or perhaps a few minutes after the store's official closing time, Nordstrom's had assembled an appropriate dress, hose, shoes, and cosmetics.

The only remaining question was who would personally deliver the $600 order to the woman, who had given her credit card number when she called in. The answer came quickly: An employee who was traveling home to the North Michigan Avenue area said she would be glad to do this good deed. So it was that by 10:00 P.M. the desperate businesswoman, who had seemed trapped in an insoluble nightmare, received everything she needed for a presentable appearance at her important meeting.

In another instance not long ago, a young man called the same store's personal-touch department and asked them to do something special to pave the way for him to propose to his girlfriend. Sure enough, the department created a scenario and phoned the lucky young woman to tell her she had been selected to receive free makeup, facial, and manicure services and a dress of her choice, followed by dinner with a companion of her choice at Bistro Banlieu in suburban Lombard. The woman happily appeared with the companion of her choice (guess who?) on the appointed afternoon and was made to look extra beautiful and outfitted in a stunning dress. Off the happy couple went to dinner, where the young woman (of course) accepted the young man's proposal. Presumably, the couple are living happily ever after and are loyal Nordstrom's customers. The point of these true stories is the lengths to which Nordstrom's will go to please customers and the ingenuity their people show in implementing unsurpassed customer service.

We can learn other customer-oriented lessons from the Atlanta-based Home Depot chain, which excels in the home-center field and in wooing the customer with exceptional service. "Every customer has to be treated like your mother, your father, your sister, or your brother," declares chief executive Bernard Marcus. He likes to greet customers personally and chat with them in some of the rapidly growing chain's 250 stores and enjoys it even more when his employees do this. Marcus launched Home Depot after being fired as president at Handy Dan home centers, perhaps for trying to cater too much to the customer and thereby spending money to do it. Handy Dan eventually went out of business.

He has created basic home centers with no frills and plenty of price-value. Each salesperson on a Home Depot floor proudly wears a bright apron, which states in big, bold letters: "Hi, I'm (full name), a Home Depot stockholder." The salespeople are trained to build relationships with customers and to learn as much as they can about home-repair equipment. Product-knowledge sessions are held weekly at every store so that employees learn every aspect of home repair and can help customers in any department.

Some of the do-it-yourself customers who thrive on Home Depot were previously unable to even install a new washer on a faucet or hammer nails straight. An essential part of employees' job descriptions is that they are to find a way for the customer to do any task for less money and spend less for needed supplies whenever possible. That is a long way from the "trade 'em up" philosophy of other retail chains—and of some restaurant chains.

Two famous legends at Home Depot are of one customer who was set to spend upward of $20,000 to renovate a kitchen and two bathrooms through Sears but did the job just as well, if not better, for $5,000 through Home Depot, and of another customer ready to spend at least $150 for a home-repair job, who was encouraged to spend only $5 to complete the project by doing the work in a much simpler way.

Marcus once refused to accept Ross Perot as a $2 million investor when Perot told him to get rid of his leased Cadillac. "If Ross Perot is already so involved in the company, to this detail, I won't be able to run the business," Marcus decided. By the way, he agreed with Perot's point that "a company car is an irresponsible expense if you're preaching value to customers" and gave up the Cadillac. Perot now can be seen shopping regularly at the Home Depot store in Plano, Texas, near Dallas and publicly says that it's his favorite store.

Typical shoppers go to Home Depot an average of 30 times

annually and spend an average of $1,100 a year, for estimated life-time Home Depot expenditures of $25,000 each. When one multi-plies these loyal repeat customers by all the friends they tell about Home Depot, the effect is monumental. The company has shown an incredible 45 percent 10-year return on investment and in a recent fiscal year achieved $363 million net income on $7.1 billion revenues.

Wal-Mart, the number one volume retailer, is another shining example of how personalized service and the implied recognition of individual customers can win against complacent, impersonal ser-vice as represented by Sears and Kmart, both of which were over-taken by Wal-Mart. Although Wal-Mart's distinct advantage seems to be low-cost assortments, its real leadership stems from superior service. An employee in each store is designated to give a friendly greeting to every customer who enters. Although that doesn't actually happen all the time, it happens often enough to bring a smile to many customers' faces and to keep them shopping at Wal-Mart rather than at Kmart or Sears.

CHANGING DEMOGRAPHICS

Chains must become more aware of the demographic implications of a far more diverse customer base, with the numbers of African Americans, Hispanics, and various ethnic groups constantly grow-ing in the United States. This may signal the need for more ethnic chain restaurants, but it also suggests the necessity of being far more customer oriented in general and with each group in particu-lar. When it comes to foodservice patronage, Hispanics are the fast-est emerging market. Of adults surveyed by the National Restau-rant Association (NRA), 53 percent of Hispanics frequented a foodservice establishment on a typical day in 1993, as compared with 43 percent of whites and 39 percent of African Americans. Almost the entire Hispanic ratio lead is established at lunch, with breakfast and dinner running close to even among the three groups in the percentage of those eating away from home.

Although Hispanics account for a relatively small proportion of the total U.S. population, they are a rapidly increasing proportion and one with major implications for the foodservice industry. Asians too are a fast-growing element, and more flavorful, spicy foods are needed to meet their needs if the chain restaurant industry is to be truly customer driven.

Customer traffic patterns also are changing as consumers seek convenience-oriented foodservice. Take-out and delivery are showing the fastest growth, while conventional on-premise restaurant traffic keeps declining. Chain operators can capitalize with more takeout and delivery, as well as using fax-delivery services and outside services such as Herndon, Virginia-based Takeout Taxi. Taylor Devine, president of Takeout Taxi, insists on providing maximum service for the customers as well as the restaurants for which Takeout Taxi delivers. "Every first-time customer gets a call to measure all aspects of satisfaction or lack thereof," Devine says, "and 10 percent of some 300,000 individual customers in our database are called on a steady basis to get their continued reactions. We get regular customers involved by having them try new menu items from the restaurants we serve."

EXCEED EXPECTATIONS

Providing service beyond expectations is the key to building customer loyalty in an age when many customers will readily switch to the restaurant across the street or down the block. As Chevys president Mike Hislop expresses it: "Anyone can provide good service. We don't think that's good enough. Our philosophy is to go well beyond that, to give our guests more than they would get anywhere else and more than they would normally expect from us."

Hislop and his managers follow through on their Fresh Mex pledges to their customers to serve flour tortillas within three minutes of baking; to blend salsa hourly from freshly charred tomatoes, onions, and jalapenos; to never serve any frozen fish, chicken, or beef; to allow no cans on the premises except those for pure olive oil;

and to use no MSG (monosodium glutamate), food preservatives, or extenders. Mutual trust results between the customer and Chevys and, it is hoped, a bond of respect.

When Chevys had to close its restaurant in Stockton, California, a loyal Chevys customer pleaded with the company to reopen there, but that was not feasible. Instead, Chevys Northern California operations vice president Gregg Landauer checked the next closest Chevys and arranged for a limousine to pick up the loyal customer and drive him and three guests to that location, where they were treated to dinner. Now the customer and his friends have found a new favorite Chevys restaurant.

Making things fresher and healthier is a customer priority. "Our symbol is an apple," says Rockville, Maryland-based Silver Diner president Robert Giaimo, "but we give customers a choice. We stress everything made fresh, lower-cholesterol items, less salt, more natural herbs, but also hot fudge sundaes (for health-conscious customers who want to splurge and for those who merely want to indulge themselves)."

Whataburger, a regional Southwestern chain, also tries to emphasize exceptional service as one of the cornerstones of its long-term success. When its drive-throughs weren't measuring up to potential in the early 1980s, the chain enhanced and enlarged the drive-through windows, illuminated them better, assigned special expediters to speed the service, and launched 24-hour drive-through service "because that's what customers wanted," recalls Alan Stoner, who retired as operations senior vice president in 1993 after a 39-year career at Whataburger.

An 800 phone number that enables customers to comment about service is advisable for any chain. Whataburger tries to phone customers directly, within 12 hours at the most, if they call to complain about such matters as French fries being served cold. The Whataburger central 800 number enables customers to express their positive or negative feelings, resulting in a feedback process that has steadily improved service. Dissatisfied customers who have no easy feedback number to call to bring their feelings into the open tend to simply not return to the particular restaurant. It is crucial to give customers an opportunity to voice their feelings.

The traditional doggie bag can tell a lot about a restaurant. The bigger a chain's bags, the more value customers are getting. Although certain customers resent large-sized portions, most—although they won't always publicly admit it—like the idea that they are getting enhanced value when they can take home a healthy part of their order. A chain has to keep this practice in perspective and balance, but offering a doggie bag can be an important image builder, ensuring consumers' perception (and perhaps the reality) that they are getting a bargain.

Customer defections are a menace that restaurant chains can ill afford in an era when consumers are more sophisticated, appreciate the difference between good and bad service, and will desert a non-caring restaurant at a moment's notice while also turning many acquaintances against the restaurant. Defections can multiply like a plague. "We want to find disgruntled customers or any that would leave us and correct the problem before it is too late," asserts Sfuzzi president Robert Colombo. "Our real goal is zero defections."

Yet we still see restaurants—of chain and otherwise—operated for the benefit of owners' personal preferences or egos. These are the restaurants where, rather than the answer being yes all the time, it is almost inevitably no. No, we can't substitute rice for potatoes. No, you can only have apple sauce with that dish.

The winners are operations driven and customer driven, not numbers driven. "You don't make money in the restaurant office, you make it in the restaurants," declares Wendy's chairman-CEO James Near. "Let's help the woman who is driving around with two children and just $12 in her pocket, by guaranteeing that we'll make it possible for her and the children to eat a full meal at Wendy's for the lowest possible price—and that's under $12." Near's persistent dedication to the customer on pricing and everything else sparked Wendy's spectacular turnaround in the early 1990s after it had seemingly lost sight of the customer.

Taco Bell's John Martin's consistent emphasis on value pricing for the customer, with a range of items anywhere from 49¢ to $2.99

for combinations, indeed has revolutionized the fast-food industry in favor of the customer, as well as touched off full-scale price wars.

Chains operated for the benefit of their customers, with the flexibility and desire to please their customers virtually every time, will win against those run for the benefit of executives and stock-holders. "Have it your way" decisively beats "Have it our way."

oooooo **Link Four** oooooo

Keep Your Eye on the Ball

Sticking to an operational focus that is not diverted by anything.

"Once you chain a restaurant, you lose the Broadway, movie-making sense of excitement."
—*Alan Stillman, founder of TGI Friday's, who prefers a group of individual restaurants with a full focus on each one (but would still love to "chain" his Smith & Wollensky steakhouse concept)*

HIGHLIGHTS

- Conglomerate problems
- Replicating no easy matter
- General Mills, PepsiCo, Inc., Brinker International excel
- Melman, Levy set the pace
- Second and third concepts proliferate
- Multiunit independents
- Mixed-brand combos
- Saturation forces multiconcepts
- Consistency a necessity
- Flexibility crucial

CONSISTENT EXECUTION

No matter how great customer service or any other aspect of a restaurant chain or group may be, it is a serious challenge to maintain consistency in all aspects from one unit to another. This is not as easy as it sounds and is one reason that chains sometimes demand that franchisees toe the mark in adhering to the company's basic menu and principles, or else face having their units taken over by the company or by another franchisee.

Initiative can be allowed within this framework, and there should be room for popular local or regional items. But a customer has to know that no matter which McDonald's he or she goes to, it will have the high standards expected. Just one bad experience is enough to turn off a customer. While McDonald's has prospered by standing for consistency, Burger King has typified uneven quality. One never really knows what to anticipate from one Burger King to the next, and that has been a major problem plaguing the chain. A business person or tourist should receive the same quality and service in Dubuque, Iowa, as in Chicago or New York City. Yet it often does not happen that way, much to a chain's and the customer's consternation.

As ARA Global Food Services chairman John Farquharson, discussing his giant foodservice management company, declares: "Meeting the client's expectations account after account, year after year, is a necessity. Measuring up to those expectations—whatever they might be—so consistently that you become recognized as the best is the road to leadership in the contract dining service business."

Eateries' Vincent Orza keeps his chain consistently focused, he says, "by continuing to upgrade and improve our product, place, promotion, and price to enhance our operations and the guest's experience." One way Garfield's fulfills its consistent family orientation is by providing crayons and full paper tablecloths so that children can remain pleasantly occupied. "This provides our guests with an unusual and beneficial tool in helping children enjoy their dining experience," Orza says.

Robert Taft, president of Papa Gino's and former Skipper's chief operating officer, thinks implementation and execution are the key challenges in maintaining consistency. "Throughout all our changes at Skipper's, we kept a consistent focus on good execution and evaluated our performance in each restaurant through mystery shoppers, feedback cards, and, most of all, our own visits to the restaurants."

Throughout his 39 years with Whataburger, former operations senior vice president Alan Stoner maintained an unrelenting focus on consistency—"hour by hour, day by day, unit by unit." He always sought the most consistent levels of service, food quality, sanitation, ambiance; it was part of his commitment to total customer satisfaction. To emphasize the point, Stoner kept a big sign on his desk, proclaiming in bold letters: "Consistency." He always shared his philosophy and the importance of consistency by giving "Consistency" signs to visitors and staff members.

However, consistency is elusive. No matter how consistent a chain might think it is or wish to be, breakdowns in food quality and service levels inevitably occur. The important thing is to keep such instances to a minimum and to recognize and correct them when they do occur. Multiunit operations, be they franchised or corporately operated, succeed in direct relationship to the consistent levels of product quality and service maintained from one unit to another.

Sonic chief executive Stephen Lynn valiantly strives to maintain consistency as the best drive-in burger chain. "We want our customers to know that every Sonic drive-in shares that desire. So at each and every drive-in, our customers will find the same look and the same menu as well as the same service, quality, value, and price." Lynn is asking for utopia but deserves credit for trying. Of the some 400 Sonic units that are in the Sonic Franchisee Association (30 percent of the chain's units), there are those that don't have quite the same dedication or quality as others.

"We work very hard to maintain our chainwide consistency," declares Lynn. "We protect it with a single voice to our consumer—our advertising, promotions, and local marketing techniques all work to build and support that consistency. We believe consistency has been and will continue to be a mainstay of our success."

Of course, a chain can be consistently bad and have consistent mediocre quality. That obviously is not what it takes to succeed.

The Cheesecake Factory's David Overton pinpoints food focus, service, location, and decor, in that order, as the four areas where consistency is crucial. If one of these falls short in any of these restaurants noted for excellence, it is enough to make customers take immediate notice—particularly in regard to the first two factors. But it is also important for a chain to project consistency in high-traffic locations that can bring in more customers, and in a decor that may be a bit individualized but makes the customer feel comfortable at being "back home at my favorite restaurant"— whether the customer goes there once a year, once a month, or once or more a week.

It is true that by maintaining a consistent focus, the chain is giving a "chain image." Within that context, it has to find ways to individualize itself so that it does not project a cookie-cutter look.

As Outback's Chris Sullivan notes: "Our Sarasota, Florida, and Cherry Hill, New Jersey, restaurants must be basically the same. But there is room for individuality as ambience and the staff may vary at each restaurant, just as individual personalities always vary."

Strategic planning is not a magic cure-all. It seems to be more successful for planning a year in advance than for the long-range, an area in which so many things are at best a calculated hunch. Flexibility and gut feel also must figure in any strategic plan. Although strategic planning was the rage of the 1970s and early 1980s, some companies grew disillusioned with it and blamed it for poor performance. Yet it can be a valuable tool if kept in proper perspective. It should not be just a list of goals, objectives, and numbers, but rather a plan of practical ideas and concepts that can work.

One problem with strategic planning is that it easily becomes bogged down in technicalities. Consider this early-1993 mission statement that took Tony Roma's three full weeks of effort to develop: "Our mission is to reenergize the concept to be more competitive within casual dining and more appealing to future guests." This was followed by a positioning statement on the menu, identity, design, and people. Soon afterward, Tony Roma's was acquired by National Pizza. If Tony Roma's did not know exactly where it was going all those years and did not know who it was, that was a problem in itself. All leaders can congratulate themselves on drafting perfect mission and positioning statements. But unless they really believe in them and are willing to do what it takes to implement their goals, these strategies are not likely to work.

A consistent focus should be spelled out in simple, direct terms. "Our focus is people," says Silver Diner's Robert Giaimo. "Hiring is the key to everything in this business, and you have to stay focused on people." The chain interviewed 600 potential restaurant general managers in 1992 just to hire 6. That 1 out of 100 ratio may be producing very special people, or the raw material for success. "We give each person a development plan geared to his or her own talents," Giaimo says.

Consistency on pricing is also crucial. Chevys Mexican restaurants president Mike Hislop lowered his prices four times in the early 1990s, and each time customer counts rose—not a coincidence. The real challenge of consistent focus is to outperform the guest's expectations in every sphere.

O'Charley's and Western Sizzlin's David Wachtel calls the ability to maintain a consistent focus "the greatest asset in our industry today. It seems that everyone is suffering from the 'grass is always greener' mentality. History proves that consistency and quality of service win out over gimmicks, promotions, and decor changes. I fight every day to keep my eye on the ball and to maintain focus."

Familiarity and feeling comfortable are important to most customers—even if they want to try new things all the time. So that customers can count on every Johnny Rockets being the same, "we put the tomatoes in exactly the same spot on the hamburger every day every time," asserts president Ronn Teitelbaum. "Baskin-Robbins makes a special Johnny Rockets ice cream for us in all our restaurants. I want all the malts to taste exactly the same too."

Ray Kroc, founder of the McDonald's chain, fervently believed that there should be no surprises for the customer—except perhaps the surprise of food quality and service surpassing expectations. His McDonald's descendants have followed this credo too, and that really is the primary reason they are still on top of the world.

The way Lou Neeb sees it, consistent focus means setting "clear goals on what you are and what you aren't. Don't try to be all things to all people. Steak and Ale (Neeb was Steak and Ale president in the late 1970s) tried to switch menus in the mid-1980s and not include so much steak. They opened the way for Outback, Lone Star, and others to climb into that niche. Meanwhile, Bennigan's cut their quality to save money and opened the way for TGI Friday's, Applebee's, and others to pour into the gap in bigger numbers."

Stephen Elmont is convinced that consistent quality and focus win the fray. "Don't confuse commitment and hard work with achievement," he says. "Don't let emotions get in the way." He fired the chef at his Mirabella restaurant on a Saturday "because the chef was not on the same focus as I was." On Sunday, Elmont did the cooking.

Quantum's Allen J. Bernstein maintains a consistent focus by keeping all his restaurants company operated and making sure that suppliers consistently remain the same. "If Victoria Station had stayed consistently focused on its prime rib," he maintains, "it could have made it. After all, Lawry's has done it."

Ann Arbor, Michigan-based Domino's Pizza once owned the home delivery market, but it lost focus and made the strategic error of trying to compete on price. It simply could not keep winning that way. Then it tried to deliver sub sandwiches and clogged its entire delivery system.

Thomas Monaghan, who founded Domino's Pizza at age 23 in 1960, kept a phenomenal focus on the chain's business until the mid-1980s, when he admittedly let success go to his head. He purchased the Detroit Tigers in 1983, and they won the World Series just a year later. He also purchased airplanes, bought some 200 fancy cars, built an airstrip and hangar, purchased two yachts and a large pier on a lake, constructed a luxury North Woods lodge, and along the way built a championship golf course, bowling alleys, a hotel, and upscale cottages. He also began building a luxury house on 27 acres as the climax of his dreams. All of this cost a cool $30 million. Then he started financing Honduras missions and moved to sell the chain so he could focus full-time on his philanthropies.

Perhaps fortunately for Monaghan, he couldn't sell Domino's for a decent price, so he returned to his chain as chairman-president in 1990 to regain focus. He then had to sell unprofitable units, close regional offices, and try to pay off much of a large company debt that had accumulated from loans. It was a classic case of taking one's eye completely off the ball and losing perspective. "I feel good about having gotten the distractions out of my system," Monaghan says. He now feels that Domino's is definitely on the comeback road, with training systems and computer systems finally having been installed in its units.

McDonald's constant pizza tests through the early 1990s may also signal a diversion of focus. "They simply don't have and can't get the proper refrigeration system to do quality pizza," insists a competitor, "and these efforts are only going to hurt them. The customer won't accept it." Still, McDonald's goes merrily on its way. Perhaps it can afford to test and retest pizza and then decide whether customer response and the potential return on investment merit a chainwide rollout or an abandonment of pizza. However, McDonald's wants to have pizza in its arsenal as potential ammunition, even though pizza on its menu could divert the burger focus.

Consistency in food quality, service, pricing, and all other aspects is a necessity for chains. Sometimes the best surprise is no surprise—consistent quality at every level.

GROUPIES

Restaurant chains are faced with the challenge of retaining some measure of individuality while replicating themselves. Throughout this process, a consistent focus on the restaurants is essential. In many cases a loss of focus has occurred when a chain tries too many different concepts or a grouping of chains takes place in what some view as a conglomerate format. Most of the corporate groupings have failed, lacking the entrepreneurship and vision to operate multichains, much less even one chain. They tend to function by the numbers, opening a given number of units annually without regard to quality and controls.

A prime example of such problems is W. R. Grace & Co. and the multitude of chains and restaurants it operated in the 1970s and early 1980s, most of which chairman Peter Grace finally spun off. Further examples are Norman Habermann's troubled Irvine,

California-based Restaurant Enterprises Group, Inc. (REGI), including Coco's, Carrow's, El Torito, Tequila Willie's, and various dinnerhouses and specialty restaurants, plus Chi-Chi's, which REGI in effect acquired in early 1994 from Foodmaker, Inc. under a new combined corporate name, Family Restaurants, Inc.; Anwar Soliman's Newport Beach, California-based American Restaurant Group, which never really hit its stride with Stuart Anderson's Black Angus steakhouses; the Spectrum group of specialty restaurants, Spoon's Grill & Bar, Grandy's fast-food chicken, and Velvet Turtle dinnerhouses. A major problem with groups of this type is that they include chains from varied market segments (i.e., dinnerhouses, casual restaurants, fast-food) that require different skills to operate.

Supplier conglomerates have never proved particularly adept at achieving their restaurant chain potential either. General Foods had the chance to make Burger Chef a fast-food power in the 1970s but did not capitalize on opportunities and finally sold the chain to Hardee's. General Foods also went through abortive efforts with GuadalaHarry's Mexican dinnerhouses. Pillsbury certainly had its chances with Burger King and with Steak and Ale and Bennigan's but could not give these chains the backing they needed. Hershey Corporation did not view the Friendly Ice Cream chain as an opportunity in its own right, but rather as an adjunct to Hershey. Quaker Oats finally gave up on its Magic Pan creperies and Engine House pizza units and sold them.

All too often—and this was particularly true of Pillsbury—the corporation does not realize that if it puts full money and support into a restaurant chain or chains, the restaurants would produce a higher return on investment than the corporation's food supplier division on which it is so focused. John Kluge's New York-based Metromedia Company conglomerate has had decidedly mixed results with Metromedia Steakhouses (Ponderosa and Bonanza) and S & A Restaurant Corporation (Steak and Ale and Bennigan's). Metromedia has consolidated all of these under the leadership of Michael Kaufman, who Metromedia says has completely turned around Ponderosa. Metromedia acted after a series of leadership crises at S & A, where the top four executives had to be fired in mid-

1992 and Steven Leipsner was ousted as CEO a year later. It remains to be seen whether Kaufman, a former Metromedia acquisitions expert, can make all these chains go.

However, there are also some upbeat stories. To date, General Mills is probably the only conglomerate that successfully started its own major chain—The Olive Garden. It endured a number of its own startup failures, such as the Betty Crocker Pie Shops and Tree House restaurants, Hanahan's steak and seafood restaurants, Fenimore's breakfast concept, and, more recently, Bringer's home delivery that it tried to start, and others that it acquired, such as Casa Gallardo Mexican restaurants, the Good Earth healthful food restaurants, Darryl's theme restaurants, and York Steak Houses. But it persevered and succeeded—in spades—with Red Lobster, which it acquired in 1970 as just five Florida restaurants and built into by far the number one seafood chain in the world.

Red Lobster succeeded in large degree because of its president, Joe Lee, who had the autonomy and vision to make it work. "We focused on just a few core ideas for Red Lobster," he recalls. "We put limits on what we could do, and we decided early in the game, after launching one Red Lobster franchise in Greenville, South Carolina, and one in Savannah, Georgia, that franchising a complex dinnerhouse operation simply wouldn't work, that we needed to control our own destiny." He also reengineered the entire supply system, got seafood suppliers to serve Red Lobster's specific needs without having to go through all the distribution channels, set up a unique shrimp and lobster supply system in Nicaragua, and was one of the first to utilize computerized inventory controls. He also established intense training programs, highlighted by the informal "breakfast with Joe" session for each training class.

It was Ron Magruder, who followed in Lee's footsteps and—with Blaine Sweatt as the creator—built The Olive Garden from the ground up into by far the nation's leading Italian restaurant chain. China Coast, also molded by Sweatt, is now making a bid to grow into the leader of the Chinese restaurant segment.

Orlando-based General Mills Restaurants did it by sticking entirely to company-owned restaurants and to its own carefully crafted casual restaurants segment. It applied expertise to each type of ethnic restaurant that it launched and expanded piece by piece, always adding nuances and improvements along the way. Each chain is operated with separate staffs so that there is a total concentration on a particular concept and no diversion of effort. General Mills, Inc., in turn, has granted full autonomy to the restaurant group rather than falling into the trap of making it part of a synergy with the supplier arms.

What's next for General Mills Restaurants? A good guess is the Mexican segment, where it previously tried by acquisition but now may craft its own casual prototype. Even in the increasingly saturated Mexican restaurants market, it might not be a good idea to bet against this enterprise.

PepsiCo is another conglomerate that has enjoyed success in the restaurant chain business. Whether it can continue so strongly, as it keeps diversifying into more chains, is a real question. PepsiCo says that in any case it now has a huge number of guaranteed Pepsi-Cola outlets in its never-ending fountain battle with Coca-Cola, still the foodservice leader (largely because it serves McDonald's, among others).

PepsiCo's chains include KFC, Pizza Hut, Taco Bell, Hot 'n Now double drive-throughs, California Pizza Kitchen, and Chevys. Taco Bell's John Martin heads part of PepsiCo's empire with responsibilities for Chevys and Hot 'n Now. He also has further ambitions to widen the reach in full-service restaurants with casual concepts—and not necessarily those with a Mexican theme. Martin feels that as viable as Taco Bell is, it also would pay to have a bevy of full-service chains.

Pizza Hut has also begun to craft its own restaurant empire under president Allan Huston with the 1993 purchase of Boston-based D'Angelo Sandwich Shops and Toronto-based East Side Mario's. PepsiCo succeeded through the early 1990s by delegating reasonable autonomy to each chain but has started to run into problems with franchisees as it tries to enforce strict conformity to "doing it the PepsiCo way."

Restaurant-based companies tend to do better than supplier-based companies because the former are more involved and familiar with the restaurant business in the first place. Norman Brinker's astounding array of varied concepts is formidable for his Brinker International, but its flagship is still Chili's Grill & Bar. Grady's American Grill, Romano's Macaroni Grill, and Spageddies are very much in the arsenal too, and a Mexican-theme restaurant concept has been launched under the name of CozyMel's. Brinker keeps winning in such diversified efforts because he knows how to choose and motivate the best people and because he is never satisfied with what is. "The race is never over," Brinker says. "Consumer trends constantly change, and you can never be complacent. You have to always look down the road to improve your current concepts and to develop new ones."

Brinker sees his concepts as appealing to a wide range of consumers from lower-middle income to upper income. "But each appeals in different ways," he observes, "and thus we grab customers who want variety and will try each type of restaurant. Almost no customer eats in the same place every day. Our biggest challenge is to balance all our multiunit concepts and to have each one keep its own individual identity. This means balancing their growth relative to size and making sure each is focusing on operations first and then on the financial aspects."

Brinker's restaurants are sometimes called "the mutual fund of the restaurant industry" because of the variety of chains and their different niches within the ever-popular casual full-service restaurant business. Chili's has a broad appeal, limited menu with an average check of $8, fast service (tables are usually occupied for just 30 to 40 minutes), rapid turns, and $2.4 million average per unit annual sales (up $1 million from when Brinker arrived in 1983). Grady's American Grill is more of an upscale dinnerhouse featuring steaks, prime rib, pastas, and fresh seafood with an average check of $11 and $3.2 million average per unit sales. Meanwhile, Romano's is an upscale Italian restaurant with a $14 average check and $2.4 million average per unit sales. Spageddies hits the lower end of the Italian-theme restaurant market with an $8 average check.

Will the struggle for dominance in the casual full-service restaurants segment ultimately come down to the battle of the two Rons? Brinker International's Ron McDougall calls this the age of "the multiconcept, casual dining powerhouse corporation." He lists the key players as General Mills (Ron Magruder & Co.), PepsiCo, and Brinker International. He advocates staying in the same segment, with parallel but separate individual concepts, and says these Big 3 corporations understand the restaurant business and have made a long-term commitment to it, have a growing group of successful expandable concepts with proven management teams and realistic expansion plans, and are poised to "explode across the United States."

A group approach gives a chain far more flexibility in site selection, diversity, and the shifting of concepts such as Morrison's converting Silver Spoons to Mozzarrella's. And a Brinker International can decide which of several concepts fits in better on a given site and make a deal for the site. Or—as is increasingly being done—it can include two or three concepts on the same site, thereby cutting costs and, in effect, building a comprehensive market area in that one place. Others, such as Quantum's Allen J. Bernstein with his Morton's, Peasant (itself split into a variety of concepts), Mick's, Bertolini's, and Santa Fe Steak House concepts, can do likewise. It also is quite possible for unrelated chains to team up on sites. Spaghetti Warehouse, On the Border, and Outback are eyeing combination sites for their mutual benefit, although they obviously are not a group.

Perhaps the best examples of diversified restaurant groups are those in which a restless entrepreneur keeps expanding with new concepts that rarely replicate each other. Tops in this category is Richard Melman, the irrepressible creator and president of Lettuce Entertain You Enterprises (LEYE), which not only entertains and dazzles with a multitude of varied concepts but rarely duplicates anything. Melman's credo is that the restaurant succeeds best "when the owner is in the restaurant." Thus LEYE has made each of its restaurants an individual corporation, with the restaurant's general manager being a managing partner and owning a large interest in it. This permits the corporation to focus on basic systems for all the varied restaurants while each restaurant is autonomous and retains maximum creativity. So far this system has worked sensationally for more than a decade, with very few of its restaurants failing.

Melman opened one of his most creative concepts, Foodlife, in May 1993 at Chicago's famed Water Tower Place shopping center. It was expected to hit $10 million in annual sales for the first year, with separate kiosks selling Asian food, Mexican food, pasta, rotisserie chicken, salads, grains, burgers, desserts, juices, wine, and beer. A magnetic debit card records customers' purchases at each station, and they pay the total to a central cashier when they leave.

As well as he has done in the Greater Chicago area, Melman is convinced that he can do just as well in other cities. Furthermore, he is no longer averse to replicating or chaining a concept—perhaps as long as there is only one of each in each city. He created Ed Debevic's Diner in Chicago, but for financial reasons didn't seem to do well outside of Chicago. He loves his Tucci Benucch Italian restaurant on North Michigan Avenue, and his customers love it, too. Inevitably, he opened a Tucci Benucch in Minneapolis's gigantic Mall of America—a city in itself—as well as in Seattle (where he also plans to open a quick-service Italian place), and two licensed ones in Japan. Tucci Bennuch seems well positioned as an expanding Melman chain with its $10 per-person average lunch check and $14 dinner average. Melman's Maggiano's and Corner Bakery restaurants may also be potential chains.

Melman's research methods in opening restaurants seem to be more effective than all the computerized analysis and printouts in the world. If he likes the feel of a potential place, he goes with it. If his friends like it, that's a double winner. And if he or his friends spot some flaws, then refinements and adjustments are made. This kind of gut feeling is especially effective in the highly personalized restaurants that he loves. For Melman, operating restaurants is fun (when things are going right), and the best concept is the one he has just opened or is working on now. He intuitively grasps the essence of what the customer will like today and tomorrow.

Among Melman's some 35 restaurants are a mix of a few fine dining places and varied casual restaurants, mostly with distinctive names: Shaw's Crab House (his best performer at $8 million annual sales), Ambria (fine dining), Avanzare (Italian), Bub City, Cafe Ba-Ba-Reeba, Hat Dance, The Pump Room and Un Grand Cafe (fine dining), Scoozi, Tucchetti, and Tucci Milan.

Larry and Mark Levy's Chicago-based Levy Restaurants has become the multipower of the "captive audience" market—fed by concessions at stadiums and arenas—by serving quality food as well as fast-food selected from the menus of their restaurants. With Lawrence (Larry) as chairman, brother Mark Levy as vice chairman, and Bill Post as restaurants president, Levy Restaurants has an arsenal of varied concepts, including Bistro 110, the Blackhawk Lodge, Spiaggia and Cafe Spiaggia, City Tavern, D. B. Kaplan's Deli, Eadie's Kitchen, a new Mia Torre concept in the Chicago Sears Tower, and many others. It also operates the Fireworks Factory and Portobello Yacht Club restaurants at Disney World, Orlando, Florida, and has gained a special niche in sports stadium feeding with facilities at Comiskey Park, Wrigley Field, and Arlington International Racecourse (all in metropolitan Chicago), the new Cleveland baseball stadium (Jacobs Field), and a foodservice contract for the new Portland, Oregon, basketball arena. Doug Roth, a partner in Chicago's Bistro 110, also operates a Bistro 100 in Charlotte, North Carolina.

Levy Restaurants garners half of its over $100 million annual sales from these concession feeding operations, including restaurants and snack bars at Chicago's McCormick Place, and has branched out to facilities in other cities. The magic might not work quite as well outside its core Chicago area, but indications are that Levy Restaurants can localize its image wherever it goes, particularly in the Midwest.

"Staying popular is tough for any restaurant," observes Lawrence Levy, who reluctantly closed the Chestnut Street Grill after 13 years. "A restaurant is a fixed investment, and you really need to keep it going as long as possible, at least 25 years. New places keep emerging. As soon as we closed Chestnut, we were deluged with customer requests to reopen it. That was not feasible."

Meanwhile, Levy opened a 350-seat Los Angeles restaurant/entertainment complex in May 1994 in a joint venture with movie producer Steven Spielberg and Walt Disney Studios chairman Jeffrey Katzenberg. Called the Dive! it is in the Century Plaza Shopping Center near Los Angeles. A second such Dive! is to open in Las Vegas.

Donald N. Smith, Tennessee Restaurant Company chairman-CEO, has fashioned a neat two-chain combination out of two family restaurant concepts: Memphis-based Perkins and Wilbraham, Massachusetts-based Friendly. First, he turned around Perkins after acquiring it in 1985, and then he turned around Friendly in a longer process that took from 1988, when he purchased it, to 1993. Both give him a wedge in the family restaurant market, but Perkins is more upscale than Friendly and has fuller meals. Together, they are a potent combination for Smith, who may finally be willing to forego his dream of creating a wide-ranging restaurant chains empire in favor of relative prosperity.

Italian cuisine looms large in a number of diversified groups' plans. Raleigh, North Carolina-based Investors Management Corporation (IMC), the parent of Golden Corral steak houses, has targeted three different casual-type Italian restaurant chains for growth—Ragazzi's: An Italian Place, focusing on pasta in a mid-price range in the Southeast; a joint venture Zia Mia pasta house in Bethesda, Maryland, based on Zia Mia restaurants in the St. Louis area; and IMC's own pasta-pizza GiLuigi's restaurant in Raleigh. Of the three, only one is likely to be developed full-scale, with Ragazzi's the front runner for any real expansion. IMC may already be diverted with its Oh! Brian's theme restaurants and an unrelated venture in Quick-Ten Lube Centers, but the entire corporation is expertly managed by its chairman-CEO, James Maynard.

The Seattle-based Schwartz Brothers group of diversified individual restaurants is expanding Cucina! Cucina! Italian Cafes as a chain to balance its costs and capitalize on the Italian craze. Former company president-CEO William Schwartz has switched his focus to Cucina as a separate company and as president-CEO there, a wise move considering that the Italian concept is averaging $4.5 million per unit annual sales. Schwartz has also launched a small Cucina! Presto! pizza-pasta-salad place in a suburban Seattle supermarket as a prototype for future retail in-store units, as well as a Spazzo Mediterranean Grill. He is eyeing a casual steakhouse concept and a possible upscale Mexican restaurant. His brother, John Schwartz, will move up to the presidency of the main company.

Meanwhile, Outback hopes to expand its joint-venture Hous-

ton-based Carrabba's Italian restaurants. Outback apparently is
hedging its bets, figuring that if its Outback restaurants ever slow
down, it would have a major Italian entry. More than likely, Outback is anticipating the possible saturation of certain markets and
sees the need for an alternative concept that can draw other customers, or the same customers on different occasions. Bob Merritt,
Outback chief financial officer, says Carrabba's own management
was retained to develop that chain, leaving Outback's management
with a full focus on its Outback restaurants. A similar refrain is
sounded by just about every company in this diversified position,
but it by no means always works out as intended and does, in fact,
often become a diversion of financial commitments and people in
the long run. With the best of intentions, too many companies take
their eye off the ball.

The venture capital approach exemplified by Outback, and in
some ways by Investors Management Corporation, seems to be the
wisest and safest for chains eyeing new opportunities. It allows a
separate chain with management already in place to carry out at least
the initial growth phases with equity from the investing chain company. This was the thinking of Allen J. Bernstein in the late 1980s
when, after having been a Hardee's and then a Wendy's franchisee,
and after trying to build up Denver-based Le Peep breakfast restaurants, he decided to go only with successfully established chains. He
formed the Quantum Restaurant Group to acquire Atlanta-based
Peasant and Mick's restaurants, and subsequently acquired Morton's
upscale steakhouses, and took over Bertolini's, which had potential
for expansion to a chain. Going with proven winners and expanding
their base each time has worked well for him.

Explaining the group philosophy, Bernstein points out, "Each
chain in our group has its own culture. The operating principles are
identical, but the interaction and execution are different. If we tried
to integrate these chains, they would lose their independence and
their individual flair. Also, we can move employees of one chain to
another chain in a different city if they so desire." He cited the case
of a waiter in an Atlanta Peasant restaurant who wanted to move to
Chicago to sing in the opera. Presto! The waiter was soon working
at a Morton's restaurant in Chicago.

Other independent multipowers include Restaurants Unlimited in Seattle, Laurence Mindel's Il Fornaio group in San Francisco, Lee Cohn's Big 4 (and more) in the Phoenix area, and Michael Weinstein's Ark Restaurants in New York. One thing they all seem to have in common is that they thrive when they stay in their own geographic areas or within the same metro markets, but often falter when they tread on unfamiliar soil.

Among various chains pushing second concepts are Applebee's International, Inc.'s largest franchisee, Georgia-based Apple South, Inc., which also is a 10-unit Hardee's franchisee and is trying to establish its own identity starting with the two Gianni's Italian restaurants that it acquired in Florida; Boston-based Au Bon Pain bakery-cafes, capitalizing on its purchase of the St. Louis Bread Company chain; Dallas-based I Can't Believe It's Yogurt, which under the Brice Foods, Inc. banner is trying a sister chain called Boxies Cafe, featuring soups, sandwiches, salads, and other offerings in a small food court setting; Los Angeles-based Sizzler International, Inc., which is putting considerable effort into a Buffalo Ranch dinnerhouse chain spawned by underperforming Sizzler Steakhouses; Nashville, Tennessee-based Volunteer Capital Corporation, a 50-unit Wendy's franchisee, which seeks to do likewise with its J. Alexander's casual restaurant concept; Bob Evans Farms, Inc., with its family restaurants and its hopes to expand its Cantina del Rio Mexican restaurants; and Chattanooga, Tennessee-based Krystal Company's fast-food units, which are diversifying with Krystal Kwik drive-throughs.

Chains often seem driven to try new concepts and to keep expanding as part of seeking greater complexity. Sometimes they are better off keeping things straight and simple.

Some of the groups operate one or two restaurants in each of a number of markets on a trial-and-error basis. The Harman-Nickolas Restaurant Group, with Nick's Fishmarket and other concepts, had opened 25 restaurants in 25 years by early 1994. Because of periodic closings, it then had nine restaurants in action, three in Honolulu, two in Chicago, two newer ones in Boca Raton, Florida, and two in Miami and Miami Beach—the latter a gigantic 1,000-seat restaurant. At $45 to $50 average per person price points, this may be the best approach for a multiunit group. "Our concepts are ideal for expansion in big cities such as Atlanta and San Francisco," says Nickolas.

Some restaurant groups are dependent on one chain but also include a number of individual companies. Detroit-based C. A. Muer Corporation under Leo Beil, who moved up from treasurer to president after founder Charles A. Muer died in a March 1993 Bahamas sailboat accident, operates some 10 Charley's Crab restaurants and at least 11 other individual restaurants, including Engine House No. 5, Grand Concourse, Joe Muer's, Meriwether's, and Pals.

To some, the fame and the fun are not in the chain. "Once you chain a restaurant, you lose the Broadway, movie-making sense of excitement," asserts New York's Alan Stillman, who created TGI Friday's in 1964 but sold it when it had expanded to 12 restaurants eight years later. He has built up the New York Restaurant Group, with its Smith & Wollensky upscale steakhouse and grill as the flagship, which also includes the Manhattan Ocean Club, La Cite, Park Avenue Cafe, and Post House. Now that he has a New York City empire of individual restaurants, what will he do? "I want to open Smith & Wollenskys around the country, and maybe some hotels too," he declares. The man who once said that chains bore him has found that even in upscale restaurants, chains may be necessary to balance costs and may provide the one way to greatly broaden revenues and profitability—if the concept works on a widespread basis. Stillman has been trying to start a Smith & Wollensky chain for years, but as of mid-1994 he still had not been able to go beyond New York City and its one location. This may have been a blessing because his focus could be much stronger in one geographic area.

If Stillman can ever make a go of Smith & Wollensky as a chain, he will join the ranks of upscale steakhouse chains Morton's, Ruth's Chris, and the Palm. It is not easy to build a chain at an average price of $50 and higher.

New York-based Restaurant Associates (RA) is a classic example of a company that overextended itself through acquisitions; by the late 1960s it had lost all focus. With ultracreative Joe Baum as president and Jerry Brody as chairman, RA launched a whole series of brilliant innovative restaurants starting in the mid-1950s—The Newarker, Forum of the Twelve Caesars, La Fonda del Sol, and the Four Seasons. Brody and the RA board thought they could conquer the world. They bought Barricini Candy, Treadway Inns, and a vending company, as well as dabbling in an airline catering business and in various fringe operations such as Zum Zum restaurants. These operations drained money from the company, forced RA to cut quality in its restaurants to make ends meet, and sent the company into a tailspin that did not stop until after Max Pine was moved up to the presidency in 1976. He got rid of all the offshoots and refocused the company on its core business—restaurants. Later, he also got RA into the chain business with Acapulco and Charlie Brown's.

Foreign ownership of American chains has generally been unfortunate. Kyotaru Ltd. of Japan bailed out financially strapped RA after it had gone private, but may be ruining it by taking the cash flow to solve its own problems and cutting off growth capital, a reliable RA source says.

Kyotaru, apparently thinking it could operate restaurant chains at will, also purchased San Diego-based Paragon Steakhouses (Mountain Jack's and Hungry Hunter), the Costa Mesa, California-based Love's Barbecue chain, and Arby's Sherman Oaks, California-based KFF Management franchisee. Skylark Company, another conglomerate Japanese retailer and restaurant company, has encountered a number of problems with its Irvine, California-based Red Robin chain.

The British have scarcely fared any better than the Japanese. Imperial Group of London went nowhere with Howard Johnson's in the early 1980s, but perhaps HoJo was too far gone by then to do much. Grand Metropolitan PLC of London has had its hands more than full in trying to turn around Burger King. However, Allied-Lyons PLC of London appears to be faring well with Baskin-Robbins and Dunkin' Donuts (which absorbed Mr. Donut), thanks to having given the full reins on both of its chains to Dunkin' chairman Robert Rosenberg. From 1989 to 1993, Rosenberg doubled Dunkin's number of full units from 1,500 to 3,000 and doubled earnings to $50 million with his integration of all the systems. The difference between a conglomerate's failure or success with restaurant chains often lies in whether it has granted reasonable autonomy to its chains, and whether the chains' CEOs with that autonomy exercise it in a positive and winning way.

Hotel-oriented corporations have, too often, not focused sufficiently on their restaurant chains. Nestlé of Switzerland owned Stouffer Hotels, Dobbs Houses airport feeding, the Rusty Scupper, and J. B. Winberie restaurants, along with the Cheese Cellar and a number of individual restaurants that were operated by the Cleveland-based Stouffer Restaurant Company. The restaurant chains finally were spun off to a separate company.

Marriott Corporation, which started in the restaurant business well before it opened hotels, finally decided to focus on hotels rather than pouring more money into its hard-pressed restaurants. It sold the Roy Rogers fast-food sandwich chain and Big Boy family restaurants while keeping its foodservice management services and Host International airport operations. Marriott then divided itself into two companies to separate ownership and management. Host Marriott Corporation now owns hotels, retirement communities, and toll road and airport foodservice, Marriott International manages the hotels and retirement communities.

On the other hand, the Minneapolis-based Carlson Companies fields two contrasting chains, Dallas-based TGI Friday's and Minneapolis-based Country Kitchen family restaurants, as well as Radisson Hotels and Colony Hotels. Juergen Bartels, president of Carlson Hospitality Group, is responsible for these chains, but each chain has a separate president.

Diverse chains within a chain within a group are not uncommon either. A TGI Friday's test of an Itali Anni's restaurant is in progress at the new Pittsburgh Airport, where TGI Friday's already has two offshoots—a TGI Friday's Cafe with salads and snacks and a TGI Friday's Pub for drinks. TGI Friday's has also tried Dalts theme restaurants with mixed results. Here it would seem that TGI Friday's still has plenty of room to grow with its main concept and should be focusing almost entirely on that, with perhaps a few downscale versions.

Groups can evolve varied formats from the same base. Pat Kuleto, a leading restaurant designer, has prospered with his own Kuleto's restaurant realizing almost $7 million in sales annually, with just 175 seats off Union Square in San Francisco, and McCormick & Kuleto's Seafood restaurant bringing in $7 million. Now he has added a Kuleto's Trattoria in nearby Burlingame and a Buffalo Grill restaurant in San Mateo. In joint ventures, he has opened the Boulevard restaurant and plans to open a Southern theater concept restaurant in Atlanta and a combination restaurant-food manufacturing facility.

The Phoenix-based Dial Corporation owns Dobbs International airport services, and Dial's Restaura Dining Services handles foodservice management accounts. It is also a Burger King franchisee and has had chances to acquire chains such as Peter Piper Pizza but has backed away in favor of establishing its own food management brands: Eatin' Easy, Faber, Grand Gourmet, Pizza & Subs, and RestauraMart. John Teets, Dial Corporation chairman-CEO since 1982, is also one of a few restaurant chain executives who has risen to a corporate CEO position. He headed restaurant chains in the 1960s and 1970s and was president of Greyhound Food Management (now Restaura).

Why all the fuss about diversifying? After all, McDonald's has proven that a one-concept focus works beautifully. Yet McD is unique in its own way, and even McD fell prey to the diversification syndrome when founder Ray Kroc experimented with Jane Dobbins Pie Shops and other concepts in the late 1960s and early 1970s. Fortunately for McD, nothing he tried ever worked except McDonald's itself. Orderly diversification into one or more chain concepts makes sense if the original concept is expected to reach a saturation point or if a chain CEO feels the necessity to offer choices of different restaurants within market areas to gain a larger overall market share. In any case, casual restaurants in Italian, steakhouse, Mexican, and other segments tend to move toward theoretical saturation over a period of years, whereas fast-food chains have a potentially limitless universe. Still, for McDonald's and others, that universe is increasingly worldwide rather than just domestic.

Diversification often fails because the initial success is so hard to duplicate. Ego somehow seems to demand that an entrepreneur prove that he or she can do it again. KFC tried Zantigo Mexican fast-food units in the 1970s, and they were a miserable failure. Sambo's tried all kinds of other restaurants, and they too failed.

Sambo's is a classic example of ego-driven diversification away from a main concept. Starting in the early 1960s, Sambo's co-owners Sam Battistone, Sr. and Newell Bohnett successively launched (and eventually closed) a Bonanza dinnerhouse, cocktail lounges, and a Congo Room, a Blue Ox steak and lobster house, and a Red Top fast-food burger unit. After that, Battistone's son, Sam D. Battistone, tried a Heidi's Pie Shop, Pullman Pie Shops, and Red Top and Blue Ox units that he purchased from his father and Bohnett. Fortunately, Sambo's board halted the diversification efforts in 1972, and Sambo's was able to focus on its own restaurants for the next several years—enabling it to grow into the largest full-service restaurant chain (1,117 units) by 1977 before its big fall.

Can an independent restaurateur be a multiunit operator? Most emphatically, yes. That is known as having your cake and eating it too. When Pano Karatassos was honored with the prestigious 1993 Silver Plate award from the International Foodservice Manufacturers Association, he was hailed as the Independent Restaurant Operator of the Year. But his company, the Buckhead Life Restaurant Group of Atlanta, operates the Buckhead Diner, Buckhead Bread Company & Cafe, Pano's and Paul's, 103 West, Chops, Pricci, the Atlanta Fish Market, and Veni Vidi Vici. Still, each of these is one of a kind.

Other notable examples of independent groups are New Orleans's Richard and Ella Brennan's Commander's Palace, Mr. B's, the Palace Cafe, Ristorante Bacco, and Brennan's of Houston; Los Angeles's Wolfgang Puck's two Spagos, a downscale Wolfgang Puck's Cafe, Chinois, Postrio, and Granita; and Chicago's Joseph and Charlie Carlucci's Vinny's, Charlie's Ale House, a potential Strega Nona low-priced pasta restaurant, and, of course, two Carlucci's restaurants.

Puck and other chefs have diversified to the point that one wonders whether they are keeping an eye on the ball while trying to balance their costs and capitalize on opportunities. Puck runs a profitable frozen pizza business. Mark Miller operates retail stores selling food and general merchandise at his Coyote Cafe restaurant in Santa Fe, New Mexico, and Red Sage in Washington, D.C. He also operates a mail-order business and has authored three books. When customers ask why he isn't in the restaurant to greet them and are told he is busy somewhere else, that couldn't make them happy. Yet many of the chefs who operate restaurants are also opening casual restaurants, bakeries, and takeout shops to help support their fine dining efforts.

Edward (Ned) Grace, president of the Phelps-Grace Company, based in Providence, Rhode Island, is launching his Bugaboo Creek barbecue concept as a small chain of four or five restaurants at first and also is eyeing a brewpub featuring beer and food, a fun-food emporium for children, a family dinnerhouse, and a family chicken restaurant. He already has seven single restaurants under other names.

Michael Weinstein, the creative president of New York's Ark Restaurants Corporation, who still sometimes bicycles from one restaurant to another or from one potential location to another in quest of low-cost sites, has a bevy of single-unit concepts, as well as three America restaurants, in New York City, Washington, D.C.'s Union Station, and Tysons Corner, Virginia, and two Sequoia Grills, one in New York and one overlooking the Potomac River in Washington with 700 seats and $8 million in annual sales. Weinstein, formerly involved with small- and medium-sized neighborhood restaurants, has incorporated his vision of size and productivity into newer restaurants as his Ark company attempts to show that there is room for all types of restaurants. That may work in New York City and Washington, but Weinstein's magic failed in New Jersey when he tried to open restaurants there.

His heavily diversified 27 restaurants, concentrated in New York City but also present in Boston, Washington, Miami, and California, surpassed $65 million in sales but achieved just a $1.9 million net income for the fiscal year ended in October 1993.

Max's is a restaurant brand throughout the Greater San Francisco area. Actually, Max is the late father of restaurant entrepreneur Dennis Berkowitz, who has fashioned an empire of Max's in honor of the man he admired. These include at least two Max's Diners, five Max's Opera Cafes, Max's Deli, three Sweet Max's, and a number of other Max's with, no doubt, more planned for the future. The name of this restaurant group is, of course, Max's Restaurants.

The ultimate in multiunit individual operations is David Tallichet's Specialty Restaurants Corporation, based in Anaheim, California. It has some 50 separate restaurants across the country with names such as Air Transport Command, 56th Fighter Group, Baby Doe's Matchless Mine, Proud Bird, Pieces of Eight, Port O' Call Village, Shanghai Reds, Shananigan's and Whiskey Joes. Most are one-of-a-kind, the one notable exception being the 94th Aero Squadron of 12 restaurants. These are themed-atmosphere restaurants, sometimes with beautiful views. Tallichet did everything he could to buy the best locations. But the eventual costs of unreplicated concepts were too high, and the company filed for Chapter 11 reorganization in 1993.

A restaurant company can succeed in diversification only up to a point. Nashville-based Shoney's, Inc. has managed to focus its main attention on Shoney's Restaurants (family restaurants) while also succeeding with Captain D's seafood shops and Lee's Famous Recipe chicken units. But its Pargo's and Fifth Quarter steakhouses have been less than sensational.

Morrison Restaurants, Inc., based in Mobile, Alabama, has done well with its more than 250 Ruby Tuesday casual restaurants. It also is holding the line with its cafeterias in the South and has launched Morrison's Fresh Cooking for food courts. Yet its L & N Seafood Grill and Silver Spoon Cafe restaurants which are both being phased out or converted, were not nearly as productive or as profitable as Ruby Tuesday, raising the question of whether it should have placed more investment dollars in Ruby Tuesday—instead of putting anything more into the other divisions. One of the hardest things in the world, for anyone, is to pull back from concepts that were founded years ago, to admit that the world is changing faster than we'd like. Sandy Beall, company president-CEO, has launched Mozzarella's Cafes to replace Silver Spoons and is trying Sweetpea's as he bids to make the $1 billion-plus volume Morrison's one of the industry's top restaurant chain groups.

David Wachtel, former president of Shoney's, Inc. and for the last several years president of Nashville-based O'Charley's, took on an overwhelming challenge in late 1993. He "succeeded" in outflanking Pizza Hut cofounder Frank Carney for control of the Dallas-based Western Sizzlin' budget steakhouse chain that Carney had nurtured for five years and that was emerging from a Chapter 11 reorganization. Perhaps this was more of a challenge than Wachtel needed. Wachtel earlier had been a Western Sizzlin' franchisee, so he presumably should know the score.

Entrepreneur Fred DeLuca, rolling along with 8,000 franchised Subway units, has started two prototype Q Burger units in Florida and hopes to franchise them. The "Q" stands for quality, and the quarter-pound burger offers a choice of fresh-ground beef or turkey on a roll. French fries and onion rings are on the menu, as well as alfalfa sprouts and salsa. DeLuca also has a majority interest in the Boston-based Cajun Joe's fried chicken chain. He has repositioned this enterprise as a roast chicken chain and is testing a new Cajoe's name. DeLuca's motivation is a fear that when Subway inevitably reaches 10,000 units within the next few years, it may in effect have saturated almost all of the domestic market—not an easy achievement in itself.

Among other mixed combinations are Atlanta-based America's Favorite Chicken Co. (Popeyes and Church's); Indianapolis-based Consolidated Products, Inc., with the Steak'n Shake chain and a number of individual restaurants; Dallas-based Black-eyed Pea Restaurants, Inc., with its Black-eyed Pea Restaurants and Taco Bueno chains and a small number of Crystal's Pizza & Spaghetti, Dixie House, and oversized Casa Bonita restaurants, which under president Ted Papit hopes to split away from parent Unigate PLC of London; and Daka International, Inc., based in Danvers, Massachusetts, a company that combines foodservice management contracts and Fuddruckers burger-oriented family restaurants.

Pittsburg, Kansas-based National Pizza Company (NPC, Inc.), Pizza Hut's largest franchisee, acquired Seattle-based Skipper's seafood shops in the late 1980s, but may have gotten in over its head with the 1993 acquisition of the formerly Dallas-based Tony Roma's chain (number one in the barbecue segment), which it is trying to run mostly with existing corporate executives. No doubt its consolidation of top executives saves costs and cuts overhead at Tony Roma's, but the net effects remain to be seen.

Group chain restaurants realistically may dominate the booming casual restaurants segment in the 1990s and beyond. Still, diversified restaurant groups must remain more vigilant than ever to maintain full focus separately on each chain and not be lured by the ego-pleasing idea that bigger is automatically better.

It makes sense to diversify into multiconcepts only when the original one or two concepts look as though they will become saturated and others are needed to allow coordinated expansion and site combinations. McDonald's probably can keep opening McDonald's endlessly around the world, but there are limits on casual restaurant chains such as Chili's and The Olive Garden; hence the diversification of those companies.

Yet given any need for diversification, each chain within a multichain company must retain its own individual focus and never take its eye off the ball.

Marketing and Merchandising Versatility

Utilizing marketing and merchandising to achieve an individualized "unchain" chain image.

"You've got to go out there and do things to promote your restaurants in the local markets."
—*Chris Sullivan, chairman,*
Outback Steakhouse, Inc., Tampa, Florida

HIGHLIGHTS

- Favorite-place image
- Long-term promos
- Specific-message targeting
- Dave Thomas and personalities
- Combo-meal and pricing struggles
- Positioning is everything
- Nonadvertising gimmicks
- The neighborhood restaurant image
- Community service
- Projecting timely, fresh image
- Research versus gut feeling
- "Wow" merchandising wins

Saturation and stepped-up competition are raising the stakes in the fierce fast-food marketing warfare. McDonald's for one intends to double the expansion of its domestic units to perhaps 450 new ones annually and to open as many as 800 annually around the world.

Being the consumer's "favorite place for something" will be the most important consideration. Menu proliferation, in effect, will continue as various restaurant locations will be virtually on top of one another. Creating a strategic difference and delivering it with a wallop will become the prime function of fast-food management. Achieving financial goals depends on this, and gains in market share will go only to chains that have this extra punch.

Short-term promotional incentives will become less effective as sales builders. Consumers are already becoming immune to price competition. More than half of all fast-food transactions are deals or coupon-related—value meals, value packages, and kids' meals, as well as advertised discounts and coupons. Skyrocketing promotional and marketing costs may become a serious threat to profitability.

Wide target audiences will be increasingly difficult to reach. It will be necessary to define the target specifically and to find more effective ways to reach the target. Marketing strategy and consumer communication should be developed simultaneously. There must be a reason, besides price or convenience, for consumers to choose a particular chain brand. Everything can be made convenient, and competitors can match any deal.

"In 10 words or less, tell me why a consumer should buy your product instead of the competitor's." This is how veteran Oak Brook, Illinois-based marketing executive Barry Klein—who literally created Ronald McDonald—likes to challenge his clients. "If management can answer that challenge with a meaningful differentiation, the chain or brand should be able to develop advertising which communicates a clear message to customers who have ever-shortening attention spans. Operational implementation of a clear, concise strategic differentiation is a hallmark of successful chains."

The strongest advertising communicates new or better tastes, food combinations, and experiences, Klein asserts. The campaign's look and feel thus may be even more important, because linkage between multiple exposures will drive home the differentiating message. "Consistency across all media, to different target groups, will have to be retained," he declares.

DAVE THOMAS

Among the best advertising campaigns in recent years is the one personified by Wendy's founder-senior chairman Dave Thomas. Although he looked a bit awkward to advertising people, he is beloved and believed by consumers—that trust is what it takes to win today. Wendy's sales rebounded and grew steadily from the time that Thomas started his personal TV advertising campaign in 1990. To the consumer, he represents better taste, higher quality, and an inspector who makes sure the consumer gets what is promised. This personal campaign has a unique touch and could serve Wendy's well for many years. Dave Thomas's message is essentially that whether it's the 99¢ menu or a large bacon cheeseburger, you'd prefer to buy it at "Dave's place."

In his early commercials, Thomas was not comfortable in front of the camera. He was the opposite of the slick, polished, overrehearsed person who tends to play this role. He gave the impression of not wanting to be on television but strongly believing in what he was saying. Thus he just had to play the role, and we believed him. But as the campaign progressed, Thomas gradually projected a pleasing personality, combining warmth and humor with the sincerity that he always had. Soon the Wendy's advertising script writers were able to make him a bit of a rogue, such as in one situation where women admired one of his "spicy" new products. He defied the conventional wisdom that says you can't do that with an amateur actor. Yet that nonprofessionalism was the key to his success.

We know he is not an actor. He is real, and he is one of us. When he is served tiny portions of unidentifiable food, we empathize with him. When he sneaks out for a burger because dinner isn't ready, we don't blame him. When a beautiful woman shows a special interest in him, we're pleased. And when he says he has created a great new taste, or that we should try the 99¢ menu, we don't want to let him down, so we go to Wendy's. He portrays the human element we all identify with, and to us he is a hero. We see him as a likeable character in a television sitcom.

Wendy's campaign is unique because it employs none of the techniques that we anticipate from big-budget advertisers. Yet it does everything that advertising is supposed to do, and more. Thomas's commercials cut through the television clutter, without visual or audio tricks, special music or stars. They extend our attention span with interesting copy and comfortable pictures, instead of assailing us with quick cuts and nearly unintelligible phrases. As we watch, we become involved with the product, and with the experience, because we believe Dave Thomas—not comparisons, research, testimonials, thirty-something language, or a rap song.

Most important, this advertising not only rings cash registers but boosts sales indefinitely. Dave Thomas and the overall concept wear well, and he finally seems so natural at it that even commercials not quite as strong as the others still do a good selling job. Just as Frank Perdue came to represent good-quality chicken, Thomas now is a symbol for high-quality, great-tasting food. This is a real campaign rather than individual commercials that someone hopes to turn into a campaign.

We should all thank Thomas for breaking the rules. He certainly has restored some faith in the proposition that great advertising can still make a contribution to a company's success.

Thomas has said: "A lot of marketing people think all you have to do is advertise to get customers to beat down your doors. They just don't know the operations end. They simply don't have the experience. You have to remember that marketing departments don't make money. Our operations—our restaurants—do, so everything should focus on them."

Thomas lauds Wendy's focused "hot 'n juicy" campaign of the early 1980s but questions the "Where's the beef?" campaign that followed. "Clara Peller was hard of hearing," he recalls, "so we had to have someone pinch her to get her to say her lines at the right time." But there was a problem with the ad: "We kind of lost our identity in the process. Customers were talking about 'Where's the beef?' instead of Wendy's. We thought we were better than we were and thus lost our real focus."

Personalization in advertising can be highly effective. It builds trust and credibility but is tricky to carry out. Colonel Harland Sanders of KFC (100 times more effective than George Foreman, KFC's spokesperson in the early 1990s), Frank Perdue of Perdue Chicken, Tom Carvel of Carvel Ice Cream, Dunkin' Donuts' "little baker" spokesperson who represented the freshness and quality of any product, and IHOP's TV spokesperson, "Cliff," all helped to establish their respective chains' brand identity. They were terrific spokespeople for their own companies. It is interesting that in the age of impersonalization these very personal campaigns stand out. They don't win awards for creative directors, but they do ring the cash register bells.

WINNING CAMPAIGNS

Taco Bell started a new playing field for fast-food chains, and its original "Run for the Border" campaign communicated excellently. It is still the lowest-priced, value-oriented chain, but some of the original campaign's sharp edges were not as evident in later commercials.

Little Caesars' carryout chain gained a wide leadership margin in its segment with a winning campaign in the early 1990s. Beneath the wonderful, humorous presentations, the clarity of the value message was almost unbeatable. By consistently telling consumers that at Little Caesars they get hot, fresh pizza ("the cheesiest real pizza") in large quantities for a great price, the chain achieved its rapid growth in the carryout niche. This is another case where a consistent strategy and outstanding commercials continued to move the business. Little Caesars also won a national award in 1993 for the best television commercial, in which it launched spaghetti with an ad featuring a pet monkey who repeatedly ignored a woman's pleas to twirl the spaghetti correctly and eat with the proper etiquette. (Humor often seems to win the day in TV or radio advertising.)

Some of the most effective ads have the simplest basic appeal. Consider this long-running slogan (through the 1990s) for the Krystal chain, which was founded in 1932: "You've got to have a Krystal, you've got to have a Krystal. It's a Southern tradition, the greatest square burger ever."

Among the best advertising campaigns ever, pegged to quick, simple slogans are the following:

- McDonald's early 1970s "You deserve a break today." This made almost everyone a fast-food customer, legitimatized the industry, and established McD as the leader.

- KFC's 1980s "We Do Chicken Right." KFC's unique competitive difference was communicated so well that it's hard to believe it abandoned the simple, effective slogan. Ditto for Burger King's "Broiled, Not Fried."

- Jack in the Box's "The Food Is Better at the Box" advertising slogan led the chain's surge starting in 1979. However, this opinion claim can't be used in today's regulatory climate. If the chain were to expand into specifics to support the claim, legal copy would take over the commercials.

- Domino's "We Deliver" was another strategic foundation for a chain, until others came along and delivered more.

- Red Lobster's "For the Seafood Lover in You" helped it to become the only national full-service seafood chain.

- Burger King's "Have It Your Way" was a perfect competitive communication to the customer. It did so well—and subsequent other advertising campaigns did so poorly—that they keep bringing it back.

- Carvel's early 1990s "Everything should be made of ice cream" campaign updated its tired image with ice cream landscapes, ice cream cakes, and ice-sculpted figure skaters circling a double-dip cone. Clearly, the brand now stood for "real" ice cream, not soft ice cream or soft frozen yogurt.

LOSERS

We can learn from losing advertising campaigns, although some chains keep repeating the same mistakes. For example, Burger King's campaign and strategy seem to change almost monthly. This is one of the classic cases of unfocused strategic thinking and out-of-control creative direction in marketing history. A 1993 Burger King campaign may have broken through to teens, but the slogan "I love this place" could not build overall business. It was far from unique and could describe almost any restaurant.

Meanwhile, the only Pizza Hut commercial that really could be remembered in 1993 was its pale imitation of Little Caesars, for the Pizza Hut Big Foot pizza. It is amazing that in all the years, with all its money from parent PepsiCo, Pizza Hut could not establish a unique strategic difference to give it a distinct edge over competition, other than total number of units.

Carl's Jr. is a lesson in how misdirected advertising can change a chain's image from highly positive to neutral. Its campaign went from a not-so-great version of Wendy's campaign to something relatively unintelligible, and sales plummeted. Founder-chairman Carl Karcher simply could not be Dave Thomas in person; his stiff delivery was obvious in his personal TV ads. But there were other factors, such as overpricing, in Carl's Jr. early 1990s sales declines during a period when staunch value-pricing was carrying the day.

Carl's tried to straighten out the marketing mess in mid-1993 when new president-CEO Don Doyle hired Karen Eadon away from Taco Bell as marketing vice president. She began pushing the 630-unit chain toward satisfying customer needs rather than simply advertising products. She also emphasized value, price, and faster service. Carl's, the first fast-feeder to expand to table service (in the 1950s) had gotten away from its roots, with too much upgrading and a price structure that was too big as it moved more toward a dinner menu in the 1980s. But even with these efforts, it still had a long way to go toward a real recovery.

THE MASS MARKET

McDonald's is proof of the idea that if you throw enough money, enough constant ads, and enough creativity at the television tube, you will win. McD has an advertising-marketing budget of 6 percent of sales, and it is hard to match McD in this crucial area, although Wendy's sometimes comes close to overcoming the dollar difference with more effective commercials, advertising commitment, and effectiveness.

"Marketing has to be superimposed on the business" (once the business has been built up, not vice versa), emphasizes McD senior chairman Fred Turner. McD reduced its national television advertising budget to less than $200 million in the early 1990s while raising its local television advertising allotment to more than $200 million. McD supports this strategy with local menu offerings such as crab cakes in Maryland and lobsters in Maine.

Still, Taco Bell's John Martin does not believe in spending 5 percent of sales in marketing. He even thinks that the Taco Bell's 1993 figure of 3.8 percent was too high. "If we're really as good as we should be," he asserts, "we shouldn't have to advertise that much." Customer frequency for the typically heavy fast-food user should be four or five visits each month. "One-third of the population gives you three-fourths of all your sales," he says.

Yet we wonder if it is a coincidence that Taco Bell's sales growth has slowed since it reduced its proportion of advertising expenditures. Heavy fast-food users tend to stick with chains that are highly visible on television. Impulse visits usually go to the chain brand that ensures the highest awareness.

Eateries, Inc. markets its Garfield's Restaurants heavily with steady television campaign on quality, price, and items, emphasizing value-priced platters. It constantly tests new products through a RHINOS program (recognition of its best sales-oriented hourly employees). It also uses mystery shoppers to help evaluate food, service, and selling techniques.

Sonic America's Drive-Ins have consistently scored critical successes with their monthly advertised combination meals. They maintain this strategy even in the face of 99¢-value menus of other chains. "We will not succumb to the allure of short-term gains from deep discounting," says chairman Stephen Lynn. "We will continue to offer a monthly deal—a generous amount of food for a promotional price, a price that is easily recognized as a good value by our customers, but which offers our operators a realistic profit margin."

Sonic goes to great lengths to offer chainwide consistency in its monthly promotional offers and advertised prices. But with some 1,300 units in 27 states, it is inevitably moving toward regional customization of its programs. Presenting a consistent image through mass media advertising has reinforced the Sonic image and built consumers' confidence about what they can expect when they pull into a Sonic drive-in. Sonic has at least 70 advertising co-ops representing 95 percent of its franchisees and at least a $15 million annual advertising budget—most of which inevitably goes to the one true mass medium—television. Virtually the entire chain is organized into purchasing co-ops, and there is 90 percent participation in chainwide promotions. "Over 1,200 units working together toward common goals have given us more media clout, greater buying power, and a momentum for success that no one unit could have achieved alone," says Lynn.

The public indeed is fickle, and chains are always trying to devise new slogans and new advertising, dismissing an advertising agency every few years (almost without fail) and trying another agency with a new approach. But sometimes the same slogan and the same basic advertising, maintained steadily over the years with some added nuances, wins the day with consistency, credibility, and a steady pattern. One of the winning campaigns was the early 1990s "No Place Hops Like Sonic," with 1950s teen singing idol Frankie Avalon as its spokesperson. This simple, readily understandable theme gave Sonic a direct competitive edge. It emphasized Sonic's speed and energy, as well as the unique delivery system personified by the carhop.

Sonic's television advertising focuses on the monthly promotional food combo—taste appeal, value, and the food items unique to the Sonic concept. In 1993, however, Sonic also started to emphasize how the drive-in concept differs from traditional fast-food concepts and how important the carhops are.

Unique Positioning

Effective marketing requires specific positioning. You need to understand what the customer wants, or else competitors will. The advantage is to the chains with local orientations and special marketing savvy in each locale.

Burger King also moved more toward local TV advertising and emphasized local ethnic programs, such as its Italian Fest in the Northeast that featured five special sandwiches. Burger King ties in heavily with local sports events such as bike races and community competitions. Menus vary from region to region. However, Burger King's marketing needs to strike a balance between experimentation and strategic focus.

John Creed, founder-president of Solana Beach, California-based 65-unit Chart House, Inc., was one of the mavericks who depended on word-of-mouth promotion for 30 years and succeeded more often than not. But in 1993 he finally launched his first national advertising campaign, via print media (mostly magazines), radio, and direct mail. The message urged customers to go to Chart House on a regular basis, rather than only for special occasions. Creed also started a frequent-dining program with points and awards for regular customers as he sought to boost sales. Like many others, he finally realized that steady sales increases are no longer a given.

Celebration themes can be particularly effective. Chart House's first national advertising campaign was pegged to customers "celebrating life's little successes" and featured the slogan "Great food, great service or it's on us."

Golden Corral coordinates its menu item promotions by taking a tray of samples to the order line and letting customers try them. The chain emphasized the theme "Come Taste Our Celebration" during its 1993 20th anniversary promotions.

In a long-running "Celebration of Food" campaign, Chi-Chi's tried to emphasize its position as "the place for Mexican food and fun." This image enabled the chain to introduce several new food products and leverage some old favorites, while reinforcing its leadership position in the full-service Mexican restaurants category. "Given our size and strength," says former president Joseph Micatrotto, "we are ideally positioned to develop and evaluate dozens of new products annually and then move quickly to implement winners that have performed well in unit and market tests." But Chi-Chi's changed advertising agencies and changed the thrust of its winning campaign. Inevitably, its sales went soft.

Some regional chains simply don't advertise. As of late 1993, Claim Jumper had never advertised. "Our advertising is in our food," said president Craig Nickoloff. "We get involved with local sports teams, the Special Olympics, and the Joswick Riding Center for the Handicapped." The chain sponsors an annual barbecue at the equestrian center, and each of its restaurants employs developmentally disabled people. (Approximately 70 disabled persons are employed by the chain.) "I have a personal commitment to that," Nickoloff affirms.

The national Entertainment Book restaurant coupons and all kinds of other coupons and promotional offerings are helping to drive restaurant sales in the 1990s as business has become a lot tougher and seats often aren't as full as they once were. These promotions, deals, coupons, and discounts are very much a mixed bag. When the excitement ends and the price has to be restored, customers often become disillusioned. The fast-food price wars driven by the challenge "Can you undercut this price?" may have done damage to the chains while helping consumers get deals.

With the coming of cable TV, some areas have as many as 50 or even 100 channels. Chains are compelled to target their advertising to key prospects with a specific and unique message that can break through the clutter.

Chains are testing "infomercials" as TV advertising vehicles. Instead of a quick 30-second product-service message, a chain can put forth a full 15- or 30-minute "public service" program on what it is doing to help the community. McDonald's did this to maximum effect by launching the Mac Report Infomercial in a news-program format on network television portraying its good deeds in local communities. This first appeared on the Black Entertainment Television network.

Infomercials have to be carefully structured to maintain their credibility lest they backfire as customers rebel against advertising presented in the guise of news. Too often infomercials are not labeled as advertising clearly enough that consumers realize without a doubt that they are not a news programs.

The chain foodservice industry's most seductive weapon has been traffic-building promotions. The top 10 volume chains, which account for as much as 60 percent of total industry sales, spend anywhere from 4 percent to 8 percent of their annual sales on overall marketing. But they are becoming somewhat disillusioned with the constant discount couponing because coupons don't achieve high enough customer-count increases to offset overall lower prices. Furthermore, when the coupons stop, traffic plummets.

Product and pricing gimmicks can be effective up to a point. Subway tried 2¢ sandwiches and various items that could be obtained through a scratch-and-win card promotion. Each customer who bought a soda from any Subway unit was given a card with winning menu items at the 2¢ price. Another 2¢ promotion was tried by a Chicago restaurant with a flat offer of 2¢ for a glass of wine. A customer could choose any vintage of wine—a great way to get customers to try wine, although perhaps they would always expect it for 2¢.

Ponderosa began an attempt to reduce all the meal deals in 1993 and position itself as "America's family restaurant where every member of the family can get what he or she wants." "We're building up the perceived value of Ponderosa with great products and service rather than with coupons," observed William Welter, marketing senior vice president. The chain also became the official training table of Little League baseball and capitalized on this in its advertising.

Pinpointed Neighborhood Marketing

Ronald Magruder firmly believes in local marketing for The Olive Garden. It has individual agencies in each region to achieve the local touch. It also uses 24 different public relations agencies and 13 of its own marketing managers around the country to ensure that the chain's restaurants have true individual approaches.

Personalized marketing is the key in neighborhood areas. Bay Street's Bill Bouffard makes it his business to meet with the concierge of each hotel in metro Dallas and other areas where Bay Street is located. He gives each concierge 25 appetizer coupons, and when those are redeemed each concierge gets $25. Hundreds of these coupons are redeemed monthly. Bouffard tells the concierge the attributes of the restaurants and invites them to the nearest one. He asks them what their guests might need at the restaurant and tailors a program for them. "We like to keep getting feedback from a hotel as to what their guests think of the restaurant." Bouffard says. "If a certain hotel hasn't been sending guests, we'll keep after them."

Concierges and taxi drivers may be the best advertising of all for any restaurant. So you've got to cultivate them and stay in touch with them. As in most matters, Nick Nickolas uses his own unique approaches instead of advertising. "Cabdrivers, bartenders, cocktail waitresses, and concierges are great sources for getting new customers to try you," he says. "The best marketing campaign is directed by my employees and strictly depends on word-of-mouth."

Local options are critical as chains increasingly project a neighborhood image. Burger King finally backed off its national dinner-basket program in 1993 and allowed it as a local option with menu items recommended from headquarters. The program, with dinner baskets and table service, was a failure nationally as it represented a confusing message to customers who were not looking for any sort of fancy dinner at Burger King, and it also diverted Burger King's focus away from its basics. In fact, efforts to boost dinner business throughout the fast-food segment have often backfired, as they seem to divert chains from the price-value basics.

A major challenge is to avoid a cookie-cutter approach. Thus foodservice chains have jumped over the $1 billion mark in total local television advertising expenditures. But some chains, sure that a consistent image is more important, allow no local variations. In today's ultracompetitive world, the delicate balance between a consistent marketing focus and local variations is of constant concern.

Ethnic marketing can be carried on locally better than nationally. KFC targets 40 percent of an entire population within a narrow 1.5-mile radius. It launched an African-American theme in 500 selected units and a Cuban menu including beans and yucca plantains in 13 Miami units. Sales were reported up 5 percent to 10 percent in these local marketing efforts. In addition, KFC targeted units in Texas and southern California for items such as ranchero beans, tacos, and yellow rice and with Western uniforms to match as it bid for the Mexican-American market.

Arby's dropped national advertising in the mid-1980s and ever since has focused entirely on local advertising through its franchising-coop system. It also varies menus regionally, such as by offering rye bread in the Midwest.

While still maintaining standardized, consistent menus, Pizza Hut allows variations for regional tastes—cajun shrimp pizza in Louisiana, jalapeno pizza in Texas, and thin-crust pizza in the Northeast.

Special promotions can be key marketing tools for chains. In the summer of 1993, Newport Beach, California-based Wienerschnitzel hot dogs staged hundreds of Schnitz Blitz Parking Lot Parties as part of its "Hit the Schnitz" advertising campaign. To entertain families with small children, the chain engaged costumed characters such as Wienerdog, Heather Hotspots, and Roger the Rhino, as well as games and drawings. It also gave away lower-priced hot dogs. A 17-van fleet transported all the equipment throughout the chain's 10 Western states for the parties at its some 300 units. Each unit hosted a party on two summer weekends. Sales increases as high as 25 percent to 50 percent were reported for the days of the parties.

David Wachtel views advertising "as a necessary evil, like accounting." He feels that advertising is simply necessary to survive and that without it a chain would lose all momentum. He emphasizes local-restaurant and neighborhood marketing, with the focal point being public relations projects that sponsor various events on a local level: "This, coupled with strong operations, will win."

But no amount of advertising can make a poorly run restaurant succeed.

Outback does television and radio advertising in 17 separate markets. "You've got to go out there and do things to promote your restaurants in the local markets," says chairman Chris Sullivan. "We help sponsor golf tournaments and charitable events." The chain has taken over sponsorship of the annual Gator Bowl football game and could gain a great deal of recognition and marketing momentum from the Outback Steakhouse Gator Bowl. But the question remains as to whether the chain has enough restaurants nationally to justify such a large investment in a network event.

Local restaurant marketing indeed is a necessity. However, Max Pine, who was Restaurant Associates Corporation (RA) president for 17 years, is convinced that he got a lot more bang for the buck by doing almost all marketing-advertising on a personal basis rather than using the highly expensive TV outlet or any other medium. RA has a door-to-door sales force in all its geographic areas, and these salespeople make personal visits to all local businesses, hotel concierges, and movie theater managers. The return on the cost involved is much higher than it would be through any media. "It's so difficult to compete on television with just a few ads," observes Pine. "You need to spend millions to make a significant impact. That's why we target our customers and have mailing lists of 150,000" (obtained from credit-card customers who eat at RA restaurants and from data bases).

RA also emphasizes its Handshake Club and has built up a total of 150,000 names of customers, who receive a periodic newsletter and all types of coupon-discounts—particularly for Charlie Brown's in New Jersey and Acapulco in California. RA also maintains a full-time sales force for this purpose in New Jersey and California.

Banquet business is a marketing win for RA too. Customers who visit RA's restaurants for banquets or parties often return to the restaurant for regular meals. These events are terrific for repeat business.

Any chain that can project a neighborhood image in each of its market areas is likely to be a winner. Customers today like to think they are going to their favorite neighborhood place. Kansas

City-based Applebee's is leaping toward the top of the casual segment partly because it constantly hammers away at the theme "Applebee's Neighborhood Grill & Bar—America's Favorite Neighbor" and follows through with neighborhood specialties on the menu and pictures of local high school and college sports stars of the last 10 years adorning the walls. San Diego-based Home-Town Buffet, Inc. is rapidly gaining in its segment with a sharp neighborhood image pegged to its name.

The Olive Garden projects a neighborhood image by offering selected regional menu items at each of its restaurants. Its individualized menus have enabled it to achieve recognition as a favorite neighborhood restaurant, even though it is a more than 450-unit chain.

Community-Service Marketing

Ben & Jerry's is a leader in community-service marketing campaigns. It offers concerts, shows, public-awareness campaigns, and sometimes even free ice cream. Its main marketing monies go to sponsoring concerts, benefits, fund-raisers, and public awareness of causes such as the Children's Defense Fund, which educates people about the poverty facing many American children. Jerry Greenfield and Ben Cohen, co-owners, always donate a percentage of profits from any event to a charity or community group.

Serving food to homeless people and pushing campaigns for adequate health care and tax credits for needy families are among their causes as they seek to raise public consciousness on the key issues of the day. Social consciousness and public service are important things for the community and demonstrate that making money is not a chain's only goal. Such an approach shows that it serves its customers in others ways and projects a friendly neighborhood image. Ben & Jerry's and McDonald's are industry leaders in this regard.

For a foodservice management company, community activities are often by far the best way to achieve recognition. "The only way our product could become known," former president Stephen Elmont says of Creative Gourmets, "is through involving ourselves in the community." This chain spends $100,000 a year on community hospitals, symphonies, and the ballet. "It is incumbent on each of us to give something back to the community and to show social consciousness," he emphasizes.

FRESH EXCITEMENT

"Fresh" is the byword for food and advertising in the restaurant industry today. Denver-based Bakers Square restaurants' new advertising theme is "Nobody goes further for fresh." "When it comes to bringing you the freshest food possible," the TV ads say, "the people at Bakers Square are truly driven." This emphasizes the chain's retail products as well as its restaurant products.

La Salsa, a 43-unit Los Angeles-based Mexican chain, emphasized its fresh ingredients in a $300,000 advertising campaign that used billboards, radio, direct mail, and point-of-purchase advertising. The main themes were short and punchy: "Play hard. Eat smart. Stay fit. Eat fresh."

Winning ads create excitement and drama, as well as present a chain's product and image. San Francisco-based Chevys Mexican Restaurants launched superinnovative television ads that are constantly remembered by customers and noncustomers alike. Chevys television crews track down customers in San Francisco by 6:00 A.M. or 7:00 A.M. each morning and interview them for television ads that are aired that very evening. This makes people think about Chevys fresh-Mex timely concept.

An extensive news story about Chevys innovative ads was featured on a San Francisco television station. With so many people talking about the excitement generated by these on-the-spot ads, Chevys got a lot of extra mileage from the entire campaign. In other types of TV ads, Chevys own managers and employees are seen racing around to deliver food in split seconds and to do anything to please the customer. This also is a morale and ego booster for the employees.

New York-based Nathan's Famous, Inc. emphasized an intensive TV advertising campaign for its some 150 restaurants in 1993.

The 30-second spot ads portrayed the "Taste of New York" and the "Home of the Hot Dog and Fries That Made New York Famous." Earlier, it used television ads for its Nathan's Famous hot dogs that it sells in supermarkets in New York, New England, Florida, Los Angeles, and San Francisco.

Strength can be spotlighted in particular dayparts to capitalize on specific identities. Elias Brothers Restaurants, Inc.'s Big Boy ads in Michigan feature a number of TV-spot meal periods and portray special menus for each, such as a $2.99 breakfast bar; a shrimp, seafood, and crab bar; a burger special; and a series of home-cooked dinners from $4.99 up. Elias also strengthens the Big Boy brand name by sponsoring the Detroit Grand Prix and the Buick Open golf tournament, as well as an annual fall food drive for the hungry called Operation Can-Do.

Network television spending is still holding its own, but chains are pinpointing closely defined lower-cost media—local spot television, data base marketing to gain repeat business, and in-house publications. Every chain with children in its target audience is specifically zeroing in on Nickelodeon, Fox, and MTV in addition to Saturday morning network TV programming.

Combination dishes or value meals are constantly being pushed by fast-feeders (Taco Bell, McDonald's, and Burger King in particular) at $1.99, $1.49, 99¢, 79¢, 59¢, and so on. McD's value meals especially have boosted sales and represent an ever-increasing share of its business. Yet sometimes value meals can backfire, in terms of reduced profit margins and negative reactions by customers when the price wars cease, at least temporarily, and sanity returns to the price structures.

Most chain marketing is targeted to maximum cost efficiency on television and radio. "But our strongest marketing is the extra service we give to our guests in the restaurant," says Spaghetti Warehouse president Lou Neeb. "We don't have enough clusters to be media-efficient so we must market as an independent would."

For S & A Restaurants Corporation, Bennigan's Extra-Special Treatment ad campaign used celebrity look-alikes to drive home the message that "you don't have to be a star to be treated like one." It strengthened sales and helped operations to implement a new service-training program. But Bennigan's needed stability to succeed with this approach, which was difficult to sustain in a high-turnover environment. Meanwhile, Steak and Ale's Legend in Steak campaign clearly positioned that concept after a disastrous experiment with menu variety. The idea was to sell the sizzle and the drama.

Hardee's stepped up its product and marketing push in 1993 with the introduction of The Ultimate Omelet Biscuit and a heavy advertising campaign pegged to this addition to the 99¢ breakfast value menu. Hardee's unique niche is breakfast, and it tends to dominate this, particularly in the South where its offerings have extra appeal.

Hardee's advertising slogan, "Are You Ready for Some Real Food?" pushed into the Italian sphere with a spicy grilled Italian sausage combination, a chicken parmigiana sandwich, and a breaded whole breast covered with tomato sauce and served on a six-inch Italian roll. Hardee's also went beyond its successful Frisco Burger with a New York Patty Melt quarter-pound burger. But the much-trumpeted "Real Food" slogan couldn't have been too successful, because Hardee's dropped Ogilvy & Mather, the advertising agency that had created it, after eight years on the account and in late 1993 selected Deutsch/Dworin Advertising, New York, as its new agency.

Marketing is a lot more than sales or advertising. The great companies and winning chains see marketing as an overall approach to new trends, challenges, and opportunities. Winning marketing programs are built around the drama and excitement of the chain's concept. In most cases the core of the concept is the menu, and a new product or product extension can provide the drama. This is better than using deep discounts to generate what is really artificial excitement.

In the mid-1980s, Taco Bell launched Taco Salad and Nachos Bell Grand combination dinners, all of which grew to be a substantial portion of the menu mix. At Perkins in the late 1980s, marketing chief Patrick Morris introduced new lines of omelets, melt sandwiches, and salads in bowls made of bread. All of these provided unique points of difference against the competition. But the most successful promotion was Perkins' salad in a bread bowl—an idea that retained its luster. This was an effort to build the lunch business by providing a unique item. Few if any of Perkins's competitors had bakeries then, and those that did specialized in pies. The salad, served in a bowl made from Perkins's own French bread, was called "salad in a bowl you can eat." As Morris recalls: "The items were appealing and unique; the point of difference was extremely obvious. Furthermore, because of the lack of particular equipment by most of our competitors, we had a technological advantage that they would have a difficult time duplicating."

Frequent-diner programs—the restaurant industry's version of frequent-flyer awards—are another means of building customer loyalty. They work especially well for dinnerhouses and groups such as Lettuce Entertain You. Big 4 Restaurants started a frequent-diner program whereby customers may enjoy a discount of 20 percent after spending a set amount of dollars. They also receive a regular newsletter that keeps them informed of Big 4 activities.

Chart House also launched a frequent-diner program, the Aloha Club, offering points and gifts based on a customer's expenditures and special incentives for anyone dining at a number of Chart Houses, ranging up to free round-the-world airline tickets for customers who dine at or at least have a drink at all 65 Chart Houses in the United States (presumably during a lifetime).

RESEARCH VERSUS GUT FEELING

"In today's environment," Patrick Morris declares, "to assume you can read the consumer's mind is the greatest mistake you can make." When it comes to a decision between your gut feeling and the use of surveys, some sort of balance is needed. Yet instinct must play a role in just about every marketing decision.

Surveys and consumer research are notorious for not revealing the need for innovation. Consumers tend to base answers on what is and what they like and feel comfortable with now, rather than what could be. In fact, if John Martin depended solely on surveys, he would not be regarded as a superinnovator who takes risks, but rather as an implementer of basics and a few new ideas. And Taco Bell would remain in the middle of the pack, regardless of PepsiCo's financial clout.

It takes vision, guts, and personal feel to really succeed in this business, not just relying on numbers. Yet surveys and research can affirm (or perhaps disavow) the perspectives that emerge from instinct.

Marketing efforts must directly illustrate meaningful differences between a chain and its competitors—unique aspects that can attract more customers to try the concept as well as bring existing customers back more often.

Mind-reading or gut-feel intuition about customers was prevalent through the 1960s and 1970s when entrepreneurial-minded chains could grow as long as they had a decent concept, reasonable execution, and good sites. Marketing was a luxury more than anything else. But in the 1980s chain restaurants grew and saturated markets. Professional executives, who had in large part replaced founders, discovered that the task was not to lure customers from independents to try chains, but to get customers away from other chains. The chaining of America had proceeded in every direction. Thus professional marketers and professional researchers were needed to target customers strategically.

"When you're large," observes Pizza Hut marketing research senior director Jeff Lawson, "the only way to do things right is to have disciplined mechanisms in place." Using the latest computer technology for data base marketing and for advanced product testing, Pizza Hut feels it can project purchasing behavior fairly accurately from its scientific input data.

Customer focus groups can also be valuable. Morris prefers this type of qualitative research. "With surveys and percentages, you don't know if people are merely telling you what they think you want to hear. But in focus groups, you hear real things from people who have to explain what they mean," he says. "If you can just do one thing, I'd say to do focus groups to get a general idea of the trend."

Many of today's new menu items are developed with the help of consumer focus groups. But Roger Williams, marketing vice president of 300-unit Columbus, Ohio-based Bob Evans Farms, Inc. restaurants, does not see focus groups as a panacea. He suggests that before considering a focus group, a chain first must probe its own mindset and those of competitors. "Then you have to zero in on real specifics to make focus groups effective." In one case, when Williams used a focus group to pinpoint desired portion sizes, he discovered that some of the portions were too small. In another focus group regarding Bob Evans's new Cantina del Rio Mexican restaurants concept, Williams used only Chi-Chi's customers and found that Chi-Chi's was setting the standards for Mexican food in Columbus.

The format of Golden Corral's buffet-style food bars was established through focus groups more than anything else. Value emerged as the key (or perceived price-value might be the interpretation). Thus a large buffet, steak, and bakery concept emerged. Perhaps Golden Corral could have saved itself the trouble of all the focus groups and realized these obvious precepts by simple gut feeling. But before spending all that money and locking themselves into these formats at some of their restaurants, they wanted specific confirmation of their hunches.

Eddie Sheldrake, president of Santa Fe Springs, California-based Polly's, Inc. family restaurant, operator and a KFC franchisee, decided changes were needed at a Medford, Oregon, Mr. Steak restaurant that Polly's operated. He felt the whole operation should be converted into a Mexican fast-food concept, but he checked his own inclination by having consultant Lowell Petrie study the major restaurants in the Medford market. When Petrie found that Mexican quick-service had reached the saturation point, Sheldrake was persuaded to launch a "country-cooking" restaurant with its own unique niche for that area—meatloaf, mashed potatoes, chicken-fried steak, and so on. He also had extensive telephone surveys carried out in early 1992 regarding his 12 Polly's to see whether his feeling, that the menus were old-fashioned and lacked variety, was substantiated. It was—in spades. The surveys indicated that the menus needed more variety, that frequent users had declined, and that the age base was skewed toward older customers. Sheldrake then checked those findings with a few expert consultants and finally moved ahead with the necessary changes.

Survey methods include in-restaurant intercepts of customers (or catching them on the way out) for quick conversational surveys, staying in touch with customers afterward, concept testing, focus groups, and mystery shoppers.

Customers like choices. One of TCBY's most successful marketing campaigns, former president Charles Cocotas recalls, was for a parfait product. "We offered the consumer the chance to choose any flavor of yogurt from among available flavors, and any variety of toppings." The campaign, called "Pick Your Perfect Parfait" was a winner.

Cocotas firmly believes in customer pretesting. In setting up an annual marketing calendar, TCBY established a series of monthly product promotions with "hero products." Focus groups are presented with a wide array of monthly product possibilities and asked which ones they prefer. Focus groups, however, do not always provide the right direction. Therefore, TCBY also conducts tracking studies every six months to monitor how well it is doing against competitors in quality, operational attributes, purchasing frequency, and repurchase intent. Research is critical to managing and identifying strategic opportunities.

TCBY also utilizes mystery shoppers every 30 days and uses the findings as input to monitor the entire consumer experience, quality perception, and motivation, and in making recognition awards for employees who deliver exceptional service.

In 1993, ARA Services launched Avanti Gourmet Coffee for 400-plus units in eight months. The program featured an award-winning logo and special design that greatly raised profitability. ARA prefers to move quickly into the market when they have a winner, says John Farquharson, ARA's Global Food Service chairman. "We use taste panels extensively in recipe development and refinement, but gut-feel is cheaper than research. . . . We leverage active menu concept/trends in the marketplace to assure success."

DATABASE MARKETING

A popular trend is database marketing aimed at getting customers to return. Chains are finding that keeping current customers is cheaper than trying to buy new ones with the discounting and couponing that destroy value. Home-delivery chains and delivery services such as Takeout Taxi are ideal for building extensive data bases.

Spaghetti Warehouse uses the *Sourcebook of Zip Code Demographics* to target marketing and demographic data about all possible aspects of each market the chain enters and see which parts of the market are the best ones on which to focus advertising and direct mail. In addition, customers at each new restaurant are asked to name their favorite radio station, and radio advertising is then geared more toward the preferred local station or stations.

The 20-unit Grand Rapids, Michigan-based Universal Restaurants simply registers each customer for a discount birthday meal and has thus garnered a more than 500,000-name mailing list for all promotions and events—an excellent way to get repeat business.

Under any conditions, database marketing is a key approach that may be more effective than anything else in the 1990s. McDonald's, Burger King, KFC, Arby's, and Pizza Hut are among those chains that are heavily invalued with it with the object of encouraging long-term customer relationships. Pizza Hut, for one, is spending as much as $20 million a year to keep updating its customer data base. This process can also yield excellent segment information. For example, it shows that of about 22 million families that go to fast-food places, only 25 percent are fast-food "addicts," but that these customers account for 55 percent of the total sales and spend an average of $1,900 annually per person in fast-food places. Chains that can identify heavy users and market consistently to them establish a major advantage.

As a result of such marketing techniques, however, very little research is directed toward "lost customers" who don't return or who never came in the first place. Such research would be invaluable to the industry and could show how to woo more customers rather than concentrating so completely on those a chain already has. Still, all the efforts to reduce marketing to an absolute science can never succeed, because the human element and individual judgments remain crucial.

THE WOW EFFECT

To win in the restaurant chain game, you have to provide more than just adequate food and service. The last thing you want to do is bore the customer or have him yawning from the sheer standardization of it all. Perhaps you are happy or relieved that the customer is not turned off, or angered, by your food or service. But for real success, you must exceed customer expectations by a substantial margin.

Nothing succeeds more than the Wow Effect, and we don't mean, "Wow, this is terrible!" What you need are plaudits for outstanding food and service. In simple terms, you want the customer to say, or at least to think, "Wow, what an incredible experience. I'm coming back here next time."

It is unrealistic to think that every customer experience is going to be a super-wow or even just a wow. But the more you can achieve an overall Wow Effect, the more you will win. Just one sensational, mind-boggling food item and/or a special act of courtesy or kindness by a server can make a customer eager for more of the same next time. Customers generally settle for far less than the best, in fact, for mediocrity as long as no disaster occurs. So you can triumph with just one big wow or a series of wows.

Don Smith created one of the great wows when, as Perkins Restaurants president in 1986, he started a turnaround effort by launching bakeries and then having them completely redesigned for attention-grabbing visual appeal. The new touches included burgundy and white tiles, neon lighting behind the counter, and fully displayed huge muffins and cookies. Customers took special notice of the eye-catching bakeries and the salad in a French bread bowl.

More than anyone else, the restaurant manager creates the Wow Effect, which really is a reflection of the can-do attitude that must be instilled. "What has got to happen is that the unit manager encourages all the employees to outdo themselves, to go far beyond the customer's expectations," says Longhorn Steaks president Richard Rivera, former president of TGI Friday's.

Alan Stoner, former Whataburger operations senior vice president, fondly recalls a London to Dallas flight in the summer of 1992, not because it was such a smooth ride or that the scenery was so picturesque; rather, because a passenger sitting close by who, when asked what he would like for lunch, told the stewardess: "What I would really enjoy most would be a Whataburger." Never one to lose a marketing opportunity, Stoner introduced himself to the passenger and gave him two VIP cards so that he and a friend could enjoy Whataburgers when he arrived in Dallas.

Stoner himself felt 10 feet tall, and this experience merely confirmed what he had known for years, that his chain's signature product—the Whataburger—and the chain's name were double winners. "There's no better way to ensure repeat business," he affirms, "than to vigorously guard the consistent quality of your food products and to work to maintain impeccable service levels."

Many executives in the industry take credit for creating the term "Wow Effect." Actually, Allen J. Bernstein, president of the Quantum Restaurant Group, may have been the one who first publicly talked about the idea some 15 years ago. "The Wow Effect makes customers feel good about the restaurant and about themselves," he says. "It's a nonnegotiable company philosophy that 99 percent is not good enough, that if you mess anything up for the customer, you'd better take care of it better than anyone else could."

In Bernstein's view, the Wow Effect reflects immensely on the chain brand name, and, in fact, is the brand. "Look at the food and the delivery of the food to the customer," he observes, "and if you can truly say 'wow,' then you're a winner. Look at the incredible desserts and the steaks, and if they're wows, you're a double winner."

He pegs In-N-Out Burger, a double drive-through chain content to shine just in California, as close to an all-time wow for its mouth-watering burgers, outstanding price-value, and impeccable service. Not far behind, in his opinion, is Outback, with its $4.50 massive portions of Bloomin' onions—more than enough for ten people but often served for two. One overwhelming item like that can win the day and a series of great items and superservice may triumph too. No matter what, you've got to offer something well beyond the pedestrian.

Bernstein's own favorite quantum wows include great desserts made on-premises and merchandised to the hilt in a special display window at Atlanta-based Peasant restaurants; mind-boggling specials for children at Mick's restaurants in Atlanta and Washington, D.C., and prime cuts of steak at Morton's restaurants in major cities around the country. "It's really all about taking care of people," he says. "Any way we can accommodate customers, we will."

One of his greatest wows in favor of the customer is to allow reservations for just two-thirds of the tables at the New York City Morton's and thereby give walk-ins a chance. This policy is predicated on the idea that the restaurant generates enough traffic to be full under any circumstances.

Chains can make an extra-wow impression with big steaks or a lot of food for a little money. This is the driving force of Morton's success, just as it is for Minneapolis-based Old Country Buffets, Pizza Hut's Bigfoot pizza, Domino's Dominator pizza, and McDonald's dinosaur-sized Jurassic Park meal. Although people talk about healthful foods, many tend to eat big meals, or at least to seek that opportunity. One case in which bigger is definitely better is in creating the wow effect.

The maximum wow may be the gigantic food bars assembled by various chains, which yield spotty financial results because of tricky economics. Yet they tend to build rapid repeat business, based on a perceived phenomenal price-value (assuming that a customer can eat the maximum amount offered at these food bars—or take the rest home in a doggie bag).

Aptly named Fresh Choice, based in Santa Clara, California, lets customers put together their own all-you-can-eat meals for $5.95 at lunch and $6.95 at dinner. They choose from six separate bars—salads, pasta, grilled foods, soups, baked goods, and desserts. Among the innumerable offerings are 20 salad toppings, at least 5 soups and at least 5 types of muffins. Cooking is spotlighted directly in front of the customers. As the name implies, the wow is a stunning array of fresh choices. "Our customers keep coming for the value, not for huge portions of food," says president Martin Culver, who estimates that many of his customers eat at Fresh Choice restaurants two or three times weekly.

Shoney's Restaurants thrives on an immense breakfast bar value-priced at $3.99 to $5.99 for adults and $1.99 for children. Almost 90 percent of all customers choose the breakfast bar, rather than ordering regularly. An endless array of eggs, pancakes, biscuits, grits, cereals, and fruits is available.

Other proponents of massive food bars have been Los Angeles-based Sizzler steakhouses and Raleigh, North Carolina-based Golden Corral steakhouses. Sizzler has backed away from food bars because, as a spokesperson says: "We want to be known for great grilled foods, but the hot bars were actually shifting business away from the grill." Still, Golden Corral continues to push huge food bars in its largest 10,000-square foot restaurants.

When Omaha-based Godfather's Pizza introduced its jumbo-sized pizza, customers were quickly wowed by this full-fledged multipizza product. Still, Herman Cain, Godfather's president, likes to call the chain's Wow Effect "positively outrageous service with a smile. We must always strive to exceed expectations. If we make any 'mistake' on a pizza, we automatically give the customer the same type of pizza free, plus a medium-sized pizza—even if it was not a definite mistake. The trick is not only to fix a real or perceived problem on the spot but to go well beyond that in exceeding the customer's expectations."

Stephen Elmont, president of Mirabelle restaurant in Boston and formerly founder-president of Creative Gourmets, recalls banquets at which customers expected the usual mushy potatoes and plastic string beans but were astounded when he and his partner-wife, Linda Schwab, were able to raise the quality to a spectacular level. He also recalls overachieving—creating the Wow Effect—at the prestigious Groton Prep Schools' 50th anniversary banquet and at the Bach Festival's 100th anniversary party.

One has to believe that customers who dine at such events never forget the spectacular food that far surpasses their expectations and would race to attend a similar event run by the same company. There is no better way to build repeat business. Once the customer's expectations have been raised far above the former low level, however, it becomes increasingly difficult to surpass these aspirations.

Elmont has set a new wow level at the Mirabelle restaurant, which opened in Boston in 1992 as the forerunner of a potential group of such restaurants. Most all of his offerings are untraditional or wow items—calves liver served uniquely and with a favorable taste (no mean trick nowadays), Ethiopian caramel ice cream, and a bevy of other unusual items. The place may seem a little nonconformist, but it has a definite wow niche.

General Mills has engineered its own Wow Effects in its restaurants. In the 1970s, Joe Lee wowed Red Lobster customers with all-you-can-eat Alaskan crab legs and popcorn shrimp. And through the late 1980s and early 1990s, Ron Magruder has been wowing The Olive Garden customers with super-breadsticks and all-you-can-eat salads, extra touches that customers don't forget and keep coming back for—especially with an attractive price-value of only a $10 per person dinner ticket average. Still, lasagna remains by far the number one seller!

Magruder's other wow in the equation is the localization of menus and sauces for each geographic area. That's why The Olive Garden focuses on local spot television "for the individual" rather than a national TV approach in its advertising. In essence, the overall customer experience is a wow, The Olive Garden having been voted the number one casual restaurant chain in food, atmosphere, and cleanliness for six consecutive years in consumer surveys conducted by *Restaurants & Institutions* through 1993.

Other wows on The Olive Garden platter include an open pasta kitchen, where all customers can see the pasta being made fresh; larger-than-usual portions, promoting the price-value image; cleverly combined Northern and Southern Italian cooking on some of the platters; the world's largest assortment of restaurant wines, with 470,000 cases sold in 1992, including a wide variety of Italian wines; production of its own sauces and keeping all menu ingredients fresh; a spectacular array of desserts, such as a New York style cheesecake with special chocolates and a chocolate chip cookie-dough cheesecake.

In its own modest way, the decor too contributes to the Wow Effect. Plants are used extensively throughout each Olive Garden, and the color scheme is decidedly burgundy and green. All elements combine for a single impressive effect.

Of course, Norman Brinker will not be outdone when it comes to a Wow Effect. Nor will Brinker International president Ronald McDougall or restaurants creator Philip Romano. The fajitas at Chili's and the huge portions (virtually guaranteeing doggie bags for almost all customers) at Macaroni Grill are special wows.

McDougall is convinced that with Brinker International executives providing employees with wows of their own, the whole effect is passed to the customers. He recalls a special simulated live television "David Brinkerman Show" (intended to represent a combination of Norman Brinker, television news commentator David Brinkley, and talk show host David Letterman), produced by Brinker executives in late 1992 for 900 restaurant general managers gathered at a triannual company convention in Maui. In the video show, Brinker, McDougall, Romano, and other executives did impersonations that wowed the general managers. This display of top executives showing that they are part of the team and don't take themselves too seriously built even more of a spirit of enthusiasm in the company.

One of the grandest wows is The Cheesecake Factory, based in California and led by David Overton, who once knew absolutely nothing about cooking—only how to bake luscious fresh pies (a skill that he learned and adapted from his mother). The chain offers large portions that enhance the price-value image and features 35 separate varieties of cheesecake, 15 salads, 14 pastas, 13 appetizers, 12 pizzas, 12 omelets, 10 burgers, 25 sandwiches, at least 11 separate seafood or steak entrees, and an endless array of specialty coffees and drinks. How this chain can control all this is another question, but it is a super-wow to the customer.

For Dunkin' Donuts chairman Robert Rosenberg, the biggest wow is the chain's exquisite coffee. He has an unstinting commitment to perfection in blend, roast, temperature, cream, packaging, and all other ingredients. The undisclosed particulars are packed into 26 full pages of a secret manual that we were unable to obtain, although much of his know-how is in Rosenberg's head. He has arguably produced the best 60¢ cup of coffee in the land, and it is no wonder that many customers and noncustomers alike pull their cars off highways to sample the coffee and try the donuts and cookies, which also have their own wow recipes.

If Rosenberg's education at Cornell University's School of Hotel Administration and Harvard Business School (where he received an M.B.A.) accomplished nothing else, it instilled in him a penchant for overwhelming commitment to quality and dominance in one or two key niches—all of which should make us cheer for Dunkin' Donuts' regular coffee in an age overwrought with specialty coffees. He achieves extra wows by merchandising the coffee and snacks in nontraditional locations such as railroad stations, airports, gasoline stations, and retail stores.

The Wow Effect means different things to different people. To Robert Taft, who was chief operating officer of Seattle-based Skippers seafood shops from 1988 to 1993, the wow factor was in the key lime pie (a real quality surprise for a fast-food chain), the English-style fish, and the all-you-can-eat offerings. A Skippers fast-food customer typically receives more price-value and quality than expected.

To David Wachtel, O'Charley's founder, the Wow Effect simply is overall consistency in all aspects of the game. "This may not be very glamorous," he remarks, "but over the long term it is very effective. After several visits to our restaurant, the consumer develops a loyalty and becomes the most valuable of all, the repeat customer." Maybe so, but he might do well with some kind of item to gain a stronger long-term niche in the already overcrowded casual restaurant field—something identifiable that sums up O'Charley's rather than just consistency, which does, of course, have merit in itself.

To California Pizza Kitchen's Larry Flax and Rick Rosenfield, it's items like their distinctive barbecue chicken pizza that bowl the customer over. And to I Can't Believe It's Yogurt chairman Bill Brice, it's offering an awesome array of 50 flavors of hard- and soft-serve yogurt.

Indeed, the wow doesn't necessarily have to be in the food. Bill Post, president of Levy Restaurants, feels that the best Wow Effects are produced by the waiter and waitress uniforms and the visual elements at his foodservice operations in baseball stadiums.

Nick Nickolas, long-time partner of the Harman Nickolas Restaurant Group, has an unorthodox view of the Wow Effect but one that seems to work for him. He feels that food is far overrated as a practical factor in restaurant success: "Great service is the only wow that really matters. We encourage our staff to let their personalities really shine. Customers always remember how well they are treated, and they're constantly talking about our great service."

Big 4's Lee Cohn recalls that the original Lunt Avenue Marble Club restaurant was famous for wow presentations. Among the top attention grabbers were a huge six-egg omelet, a grilled cheese sandwich priced at $6,000, and an Awful Burger created by cooks to be as ugly as possible. The Wow Effect wasn't strong enough, however, as the restaurant did not survive. Or maybe there was too much glitz and not enough price-value.

TGI Friday's wows its customers with frozen margaritas and other special drinks and is also developing a line of signature desserts. "Quality is really our biggest wow," TGI Friday's president Lou Neeb asserts. "The sophisticated consumer today won't spend money for anything else."

The Wow Effect is not necessarily a panacea. Nor is it always achievable. In the opinion of Max Pine, former RA president, seeking the Wow Effect is "like chasing the Holy Grail. You never quite get there in these efforts to woo the customer." He recalls tremendous success in the early 1980s with his New Jersey Charlie Brown's steakhouses when fajitas captured a full 15 percent of entree sales. But that was a unique situation that did not recur after the novelty had worn off.

Pine would rather shoot for a consistent series of singles and doubles than a short-lived fajitas home run. "We kept introducing different items that could achieve 3 percent to 4 percent of our total sales at Charlie Brown's," he says, "and it all added up to customer excitement and higher volumes." Fried calamari, coconut shrimp, and a variety of chicken dishes each had this effect.

After all is said and done, trust may be the key ingredient of a Wow Effect. "Time and time again, customers in general feel they have been misled," declares Sonic's Stephen Lynn. "More often than not their expectations are not met, or are met with mediocrity at best." He says Sonic never promises "what we cannot deliver and always strives to deliver more than we have promised."

As part of a check-back program, Sonic carhops go to the cars with fully-stocked courtesy trays to see whether a customer might need an extra napkin, salt, ketchup, or something else, and then give the customer a mint. This little touch often elicits a specific wow from the surprised customer, who tends to become a loyal repeat visitor. Lynn promotes trust by delivering food before asking for money. Above anything else, though, he loves the visual Wow Effect of "Sonic neon alive against a night sky, where the customer pulls the car into a stall and within three minutes can be enjoying our onion rings, an extra-long chili-cheese coney, and cherry lime-ade, all delivered fresh to the car by a smiling, courteous carhop at a value price." Sounds like utopia, but the Sonic system mostly works that way.

Emphasizing an extra-product line for special occasions is also a valuable tool. TCBY's Charles Cocotas says the chain developed an add-on sales program called Pie & Cakery. A frozen display case merchandised 150 different soft-serve frozen yogurt, special-occasion decorated cakes for customers to choose. This bid for incremental sales in the fiercely competitive soft-serve frozen yogurt market had TCBY customers sighing, "Wow, what an opportunity."

The ideal Wow Effect is one that "blows somebody away." This is created at Johnny Rockets where, observes president Ronn Teitelbaum, "when you walk in and order fries, they'll bring you a separate plate, pour the ketchup and give you a straw for your drink. Then the jukebox comes on, and people sing together."

This can be the greatest wow, but we can attest to the fact that the ideal doesn't always happen, at Johnny Rockets or at other places. The training programs and field manuals say that this is the way it should be, but even the best programs simply don't always work. Still, it is crucial to strive for the excitement and uniqueness of a Wow Effect, to establish a winning signature and niche for a chain.

The Economic-Focus Dilemma

Solving challenges within the parameters of the restaurant chain industry's economic realities.

"There are so many closed restaurants in the United States that it's a tremendous chance for chains (to acquire the shuttered sites)."

—*Frank Carney, Pizza Hut cofounder,*
former Western Sizzlin' chief executive, Wichita, Kansas

HIGHLIGHTS

- Don't cut corners
- Eschew price increases
- Utilize smaller kitchens
- Seek economical sites
- Scale down sizes
- Reduce initial investment costs
- Boost sales to raise margins
- Beware of overexpansion
- Look at franchising alternatives
- Investigate overseas expansion
- Beware of LBOs

With costs of occupancy, food, and labor constantly rising and cutting into profit margins, how can a restaurant chain cope? If it raises prices, it risks losing customers—something that it can ill afford in these perilous times. But if it holds the line on prices and absorbs cost increases, it may be hard hit on profits. Of the two alternatives, we think the latter is better, because it is customer oriented and in the long run keeps the customer. Once a customer is lost, the damage is done.

But there are other alternatives. A chain could realign its menu mix and its combination offerings so that prices vary, but retain the same average ticket and woo the customer with variety and enhanced value while still reducing the food and labor costs through the menu combinations. Or perhaps money can be saved in the area of real estate through lower-cost sites, by taking over existing restaurants, gas stations, or stores rather than purchasing new sites at higher costs. Still another alternative is to locate in shopping malls, hotels, airports, or tollway sites and, in effect, let the landlord help to pay.

Golden Corral and other chains are doing it with smaller prototype restaurants that yield better rates of return on investment, although total sales are lower. Or fancy decor and other costly frills can be eliminated while the food concept is emphasized. Often the customer does not mind this approach and even appreciates it as indicating a restaurant strong on basics. Still, whatever happens it is inadvisable to cut corners on purchasing or food quality.

Clearly, the best way to offset rising costs is to build up customer counts and increase sales, which will ultimately affect the bottom line. Costs will continue as a fact of life, and the challenge is to find ways to generate incremental sales. This is becoming increasingly difficult because of the intensely competitive environment. Unless sales climb, rising costs eventually tend to be passed on to the consumer. The basic standards still apply: The highest quality locations with the best operational standards in service, cleanliness, and value will win.

Outback has become a pacesetter by going all out in food quality with an estimated 39 percent food cost, as compared with an average of 33 percent for other casual midscale restaurant chains. "We've achieved a $17 average per-person ticket (a high price for a casual chain, but one that seems to be working)," says Outback's Chris Sullivan, "and that balances out and makes it OK to be six points higher on food cost." Outback also shines in its site selection, specializing in rehabilitating old buildings and often locating in shopping centers.

This is an astute balancing act, as higher food costs represent quality and encourage higher customer traffic. The opposite is also true in that lower food costs could mean lower quality and cause a decline in customer traffic. Yet that does not have to occur, as evidenced by The Olive Garden's steadily rising customer counts with only a 30 percent food cost, achieved through purchasing efficiencies and excellent menu balance.

Among the various methods of coping with rising costs are creating lower-cost prototypes, constant line-item cost reviews, smarter purchasing, research and development partnerships with major suppliers, and—the least attractive option in terms of future development—cutting back on the staff and perhaps "accomplishing more with less."

Sonic is another chain that has boosted traffic and volume to offset soaring fixed costs. Average per-unit sales jumped from $272,000 in 1983 to $562,000 10 years later, and average per-unit profits rose 181 percent in the five years through 1993.

Putting more effort and space into the front of the house greatly helps overall productivity. In previous decades, kitchens took up as much as 50 percent of total space, whereas now the back-of-the-house space ratio is running closer to one-third. What may be needed for many types of operations is to chop kitchens to 20 percent, giving 80 percent of the space and emphasis to the front where the sales dollars flow. Besides, kitchens can usually be operated more efficiently in a streamlined space. It wouldn't be wise for most chains to go the route that Taco Bell chairman John Martin foresees—"virtually kitchenless restaurants," helped by robots and automation—but some moves in that direction are advisable. And such a step could work well for Taco Bell.

Smarter purchasing also helps tremendously. "We've been able to save money through bulk purchasing and barely have ever raised our prices," says The Cheesecake Factory's David Overton. Nor does he put any money into advertising. "We put everything we have on the plate only," he affirms.

Yet there are times when a chain has no choice but to raise prices. Then it becomes a question of degree. Nick Nickolas thinks that at times a chain or restaurant has to take this action to protect profit margins. "I recently raised prices a tiny bit," he notes, "so that the average per-person ticket went from $45 to $46, and to me it meant that we just have to keep giving better service."

"The great thing about our industry," observes O'Charley's president David Wachtel, "is that the sales price usually reflects the inflation rate, and we historically have been able to pass any cost increases along to the consumer. Those of us who have been successful have done this and been able to maintain margins." But customers won't necessarily accept this anymore—not with all the options and choices there are. "We will improve our profit margins by the dynamics of growth, bolstering our menu with selective price hikes, and continuing to increase our comparable unit sales," declares Wachtel.

Simply lowering prices builds traffic and can improve profit margins in the long run. "We dropped our prices 20 percent to 25 percent," says Bay Street Restaurants president Bill Bouffard, "and our sales rose considerably. We put in lower food-cost items to balance this." For example, Bay Street is serving four shrimps on a bed of pasta rather than five shrimps on rice.

Chi-Chi's has been downsizing in some of its new restaurants to obtain better rates of return on investment even though sales at the smaller units inevitably are lower. It also has been able to maintain full purchasing quality through more aggressive contracts and partnerships with key suppliers. "We continue to hire to fully staff the restaurants," says Chi-Chi's former president Joseph Micatrotto, "but are focusing on cross-training and delegating responsibilities to our best hourly employees."

Sales and gross-profit dollars are more important than food-cost percentages in the equation. "We must get away from this type of percentage thinking and instead think in terms of the income from each menu item," suggests Silver Diner's Robert Giaimo. "The whole idea is to get people in the seats." Serving more customers faster is a great way to boost sales, although one does not want them to feel rushed—except possibly in fast-food places. "You receive any meal at our restaurants within 10 minutes or else you get a free meal on us," is Giaimo's slogan, and he rarely has to pay off on it. Years ago customers would trade speed for quality, he says, "But today you have a vastly more sophisticated customer, and you must provide the quality as well as the speed when necessary."

Garfield's has fashioned lower food-and-labor cost to sales ratios every year it has been in business, without any price increases. "We also have developed what may be the industry's best sales-to-investment ratio by, and because of, our inability to finance our growth any way other than through cash flow during our early years" (in the 1980s), Vincent Orza says. He has a particular aversion to debt and prays that Eateries, Inc. will remain debt free.

The way former Whataburger operations senior vice president Alan Stoner sees it, maximum efficiencies can combat rising costs. Streamlined kitchen design with increased productivity, robotics, and computer systems all help. "Reposition or redeploy people to spend more time in the front of the house," he suggests. "Nobody in the industry can really ever afford to cut corners by cutting people. That is long-term self-destruction. Instead, service and quality must be constantly improved." Many other executives echo those words but in practice take the easy route by eliminating staff instead of training employees and building for the future.

LOWER SITE COSTS

In Norman Brinker's view, the initial land, building, and equipment package needed to open a restaurant today costs three or four times as much ($1.2 million to $2 million), as it did in the late 1970s ($400,000 to $500,000). "This will be enough to put a lot of people out of business who can't sustain the necessary volume," asserts Brinker, who foresees a major shakeout in the restaurant chain industry, with only the strongest surviving.

Applebee's International is achieving $2.1 million average per-unit sales and has four different types of sites to give it flexi-

bility in site selection and to serve varied market areas. Its prototypes range from 161 seats in smaller markets to 250 seats in
larger ones.

Chains are increasingly developing alternate prototypes to serve
different markets and to create flexibility in site selection. Golden
Corral is an excellent example, with prototypes ranging from 5,000
square feet to 10,000 square feet (with super-food bars). But the
general trend is to maximize productivity and offset costs by going
with the smallest feasible no-frills unit where possible, rather than
the largest. If customers frequently wait in line, that could be a
plus in image building and might be controlled by strategically
varying the prices.

For the rest of this decade, chains will typically scale down restaurant sizes to achieve higher productivity and provide a more feasible operation for smaller and medium markets. Take-out and
home delivery, kiosks and carts, and double drive-throughs loom
large in the equation as well.

The Olive Garden is astute in saving money on site selection
and still getting the highest traffic sites. It has purchased all kinds
of old buildings and transformed them. "We've successfully converted everything from tire and battery stores to the old City Hall
in Spokane, Washington, to The Olive Gardens," Ron Magruder
declares.

While downsizing and streamlining are potential solutions for
many chains, Spaghetti Warehouse needs a big building for its restaurant to accommodate large groups of customers. "We simply
couldn't downsize," says former president Lou Neeb. For years the
chain specialized in converting old buildings but found this costlier
in the vast renovations that had to be made. To sandblast one of
these buildings could cost $100,000 alone and then take a year to
redesign. "So we looked at new buildings and paid the price, hoping to generate more volume," says Neeb. "We did the best we
could without raising prices."

Pizza Hut founder Frank Carney, who was trying to revitalize
Western Sizzlin' after emerging from Chapter 11 in 1993 and then
fought a losing battle for control of the chain, saw a vast opportunity to use shuttered restaurants as sites. "There are so many closed

restaurants in the United States," he says, "that it's a tremendous chance for chains." This trend creates alternating cycles of stability and chaos.

Finding a unique niche is crucial in site selection. "I go where others don't," says Vincent Orza, who by mid-1993 had 33 Garfield's units averaging $2.5 million to $3 million per-unit sales, with seven others under construction. "We've concentrated on mall sites, but now we will go for free standers." He concedes that the chain initially grew too fast, jumping from 5 units to 12 in 1987. At that point he called everyone into his office and declared that no more restaurants would be built until costs were brought into line and more sales were generated in each existing restaurant.

Tony Roma's has always been unconventional in its site selection. "We somehow would find the right location at a reasonable cost," recalls former Roma's president Ken Reimer. "We took over existing restaurants or other types of structures. We were in Nevada casinos, shopping centers around the United States, and basements in Japan."

Emeril Lagasse, a leading New Orleans owner-chef whose Emeril's restaurant is in a remote section of the New Orleans warehouse district and who more recently opened his Nola restaurant in a historic French Quarter townhouse, is convinced that site selection is overwhelmingly crucial in the restaurant equation. "What's the deal?" he always asks. "The price per square foot or the rent has to make sense." The variables of how many seats and what the menu is all about have to enter into what type of site is desired for a particular restaurant. "The bottom line is that annual sales have to justify the deal very quickly."

The type of deal is important, but the actual location may not be in some cases. Commander's Palace, a prize-winning restaurant, is across the street from a New Orleans cemetery. But the greatness and renown of this restaurant have made the location a high-traffic one. And Lagasse's remote Emeril's restaurant was *Esquire* magazine's 1992 Restaurant of the Year.

The type of location and the size should be predicated on a plan. "You have to think of parking, access, foot traffic, and who the audience is," asserts Lagasse. Once the restaurant is open, he says, you need at least three months of money reserves, and you need to keep negotiating everything. "Be prepared for a year of 16-hour days—every day," he advises. "If you don't want that, don't try it."

Letting franchisees pay for sites is another way to reduce costs. "Franchising can work when you have great general managers or a tight rein on systems control," says Frank Carney. "But a lot of companies have unfortunately taken the incentive out of franchising, locating kiosks and other units in direct competition with their own franchisees and putting products in the supermarket that also compete with their own franchisees' products." This type of assertion is currently the subject of much debate in the industry.

Each chain is in a battle to target the maximum number of units it feels the market will bear and then to try to grab the necessary sites as quickly as possible, before the high-traffic sites are gone. There always seems to be something available—but for a price. Being first into a market and getting the prime sites is critical, as the double drive-throughs battle among Rally's, Checkers, and Hot 'n Now shows.

Big 4 Restaurants have been forced to lower their investment and occupancy costs. Instead of the previously sought initial investment packages of $1.5 million per restaurant and rents of 8 percent of sales, Lee Cohn is searching for smaller or medium-sized restaurants without frills and with an initial investment cost under $500,000 and rents in the 4 percent to 5 percent range to offset skyrocketing costs.

Robert Colombo, Sfuzzi president, asserts that practical experience is the best way to learn how to pick low-cost sites. "If you never picked a bad site, you wouldn't know the difference between a bad site and a good one," he notes. "The real goal is to do the complete demographic and traffic-flow studies in advance and choose only the best sites. This country became overdeveloped with restaurants because everybody thought that any type of site will be a home run." Sfuzzi focuses on free standers, shopping centers, and sites adjacent to store developments, depending on the requirements and availabilities in each market.

Fast-feeders will go to more nontraditional sites to capitalize on the large numbers of convenience-minded customers. Prime site candidates include college campuses, schools, department stores, supermarkets, zoos, parks, hospitals, health care facilities, senior residences, toll roads, railroad stations, airports, fairs, and other temporary sites. McDonald's, Pizza Hut, and Taco Bell are early leaders in the current surge to nontraditional locations.

Smaller companies and chains, though, should have an advantage against larger companies, because they are closer to marketplaces and more flexible in site selection and in other aspects. Yet it doesn't always work that way, as attested by the clout of General Mills.

If a chain carries enough power, it may not even have to pay for a site. When Morton's opened its first New York City steakhouse in midtown Manhattan in September 1993, the building's landlord arranged a lower-than-usual rental cost and rebated Morton's site costs, because he felt the upscale Morton's was prestigious enough to bring tenants and business to the building. "We enhance the properties," says Allen J. Bernstein, president of Morton's parent Quantum Restaurant Group, "and people in effect have been paying us to come to various major cities."

The Cheesecake Factory's David Overton figures the investment cost at $300 per square foot, and with restaurants ranging from 8,000 square feet to 14,000 square feet, this means an initial investment cost of $2.4 million to $3.2 million. But Cheesecake gets back $1.5 million from the landlord on many of these deals. Overton is more than willing to pay for a high-traffic site, saying he prefers to "let the site drive the deal."

However, occupancy cost reduction can also be a restaurateur's enemy. Too often, restaurant companies—particularly franchisees—accept a large contribution from the landlord, sometimes getting into a restaurant for pennies or for nothing. In return for that consideration, the restaurateur is saddled with a heavy rent or debt service to finance all or most of the up-front costs. Although everything seems great during the honeymoon period after opening, if sales should slow or the restaurant encounters tough times because of competition outpositioning it, a franchise can suddenly be in serious financial straits with no help in sight.

PROFIT-MARGIN PRESSURES

Max Pine, former Restaurant Associates (RA) president, points out the big challenge now being faced because of declining liquor sales. Liquor has higher profit margins and thus could improve all the ratios. But with a growing public aversion to liquor, the liquor ratio at RA's Charlie Brown's restaurants slumped from 30 percent to 20 percent of sales. Thus the chain's entire profit structure was thrown out of kilter.

"We had to find a way to raise the average check by adding in a few higher-priced items that customers can order if they want, without hurting the majority of customers who want to retain price-value," Pine recalls. A T-bone steak was added for $15.95, well above any other entree price. This certainly is a quality steak, but many customers may not choose to spend that kind of money very often when the original idea was to get a full dinner at that restaurant for $10 or $12.

Charlie Brown's and most other steakhouses are open for lunch and dinner. Perhaps the solution is to open only for dinner—if one can achieve a high enough volume. Outback is open for dinner only and manages to outpace just about everyone in both volume and return on investment. Outback has been showing an astronomical 22 percent to 27 percent profit return on its investment, while Charlie Brown's has been in the 11 percent range. Pine feels that 15 percent, which Charlie Brown's achieved in 1989, is a realistic goal. "They must reengineer all the elements and climb back to where they were," he declares.

Sales are still the key to profit margins—and to the whole business. "We've taken the cost out of our business structure," says Longhorn's Richard Rivera, former TGI Friday's president. "The challenges are overwhelming—higher energy taxes, income taxes, a higher minimum wage. The real estate market is down, and we have to be stronger in our site negotiations."

TGI Friday's survives and prospers because, if nothing else, it is topping $3.5 million average per-unit sales. With all the fancy slogans and ideas to maintain or raise profit margins, the battle is still won in the trenches of sales warfare, determined by which chains can keep their seats fullest.

S & A Restaurant Corporation was hamstrung with debt from a leveraged buyout and did not grow much in the early 1990s. "Our industry depends upon inflation to bring occupancy costs in line with sales," says Steven Leipsner, former chairman-CEO. Because inflation was minimal for several years, the cost of developing restaurants became a far more significant issue. Conversions and rehabilitation projects were the order of the day. "You've got to constantly look at the sales-to-investment ratio of new buildings and explore less traditional locations such as closed restaurants and shopping mall sites," suggests Leipsner.

Tony Roma's completed a plan for new labor standards in 1990, and this directly led to improved menu management and food-cost controls. "We were able to give more and better service," says former president Kenneth Reimer. "I affirmed that every manager must visit every table at least once for every dining experience in his restaurant." (If that actually happened even half the time, that's a good record in the restaurant industry.) Still, much to Reimer's consternation, labor costs kept rising and defied solution "no matter what we did."

Patrick Morris, who was Tony Roma's senior vice president under Reimer, sees the challenge as one of balance. "Just as we have to balance the menu by ensuring that the core products on which the concept is built stay consistent and true," he says, "new products should be added to meet the needs of a changing marketplace." From an economic standpoint, those aspects of the business that are central to the concept can't be compromised in any way. Chains can go to shopping mall locations and use other means of reducing occupancy costs as long as they don't cheapen the concept or blur the identity.

EXPANDABILITY

A chain indeed can win against larger competitors by projecting an individualized neighborhood restaurant image that, behind the scenes, also achieves economies of scale. But if it wants to gain the necessary marketing and advertising clout, it must admit to being a chain and act like a chain—unless it depends strictly on word-of-mouth (which is the best form of advertising anyway).

More chains than anyone can imagine have literally overexpanded themselves right out of the business. Sambo's and Victoria Station are two notable examples already cited. Yet others have shown themselves capable of controlled expansion in varying degrees—Levy Restaurants, LEYE, and McDonald's, to name a few. The ability to expand in an orderly manner from one market to another, with capable unit managers in place, is crucial to any chain's success as it goes through various phases up to the maximum it can handle.

The toughest phase is encountered in expanding an original entrepreneurship of 10 units and then moving to 100 units. It takes astute management, intensive training, complete dedication, and a gradual delegation of responsibilities—without creating an unwieldly bureaucracy as one advances beyond that—because the odds for success are tougher than ever against any chain as it keeps growing. Competition in every segment is increasingly stiffer during such a phase.

With 450 restaurants by early 1994, just a decade after it was conceived, The Olive Garden can trace its success to General Mills Restaurants' initially putting in charge a financial person who understood operations. Before General Mills ever launched The Olive Garden in the mid-1980s (or China Coast in the early 1990s), it conducted extensive research to guarantee that the respective concepts would work. Although the outcome is still really a roll of the dice, it is far less chancy when accurate research has been completed. When consumers spotted negatives before The Olive Garden was expanded, these could be quickly corrected. For example, research showed that customers did not want to be crowded together but desired more space. Within the context of maximum utilization of space, The Olive Garden devised a series of tables on wheels that could easily be rolled around and strategically placed where needed at any time. This type of flexibility is what consumers like about The Olive Garden.

Although some might call this approach overcautious, Blaine Sweatt tested China Coast for at least three years in Orlando, Florida, before General Mills gave any signal at all to move it into other markets. Numerous adjustments were made during the test period to ensure that China Coast was the best it could be. Even after that, several China Coast units were tested in Indianapolis before General Mills finally committed to going national with the chain, and this expansion will proceed in stages that can be cut off at any point.

The Olive Garden opened clusters of two, three, or more restaurants in a given market within a few months of each other so that it could gain recognition and an advertising advantage quickly. It also utilized General Mills to decide which concept was suitable for a particular site or perhaps would be located next to sisters Red Lobster or China Coast on a particular parcel. The Olive Garden's biggest market is greater Los Angeles, where it capitalized on the wide sprawl and dense populations, with 30 units open by 1993 and a projected eventual 60. This would virtually saturate the area with The Olive Garden and provide far greater visibility than any other Italian restaurant or chain could aspire to in greater Los Angeles.

Ron Magruder targets The Olive Garden to reach 600 units and $2.2 billion annual sales by 1996. This would more than double the $1 billion sales of 1993 and would be achieved through expansion and a substantiated increase in the average per-unit volume as customer traffic proliferates—if The Olive Garden does not cannibalize its volumes by locating units too close together.

Although large companies are gaining greater dominance in the restaurant business, the main expansion opportunities through the 1990s are in steakhouses and Italian, Mexican, Chinese, and other ethnic cuisines, as well as Southwest and Tex-Mex. Italian and Mexican are the types that are most popular with consumers, as well as with chain operators, because of the basic simplicity and spicy taste of the food (not too spicy, it is hoped, for most palates) and their low food costs. Healthful foods are still "in," but they seem to do better in the context of another concept rather than on their own. Consumers tend to talk about healthful foods for their hearts and then eat to satisfy their stomachs.

Commensurate with a chain's growth should be its development of management and financial strength. When a chain outstrips its ability to continue to appoint quality managers, it gets into real trouble. In addition, a chain must attract better managers of higher caliber, reward them financially and with a piece of the action, and give them a chance to move up in responsibility if they so desire.

Although a growing chain should attract stronger managers, it should be kept in mind that many of them are not satisfied unless they can advance. The trend is toward horizontal management, overstaffing units with promising people. Sometimes it takes 8 or 10 years for unit general managers to move up as district supervisors or area managers.

"The Cheesecake Factory could open in all of America and worldwide, but right now we're looking at Chicago, Boston, and Miami," says president David Overton. This is an urban concept. It is filling out the greater Los Angeles market with perhaps four restaurants, but owing to the huge scope of its restaurants and their $8 million average unit volume (which could reach $10 million or more eventually), The Cheesecake Factory may need only one or two restaurants in some of its future urban markets, including its singular unit on the outskirts of Washington, D.C.

The Cheesecake Factory finances its restaurants by making each a separate corporation, as is done by quite a few chains. It is looking at a 25 percent annual growth rate, or 4 or 5 a year and an eventual 100 (perhaps meaning 100 separate corporations) in the United States. However, the industry is littered with the corpses of fledgling chains which, after opening a few units in one or two market areas, proclaim that it soon will be a 100-unit or 1,000-unit chain. Many of these never get beyond their 20th unit at best. All the copycats and ripoffs of Wendy's in the 1970s, Judy's and others appropriating the idea of using a woman's name, faded very quickly. You must have a direct feel for, and belief in, a concept to make it work. You can't just initiate a concept and expect it to succeed automatically.

The Cheesecake Factory had nine restaurants by early 1994, located in Atlanta and the Washington, D.C., areas as well as in its southern California stronghold. The economics at the Beverly Hills Cheesecake unit make it exceptionally productive, there are constant lines (no reservations taken) at that smaller 5,400-square-foot restaurant, which realizes $1,100 in annual sales per square foot, or $6 million annual sales in half the space of other Cheesecake restaurants. To drive the projected expansion, Overton is also enlarging the company's Calabasas, California, headquarters to 60,000 square feet, including a central commissary and a bakery.

Boston Chicken, Inc., the rotisserie chicken chain originally based in Boston but which moved its headquarters to Naperville, Illinois, launched a $50 million expansion program in 1993 to move through the West with an initial cluster of several units in and around Denver. Its strategy is to penetrate Western markets quickly, one at a time—but with numerous initial units immediately in each target market—and to double the chain to 450 or even 500 units by late 1994, based on its successful 1.6-million share initial public offering and heavy franchising.

FRANCHISING

There are various ways to franchise, and this is a key method of financing steady growth. Some organizations, such as General Mills, which can afford to have all units company-owned, won't franchise at all. Others, such as Subway and International Dairy Queen, must franchise to expand and to get the experienced operators they need locally. Mom-and-pop franchisees are becoming less prevalent than they were, as larger professionally run franchisees hold sway—to some not only a regrettable development and loss of entrepreneurship, but also a financially necessary one.

Among various financing vehicles suggested for expansion is capital from public offerings or loans. But franchising can be an effective growth vehicle—a way to gain solid growth with local entrepreneurs. The king of all franchisees in diversity is The Riese Organization, which seems to have a restaurant or two, or three or four, on almost every major block in New York City. Among the multitude of brands it franchises from chains are Del Taco, Dunkin' Donuts, El Torito, Haagen Dazs, Houlihan's, KFC, Nathan's Famous, Pizza Hut, Roy Rogers, Sizzler, and TGI Friday's. "Customers can find every type of casual restaurant and fast-food chain in our mix, including some of our own units (such as Charley O's and Toots Shor)," says president Dennis Riese.

Chains today prefer professional franchisees over the mom-and-pops. "We franchise only to experienced business people or locate only with experienced hotel operators (Marriott)," says Howard Berkowitz, president of San Francisco-based Oh-La-La gourmet coffee shop chain. "We manage our growth very carefully."

Applebee's International, a franchising leader in the casual restaurant segment, opened 16 restaurants in just one month, August 1993, as it launched an all-out expansion push. It was in 38 states then. The push is spearheaded by 60 different franchisees, which as of early 1994 operated some 300 units. Some 70 units were company-owned. "We're only 20 percent developed," says president Abe Gustin, who hopes to have 700 restaurants in action in 1995 and to be the leader of the casual restaurant segment (assuming that some of the other biggies stand still). Gustin feels there is potential for 1,500 Applebee's. They are in the mainstream for today's consumer, projecting their image of being local neighborhood restaurants on the outskirts and in the suburbs of cities. There are 14 Applebee's within the Kansas City headquarters market alone.

Still, many don't see the need for franchising. Seattle-based Starbucks gourmet coffee shops and General Mills Restaurants are among the companies that have eschewed franchising in favor of complete company-owned control. Significantly, each has considerable capital available for steady growth.

Eateries' Vincent Orza is also one of those focusing on company-owned restaurants. "Franchising is minor and will be less important because of the growing success of company units." This chain grows on a pay-as-you-go basis, utilizing cash flow and landlord-tenant allowances. (Orza also plans to accelerate expansion with a secondary public equity offering.)

Given the size of S & A Restaurant Corporation, Steven Leipsner said when he was president, "We believe that if we come up with a reasonable investment opportunity, we will be able to find the capital to expand it. We currently are using available credit lines." Other options are public equity and franchising. "We have not franchised so far because we believe opportunity exists for expanding corporate ownership of restaurants." S & A was also eyeing joint ventures in the international market. Still, it intends to stay away from franchising—especially since the federal franchising laws are getting tougher all the time.

Significant risks occur when expansion outstrips internal cash flow and the number of units opened is large in proportion to the existing base. This is of particular concern with new concepts, inasmuch as their staying power is untested. "We believe we have a tested concept, and the expansion risk is minimal," Leipsner said about new concepts being tried under Steak and Ale and Bennigan's brands.

Nevertheless, franchising offers the advantage of developing a concept rapidly with little investment and obtaining a healthy return in royalties and advertising awareness. It does present challenges in maintaining control over both the concept's identity and the menu. Most chains prefer not to franchise unless they have to— which is often necessary in order to penetrate markets. It is difficult for franchisees, more particularly if they are investors rather than actually managing the business, to stay focused on the concept and to consider the welfare of the entire franchise system. They often get caught up in their own market and their own restaurant, worry about their own problems, and try to get other franchisees involved in their own problems. The result is numerous chain franchisee associations that are sometimes in opposition to the chain. Court battles between franchiser and franchisee are not uncommon.

Eventually the franchisee can lose focus, and when a series of franchisees do this, it can cause the whole chain to lose focus. The best way to franchise properly is to make sure there are strict rules about concept integrity and that these rules are never compromised. McDonald's leads the way in this regard.

CONTROLLING EXPANSION

A real gauge of how fast a chain can profitably grow may be the financial results of its expansion restaurants and to what degree they show consistently higher volumes, or at least equal volumes, in each new market. Year-to-year same-unit sales results are the best guide.

It is one thing to succeed in an initial home market where the concept is well known and especially popular, and quite another to keep expanding with it. Bojangles' Chicken & Biscuits was a smash hit when it first opened in Charlotte, North Carolina, and was doing $1 million annual volumes in the late 1970s in that market. But as it expanded to other areas, its sales and appeal dramatically slowed. After Bojangles was acquired by New York-based Horn & Hardart, it seemed to lose entrepreneurial drive without founder Jack Foulks.

Al Copeland's Popeyes never really reproduced the magic of its New Orleans debut and its ultraspicy chicken after it enjoyed popularity in its own market. Copeland was smart enough to offer a version with less spice in Northern markets but still—plagued by debt and troubles that he acquired in a leveraged buyout of Church's—had to file for Chapter 11 in 1991 and eventually was ousted from the operation (while remaining a franchisee and supplier) when the two chains were completely reorganized as America's Favorite Chicken Co.

The transition stage from operation by a founder to the next generation is tricky too. When the late Leonard Rawls merged Hardee's with Jack Laughery's Sandy's operation in the Midwest in 1973, Laughery, a former insurance salesman, took complete command a few years later and Rawls disappeared from the scene. This also happened to Marie Callendar's founder Don Callendar after he sold the California chain, which he built from a pie shop to a widespread full-service restaurant chain, and to CKE's veteran founder Carl Karcher when he was ousted by the board in late 1993.

Thomas McFall, former chairman of Hamburger Hamlet Restaurants, which started in 1951, views the chain as a "high-use, high-repeat operation." He sees the only limitation on each unit as a productive maximum of 7,000 square feet and $3 million sales. "We can open 10 a year and be a 100-unit chain." He describes the chain as "casual non-theme restaurants." Certainly the days of the theme restaurant and the gimmick are just about gone, as customers seek a genuine place with true values and no hype.

There is a 97 percent awareness of the Hamburger Hamlet name in Southern California, but most people think of the chain as The Hamlet. Many of the restaurants are old and need remodeling. Sales of older Hamlets were down an average of 4 percent, but those that have been renovated are selling considerably better. McFall was hoping to open a new concept called Hamlet Grill as a test of a French-like New Orleans-oriented menu with a 20 percent lower price than Hamburger Hamlet. This would put another weapon in the company's arsenal but might also divert it from its main Hamburger Hamlet objectives. There's always the chance that the chain will take "Hamburger" out of the name as it keeps diversifying the menu.

As president of Bennigan's in 1981–82, Chris Sullivan got the financial support to build a lot of restaurants. "We didn't have management teams," he says, "and we had to get people ready quickly." But his challenge as Outback chairman in the late 1980s was how to go beyond 5 units to 15, then from 15 to 30, and so on— especially tough when credit was so tight. To obtain the financing for Outback, he and partner Robert Basham, president, sold 20 percent of the company for $2 million cash and went public in mid-1991. In addition, they were getting 10 percent ($25,000) investments from each restaurant's general manager.

Sullivan's next challenge was handling the change in culture when the company grew into a successful chain. "We had to balance the proper growth with long-term development and evolving the business," he recalls. "Opening 60 restaurants a year is a huge challenge. Managers have to be trained, and principles and beliefs loom ever more important."

Bay Street Restaurants' Bill Bouffard is eyeing a steady expansion rate of two or three new restaurants a year. "We can finance them from our own cash flow," he asserts, "and can groom good managers by bringing in a couple of manager-trainees each month." He says Bay Street is getting managers and manager-trainees from Outback, Brinker International, and others "because they know they can grow just by staying in the same restaurant as general manager." The average Bay Street restaurant manager is 34 years old and knows that it is possible to grow in the same restaurant under a five-year contract.

If most of the chains that say they will launch so many hundreds or thousands of units by the end of the decade were to succeed in that endeavor, the entire nation and much of the world would be overpopulated with restaurants. And if most of those who say they will keep diversifying into new concepts succeed, then restaurant overpopulation would be far worse. However, only a handful of the strongest chains will achieve their goals and the population won't find itself overwhelmed with too many restaurants, although the chain strips that are building up on the outskirts of many cities are trending in that direction.

Ronn Teitelbaum, who started Johnny Rockets malt shops in Los Angeles in 1985, had 10 company restaurants and 48 franchised ones, including five outside the United States, by mid-1994. He anticipates average unit volumes climbing to $1 million on only a $400,000 initial investment as he pushes to turn Johnny Rockets into the "neighborhood malt shop" everywhere in the United States and, perhaps, almost everywhere else in the world. Approximately 20 of his units are in southern California, and he thinks there is a great deal of potential elsewhere. There's a real question as to whether Johnny Rockets, or any regional chain trying to become a national one, can maintain an expansion pace of 20 new units annually from a base of 58. Finding the financing and quality unit managers are the biggest problems.

Yet Johnny Rockets hopes to launch at least 30 units a year in the future and to keep expanding geometrically until it has 1,000 units by the year 2001. Good luck to Ronn Teitelbaum. If he makes it, that will truly be a surprise. Still, nothing is impossible either way in this business. (Teitelbaum was operating as a private company with a group of stockholder-partners helping to fund his expansion. As he tries to sharply accelerate the expansion pace, he now has the backing of a Boston-based investment group.) He projects a big international expansion too, moving into Australia, Japan, and Mexico, among various other countries. Any area, from

Mexico City to Melbourne, may be developed in this industry, but it's wise to remember that the grass is not always greener somewhere else.

Growth, just for growth's sake, often becomes an ego-ridden mission to nowhere. Controlled growth to extend quality reach is a healthy endeavor. Western Sizzlin's David Wachtel observes, "Many people get hung up on building new units and not tending to business, opening more and more restaurants year after year." What is really needed is increased customer counts year after year. Then new capital will most likely always be available, and managers will be too, because strong comparable unit sales tend to lead to strong management—reflecting the self-fulfilling prophecy that success breeds success (unless it leads to complacency and then failure).

Outback's Chris Sullivan is gradually stepping up the expansion pace. He opened three restaurants in 1993 and is accelerating that pace to at least six in 1994. He is expanding heavily in the chain's home state of Florida and is going into various Texas markets as well. This could become a geometric progression, and the point at which a chain may be in real trouble is when it starts trying to open 50, 75, or 100 units annually. Outback's average check per person has climbed from a former $12 to $15 to a new $17. We wonder if the price-value image of this casual chain will be lost if the average check hits $20, no matter how much hoopla accompanies it.

Raids and counterraids are not at all uncommon in the chain restaurant industry, as operators vie for the best managers and executives. Often the answer lies with a direct competitor. Outback woos other casual-restaurant chain general managers with its package of investing $25,000 in the restaurant for 10 percent ownership and five years later, when their contract expires, getting back perhaps $100,000 more, based on an independent evaluation of the restaurant's appreciation.

Lou Neeb, Spaghetti Warehouse president from 1991 to 1993, hoped to have 45 company-owned and 13 franchised Spaghetti Warehouse units by 1994. He was further developing the Chicago and Atlanta areas and is eyeing sites in Baltimore, Harrisburg, Pennsylvania, and Hartford, Connecticut, as he hopscotched from one area to adjacent areas. He also wanted to develop Arizona, Ne-

vada, and California. It is necessary to have an organized, sensible
pattern like this for a chain to succeed in its expansion. Too often
the pattern has been catch-as-catch-can, with disastrous results, as
California's Acapulco Restaurants discovered when they expanded
into Kansas City and other Midwest markets in the late 1970s.

A number of chains are moving into second- and third-generation ownership, which presents very different challenges. "We really started to succeed once our unit managers had their own children," says Vincent Orza. "Then they realized that you've got to
deal with the customer in an empathetic, understanding way.
We're going for it. Our eventual goal is to have a few hundred
Garfield's units." But he is also thinking about possible diversification within the Eateries corporation. "We're building our own corporate culture. The challenge for everyone is to do what people say
you can't do," declares Orza.

John Martin would like to have a total of 300 Hot 'n Now
double drive-throughs in action (there were 150, after some closings as of mid-1994) and then evaluate them as to whether they are
worth expanding nationally. "We could open 700 of them whenever we want," he says, "But I want to make sure we can dominate
the double drive-through market just as we dominate tacos." It
would be no simple task, with Rally's and Checkers already well
ahead and with the big burger chains cutting prices at will. Much
depends on whether drive-throughs turn out to be the smartest investment for a given amount of dollars or whether the money should
go to other areas with potential for higher returns on investment.

Martin is eyeing the possibility of thousands of Taco Bell carts
and kiosks through this decade and is thinking of a potential
220,000 "points of access" under his jurisdiction, doing $20 billion
volume by 1999. That would still trail McDonald's 1993 volume
but presumably would put Taco Bell in a clear second place for sales
among all foodservice chains. If one were then to add PepsiCo's
other foodservice chain holdings, it is possible that total sales could
overtake McDonald's.

Just as Sears once had what seemed an insurmountable volume
lead and was then overtaken by Kmart, which seemed to have an
unbeatable lead that has now been surpassed by Wal-Mart, so can

McDonald's be overtaken, although its bottom-line performance might continue to be as great as ever.

Taco Bell's carts and kiosks would go in every conceivable location—schools, colleges, airports, office buildings, factories, museums, hotels, department stores, street corners, and so on. We wonder if ego and ultra-ambition will finally cause Martin to overextend and overdiversify the entire operation. "We need the franchisees to get out there with 5 to 20 alternate points of access for each Taco Bell unit they have," he says. "Contrary to what some of them may think, these carts, other points of access, and the sale of some of our products in supermarkets will help them immensely in product and name recognition."

The "Let's open 100 units a year" philosophy can kill a chain unless there is a real belief in the concept. With the economy so tight in this decade, there is a tendency to place too much reliance on systems and assume that those systems will support any type of expansion when, in fact, only people can do that.

INTERNATIONAL EXPANSION

Chain expansion will be vastly accelerated in Western and Eastern Europe as well as the Pacific Rim and the Far East. In 1994, McDonald's was achieving almost half of its projected $28 billion total sales and an estimated 60 percent of its total profits from overseas units in 75 countries. Burger King, Wendy's, KFC, Pizza Hut, and other fast-food chains are pouring into these markets too.

Meanwhile, Spaghetti Warehouse entered the international market in 1993 by having TGI Friday's become its master overseas franchisee. TGI Friday's will operate Spaghetti Warehouses initially in Malaysia, Tapei, and, possibly, London.

FINANCING

Methods of raising money for expansion, remodeling, or other purposes vary according to circumstances. Prime options include going public with an initial stock offering, secondary offerings, loans, leveraged buy-outs, joint ventures, private placements, restructuring, and franchising.

Landry's Seafood Restaurants, a 23-unit Houston-based chain as of mid-1994, raised $24 million on a 2 million-share stock offering in 1993 for projected major expansion purposes. Furr's/Bishop's of Lubbock, Texas, a cafeteria chain, was trying in 1993 to refinance as much as feasible of its $193 million debt. It was considering various deals that could bring more equity and pave the way for expansion in a chain that had not opened any new restaurants in the past few years under Michael Levenson, the previous owner. A restructuring was in the offing to cut the interest costs on the debt. The change in thinking occurred when Kevin Lewis purchased a 10 percent ownership and he and president William Prather began working on ideas. The company had paid $21 million in interest to lenders on a $200 million debt in just six months and was hamstrung. Thus, they moved to restructure the company.

Vincent Orza recalls Eateries starting "small, poor, and aggressive" in 1984. "Our personal and financial investment made it mandatory to succeed. We've avoided debt to keep bankers and other outside forces from 'helping' us manage our business. Today we are publicly held and try to conservatively project our future to Wall Street. While not as glitzy as some publicly held competitors, we've also never disappointed Wall Street with overzealous earnings estimates."

Orza hopes that the conservative, "honest" approach is appreciated and that it literally will pay dividends. "Our single focus is working well enough that it seems prudent for us to maintain the status quo until such time as we employ the resources and people to do more than one thing at a time."

Capital is extremely difficult to find for a small restaurant chain. "Our only growth vehicle is through limited partnerships and landlord-funded operations," says Big 4's Lee Cohn. This is why the stock market is so attractive—to raise expansion money by going public.

Stephen Elmont recalls that Creative Gourmets kept growing through interim cash flow. Clients would pay a month in advance, and thus the chain did not need to borrow. "We easily kept expanding because we had values—we all believed in what we were doing—not just because of the money and the management," affirms Elmont.

Chief financial officers were long regarded as "bean counters," but today many have moved up to run a number of chains. Taylor Henry was Shoney's, Inc. chief financial officer for 18 years and made the transition to CEO smoothly when "newcomer" Leonard Roberts was ousted in 1992.

Stephen Bollenbach, chief financial officer of Marriott Corporation, had a huge influence on its dividing into two companies and on its possible financial turnaround. He earlier accomplished turnarounds at the Trump organization and at Holiday Corporation. Yet today there are still suspicions about the "bean counter" mentality.

In the middle of a recession and with a large debt, Marriott owned numerous hotels that it could not sell. But by 1993 it had reversed its financial situation, and CEO J. Willard Marriott, Jr. moved to solve its problems by dividing into two companies, Marriott International, which controlled the Marriott name and management contracts for 750 hotels and resorts that Bill Marriott would head, and a smaller company, Host Marriott, which would have about 150 lodging properties and foodservice concessions at 70 airports and 15 tollways. Bill's brother, Richard Marriott, would head the latter company, which would be responsible for some $3 billion in debt. Bill Marriott says Marriott solved its problems by instructing the operations people, "Cut staff, cut costs, do what you have to do, but nothing that will affect the guest."

Chains often delude themselves by trying to gain the approval of Wall Street rather than working to please their own customers. Public companies get too involved with the stock prices and Wall Street's expectations. When Wall Street's expectations exceed a company's earnings, or when a company's earnings predictions are not fulfilled, the stock value tends to drop even if earnings keep rising.

One of the worst examples of a leveraged buy-out was that of Copeland Enterprises (Popeyes) acquiring Church's in 1990. In effect, one company gained control of two competing chains specializing in fried chicken. This was Al Copeland's move to try to gain dominance in the fried chicken market, or at least become number two in volume after KFC. This was a blueprint for failure, as anything the parent company did to promote one chain was competitive to the other. Franchisees inevitably filed suits because they felt the company was competing with them. The lenders finally got control of the debt-ridden company, and Frank Belatti faced a challenge of two competing brands as president of the corporate outgrowth, America's Favorite Chicken Co.

Often the basic issue is whether to stay private or to go public, or vice versa. Being private has certain advantages in enabling a company to concentrate on the chain and its customers, rather than on pleasing stockholders. Ownership then does not have to justify its daily existence based on stock value. In addition, a private company has more options to raise money—borrowing from banks, obtaining venture capital, and so on. Nevertheless, the pressure of public ownership can generate higher performance levels, and going public immediately raises growth capital from an initial public offering.

Sonic went through a leveraged buy-out (LBO) during Stephen Lynn's 1980s efforts to get the franchisees united. A small group, mostly of franchisees, had controlled 72 percent of the company, and thus there was a perceived built-in conflict of interest. Therefore, Lynn carried out an LBO and then in early 1991 took the company public and broadened its stature.

Abe Gustin, who in the early 1980s was a nine-unit Taco Bell franchisee, owns 13 percent of Applebee's International and has always been concerned about a possible takeover. As a franchisee, he borrowed $22 million to acquire Applebee's in 1988. Gustin paid back $5 million and went public with an initial public offering in 1989. Then he continued franchising, partly to protect Applebee's from a takeover, as heavily franchised companies are difficult to acquire because of all the separate interests of the franchisees.

Franchisees are sometimes the best qualified to buy and run a company, and some franchisees become powers themselves. Boddie-Noell, Rocky Mount, North Carolina, a major Hardee's franchisee, tried to develop its own fast-food units too; Flagstar's Spartan Foods Systems is the largest Hardee's franchisee; and National Pizza Company, a leading Pizza Hut franchisee, owns Skipper's Seafood Shops and has acquired Tony Roma's.

Many people keep score of restaurant chains' performance based on stock prices rather than on whether customer counts are increasing. The latter is a much better barometer of true performance and of a chain's capabilities. Employees worry about the stock, and stock analysts greatly influence the stock and the company. Shortly after Chevys was acquired by Taco Bell, Chevys' headquarters executives—with their new stock holdings in PepsiCo as a result of the deal—spent a definite portion of their thinking and listening time each day finding out how PepsiCo stock was doing. That was actually a morale booster as the stock kept rising and generated even more enthusiasm, but it is easy to see how focusing on stock prices can also divert efforts away from the main objective: to work as hard as possible to keep boosting the traffic counts and performance of one's own chain. (Perhaps these are mutually compatible objectives, inasmuch as when the performance of a chain improves, that presumably helps the parent company's stock.)

When Chi-Chi's was a Foodmaker, Inc. subsidiary, it was not directly influenced by Wall Street. "But indirectly we felt the pressure for increased sales and profitability," recalls former Chi-Chi's president Joseph Micatrotto.

Leveraged buy-outs are risky and often not in the best interests of the acquired company—only in the interests of the buy-out group that has taken ownership. Furthermore, the added debt and interest greatly limit the acquired company's focus and expansion possibilities. Debt service and trying to reduce the debt as fast as possible tend to become the new priorities.

LBOs also tend to leave a chain strapped. ARA's 1984 LBO was one that was priced right. It was less than five times the price-value, and the executive principals could operate the business at maximum efficiency. But the American Restaurant Group and the Restaurant Enterprises Group buy-outs in southern California were priced far too high and created substantial debt. Life was a constant struggle to somehow pay off these debts, which required higher and higher volumes that could not always be produced; hence the executive turnover at top levels.

Creative Gourmets was one of those that stayed private. "Our company really didn't have the glamorous appeal whereby it would make sense going public," observes president Stephen Elmont. "Most of the companies that went public had problems."

Steady growth provided by a chain's own system is also quite possible for some. Cousins Sub Systems, a Menomonee Falls, Wisconsin, chain, which by mid-1994 had some 75 submarine sandwich shops, has enjoyed steady franchising growth in the Midwest and in Arizona through a corporate sponsorship program that gives discounted franchise fees and other support services to employee or franchise-manager groups.

Another financing method is illustrated by Burlington, Vermont-based Bruegger's Bagels, which had grown to some 80 units by late 1993. The company sells zero coupon preferred stock to franchisees instead of charging them a franchise fee. The preferred stock accrues 10 percent interest and becomes convertible to common stock if and when the chain goes public. This enables Bruegger's to make money operating a restaurant chain, rather than from the sale of franchises. Most significantly, this method encourages togetherness between franchisors and franchisees—a pleasant contrast to the court battles that too often permeate franchisor-franchisee relationships.

Yet some feel that public ownership has advantages over private ownership because a public company focuses on growth and building equity for its stockholders. Of necessity, greater emphasis is placed on the accuracy of results and projections. Boston Chicken, Inc., Starbucks, Backyard Burgers, and Oh-La-La were among chains using an initial public offering in 1993 to finance a sharp expansion step-up. Boston Chicken, Inc. in early 1994 also issued $100 million in bonds to help finance a projected doubling of the chain to 450 units by year's end.

The 11-unit Dallas-based Tia's Tex-Mex restaurants, owned by Chili's founder Larry Lavine, took a different route and obtained a loan agreement from Morrison Restaurants, Inc. to double Tia's chain by 1995 at an estimated $1.9 million cost per unit. The key aspect of a deal like this is that the lender (Morrison) now has a five-year option to buy Tia's and thereby add to the diversity of Morrison's foodservice operations. Meanwhile, Sfuzzi and Silver Diner were among chains taking the venture capital route.

To operate a public company, one must put a proper focus on what is really success. By no means is success how well the stock performs. In Shoney's, Inc.'s early days as a public company, its price-earnings ratio sometimes dropped as low as 5 or 6, but it was still a well-run company. "It was just a matter of letting the investing public know," says David Wachtel. "The same holds true for O'Charley's. As we continue to grow and our margins improve, the investment community will appreciate what we are doing. The best way to take care of our shareholders is to take care of our restaurant customers."

Wall Street can be both a blessing and a curse. It is a source of capital and input for the analysts' reactions to the industry and to particular chains. Yet it can be a bad influence if you let it run your business.

General Mills Restaurants was big enough and strong enough not to let Wall Street and stockholders dictate its actions. "We refused to let them push us around," says Joe Lee. "They wanted us to go much faster with our new China Coast restaurants, but we just did it our way, slowly and gradually building it up until we were sure that it was ready to expand speedily." With Red Lobsters and The Olive Gardens in operation everywhere, General Mills could afford to wait until the proper time for China Coast to really roll.

Neither is going public a cure-all for leveraged buy-out woes or for private companies on the way up. "It should be a market-share battle today, not a stock-share battle," declares Godfather's Pizza president Herman Cain.

Jim Peterson, Whataburger president from 1974 to 1993, thinks a private company has a distinct advantage over a public company. (Whataburger is owned by Grace Dobson.) "A private company can always make its own short-range and long-range decisions without worrying about shareholders' quick reactions or Wall Street," Peterson says. "The idea is to keep building for the future, not necessarily pleasing stockholders today."

In 1988, Bill Bouffard helped lead a management buy-out of Bay Street restaurants from Pillsbury. "We wanted a management buy-out," he recalls, "but Pillsbury insisted on taking bids and keeping it for a year. Finally, we bought it. After Norman Brinker left, Pillsbury didn't know why they were in the restaurant business (if they ever did know). Pillsbury actually tried to show that restaurants were a prescription for failure."

The big mistake in the 1980s was that, because it was so easy, investment bankers allowed projections to get out of hand, even though they did not know what would happen a few years down the road. Wall Street and investment bankers priced leveraged buy-outs higher than they merited. Deals were forged with heavy payments on the front end. Projections were way off, because they were based on the assumption that every restaurant in a chain would be profitable when actually one out of four would be a loss. Fortunately, in the 1990s there appears to be a healthy, balanced skepticism in the marketplace.

At the end of 1993 there were more than 100 public chain restaurant companies. Wall Street, which is mainly interested in one-concept, successful chains that can be endlessly replicated, was having a field day.

Leveraging to Win

Leveraging the natural advantages of a chain
without overcentralizing.

"I'm afraid I'm going to wake up one day and find a Taco Bell in my bedroom."

—*A competing chain's president*

HIGHLIGHTS

- Chain-name power
- Logo clout
- Double-branding combos
- Riese "owns" NYC's brands
- Brand cross-fertilization
- Chains and suppliers working together
- Retail combos
- Branding out of the box
- Chains as neighborhood restaurants
- Purchasing and distribution leverage
- Pricing leverage

THE BRAND ADVANTAGE

A crucial challenge for chain restaurants today is to leverage their positive attributes and strengths to the hilt while at the same time showing individuality in their restaurants. For example, a chain can leverage bulk buying and distribution power to maximum advantage to lower its costs and raise volumes. Yet it must always remain customer friendly so that it is not perceived as a cold corporation.

Perhaps the most valuable form of leveraging is the chain name alone—a tremendous plus when it stands for quality and service. The public generally no longer looks with disdain on a chain, and the chain brand itself is often more impressive to the consumer than are brand-name products.

A chain's logo often establishes a brand identity as important as the name. This is why it is crucial to put time, thought, and zing into a logo. McDonald's Golden Arches, Big Boy restaurants' Big Boy shown eating a burger, and Outback's Australian-oriented theme are excellent examples of how logos can propel chain identities.

A chain brand name is overwhelmingly crucial in terms of familiarity to the consumer and in projecting a consistent image. However, its value can vary, depending on the chain's actual performance and consumers' perception. If they find performance consistent and reliable, then the brand name is a plus. But if enough units of a chain are perceived to be weak, the brand name becomes a liability rather than an asset.

The significance of a chain brand is becoming more pronounced, observes former Spaghetti Warehouse president Lou Neeb, "But it only works when the concept is correctly executed in all its elements and at all locations."

To former TGI Friday's president, Richard Rivera, a winning brand identity carves out a distinct niche in value perception. "TGI Friday's brand stands for fun, quality, be yourself as a server, and take a positive approach with the customer," he declares. "We worked hard at making TGI Friday's fun. It's the way people dress, the decor, the variety, a bigger and better menu."

In the restaurant business, the point has been reached at which a chain name is its brand name and is more of an asset than specific product brand names. Product brands have not been emphasized in restaurants, because restaurants tend to depend on ingredients to make their menu items rather than merchandising actual branded products, which have become indispensable to supermarkets.

Yet when a strong product brand is emphasized in conjunction with a strong chain/brand name, a process called double-branding, it can create a dynamic combination. Such products should be promoted more often, but the choice is up to the chain inasmuch as suppliers are more than happy to promote their brands in conjunction with the chains they serve.

Can a chain name be successfully changed if drastic surgery is needed to revamp an entire image? Only if the concept itself is a solid one and a new name can be promoted over a period of time. Homestyle Buffets, a 35-unit Palm Harbor, Florida-based chain that had undergone a sweeping management change, switched its name to Stacey's Buffet in early 1994 after Homestyle's acquisition of the 11-unit Largo, Florida-based Stacey's. This change may give Homestyle a stronger distinct image, as well as more units in a field crowded with names such as HomeTown Buffet and Old Country Buffet.

In any case, for maximum effectiveness and full leverage, a chain name should be one that has a certain zing, that consumers can latch onto and easily remember in the midst of thousands of chain and brand names, and that is not insulting to any group. This is no easy task in a business jammed with almost every conceivable type of name. It is an extreme challenge to devise a completely new name or concept today, and that is one reason chains copy existing concepts to the extent that copyright suits and trademark infringement cases have moved through court battles all the way to the Supreme Court. The Cannibal Cafe and Jekyll and Hyde—actually two New York City independents—are examples of names that grab the consumer and are easy to recall.

When Sambo's suddenly switched its restaurants' name to All-Seasons as a desperation measure in the early 1980s, it ran out of money within a few months of the remodelings and the name changes and had to close virtually the entire chain. Sambo's did not have the latitude to wait long enough to determine whether it could be successful. Still, the deck was stacked against it because customers were saying, "Isn't this the place where Sambo's used to be? It must be terrible," rather than, "An interesting new restaurant has opened here." By then it was almost certainly too late to succeed with just a name change. Sambo's carried connotations of racial

discrimination in its name, even though cofounders Sam Battistone, Sr. and Newell Bohnett said the name was strictly a combination of Battistone's first name and Bohnett's last name.

On the other hand, to use a prominent retailing example, many
were skeptical in the early 1970s when a group of Shop-Rite co-op
supermarkets in New Jersey decided to split off from their well-
known successful Shop-Rite parent and start an entirely new supermarket chain under the name Pathmark. It took only a year or two
for the Pathmark name to become as well known and respected as
Shop-Rite in the New York–New Jersey area, and that gap has
steadily widened in favor of Pathmark over the years. The name
itself was no doubt sleeker and more modern, but the real advantage
was that Pathmark stood for quality and depth in national brands
and in its own private brands.

Another example is the highly successful transformation of the
old Esso gas stations to Exxon—again, going against the conventional wisdom assuming that Esso had built such a stake in its name
that it made no sense to change. The reality is that 30 years later,
there aren't many people who really remember or care about the
Esso name (except in Canada, where it is still used). Most everyone
thinks Exxon is fine. It just shows how quickly brand equity can be
enhanced with a good product.

What happens when two chain brands collide with each other
in the same company and in some of the same markets? The two
don't necessarily wield twice the overall clout; nor do the two cancel
each other out. Popeyes and Church's combined under one parent,
called America's Favorite Chicken, were still two, almost parallel
concepts competing with each other.

Other chain combinations may be an effective form of double-
branding in their own right. The sister chains of Dunkin' Donuts
and Baskin-Robbins ice cream feature different appeals within the
same snack-treats category, giving them a far stronger combined
image. Dunkin' also has a double-barreled branding image with
ARA, Marriott, Morrison, The Riese Organization, and numerous
others.

Chain brands offer speed, convenience, and value. The Dunkin'

Donuts system also includes Mr. Donut under its Allied-Lyons umbrella. "These are world-dominant brands," says Dunkin' chairman Robert Rosenberg. He tried to team as a franchisee with Chili's, but that attempt did not jell and Dunkin' had to sell the franchising rights. Even with Chili's Northeast a separately run division, Dunkin' Donuts simply did not have the feel for the casual restaurant business—the feel that it has for the snack or treat business as something unique.

After Allied-Lyons acquired Dunkin' in addition to Baskin-Robbins, it focused heavily on promoting the two brands both in unison and separately under Rosenberg, who also became Baskin-Robbins chief executive. He pushed to promote the two brands with a number of combination Dunkin' and Baskin-Robbins units in a double-branding push—in effect, the customer could get two brands for the price of one.

Rosenberg also pressed for more pacts in which brand-name foodservice companies themselves became licensees of Dunkin'. These include Morrison, Marriott, and ARA, which provide a double-plus for branding. The idea is to repeatedly hammer home the name of Dunkin' Donuts as a mecca for donuts and coffee and Baskin-Robbins for quality ice cream. Rosenberg feels that bridging the generation gap is important and that any franchise chain "must bring sophisticated consumer-brand marketing to the business."

Dunkin' Donuts and others team for multiple-branding within The Riese Organization's locations. New York City's Penn Station is overwhelmingly crowded with chain brands under The Riese Organization as brand alliances grow at a rapid pace. The ultimate in brandability and multi-chain brands is offered by The Riese Organization in New York City, where it has four different brands on some corners, multibrands on many blocks, and its own "food court" clusters of four or five different restaurant brands in many locations. Among franchise chain names and its own brands in the Riese "stable" are Bagel Factory, Beefsteak Charlie's, Brewburger, Charley O's, Del Taco, El Torito, Haagen Dazs, Houlihan's, KFC, Leo Lindy's, Nathan's Famous, Pizza Hut, Roy Rogers, Sizzler,

TGI Friday's, Tequila Willie's, and Toots Shor. The Riese Organization even offers two directly competing brands in New York City, Houlihan's and TGI Friday's.

Marriott combines a series of different brand-name chains at its travel plazas along highways and parkways. A typical such plaza off the Garden State Parkway in New Jersey comprises Big Boy, Burger King, Mrs. Fields Cookies, Nathan's Famous, Roy Rogers, Sbarro, and TCBY.

Marriott also features a wide array of its own hotel chain brands, each standing for something different: Marriott Marquis (top of the line), Marriott Suites, Residence Inns, Courtyard by Marriott, and just plain Marriott. Each has its own price schedule and different facilities. This raises the question of how many niches one company can have and when it reaches the saturation point. The reality may be that if one chain brand goes almost as far as it can in expansion, a new one can gain another share of the market in a slightly different segment. Such is the case with General Mills, Brinker International, and others with a diversity of restaurant chains.

General Mills has three chain restaurant brands—Red Lobster, The Olive Garden, and China Coast, each with a separate identity. The consumer tends to identify each chain with its own individual name rather than with General Mills. The same is true of Brinker International's multiplicity of brands—Chili's, Grady's American Grill, Romano's, Spageddies, and so on. Interestingly, Brinker International tried to change the Grady's name to Regas (the original owning family) to avoid any confusion with Lewisville, Texas-based Grandy's fast-food, but then changed it back to Grady's by popular demand.

A chain brand also provides far more purchasing leverage. "Because of the economies of our chain," says Bay Street Restaurants' Bill Bouffard, "we're far ahead of independents on pricing strategies and margins." Bay Street has a 34 percent food cost, as compared with a 42 percent average for most other seafood restaurants. It has the advantage of bulk buying, using 40,000 four-ounce chicken breasts a month at lower prices and locking in a $300,000 purchase price on crawfish for the whole year.

What's really in a name? A great deal. The way veteran chain executive Howard Berkowitz sees it, a chain brand is all-powerful and all-important. Over the years, he has been an executive with various brands, including Sky Chefs, Jerry's coffee shops, Long John Silver's, Straw Hat Pizza, and A & W restaurants. "Independents don't have a chance or a clue," he declares. He does not view their individual identities as such an advantage. "They don't have the wide vision and competitive edge on marketing, purchasing, or people that brand-name chains have," he asserts. Most of all, Berkowitz, Oh-La-La president, thinks it is an unparalleled advantage to be a branded concept in someone else's branded concept. He is putting Oh-La-La kiosks in some 50 Marriott hotels across the country, giving him a double hit on brand-name identity.

One of the most astonishing double-brand combinations is Oh-La-La's Stinking Rose sandwich at its Candlestick Park, San Francisco, snack stand. "The baseball fans love the sandwich and love its name," says Berkowitz.

John Y. Brown, so often ahead of his time, stationed an Ollie's Trolley in downtown Louisville as a mobile fast-food place in the 1970s. The name alone, based on a real person named Ollie, and the Ollieburger that he introduced at his Miami Beach snack bar and that later was the leading item of Brown's Lums chain and then of Ollie's Trolley, intrigued consumers as much as or more than the food.

Branding also provides chains opportunities at schools, college campuses, shopping centers, hospitals, railroad stations, airports, military bases, gas stations, supermarkets, department stores, fairs, and almost any other imaginable place. "I'm afraid I'm going to wake up one day and find a Taco Bell in my bedroom," says one chain president.

Nathan's Famous is capitalizing on blending brands by locating at Marriott Service Centers off highways, as well as in airports. Marriott's Host International has brought Nathan's Famous, Pizza Hut, and other brands to its airport terminal foodservice operations, and A & W Family Restaurants food courts are in CUB Foods grocery stores.

Little Rock, Ark.-based TCBY has an exceptionally high 70 percent awareness level nationally. This brand-awareness advantage has helped TCBY establish itself in airports, travel plazas, universities, and other nontraditional sites. "Consumer preference for recognized chain brands has been a tremendous advantage and asset for many years," says former president Charles Cocotas.

IHOP has achieved what marketing vice president Stephen Pettise likes to call a brand-name "treat appeal" in a "treat segment" that also includes Bakers Square, Marie Callendar's, Coco's, and the sister chains Dunkin' Donuts and Baskin-Robbins. Pettise is counting on IHOP's chain-brand appeal to help expand it from 575 units in late 1993 to 1,000 by the end of the decade. He is using a double appeal, with the name IHOP scoring a 45 percent awareness among consumers and the preferred name, International House of Pancakes, hitting a 90 percent recognition level. "We like to use both names for the same restaurants to gain maximum customer awareness," he explains.

When both names are combined in the same chain, they also become a type of double-brand. Whatever the name, the chain is thriving on items such as its basic pancakes, new country griddle cakes, blintzes, omelets, Rooty-Tooty and other breakfast brands, and Rooty Tooty strawberry-peach drinks. It does not pretend to be a healthy-foods place and therefore is generally mobbed—at least for breakfast during the morning.

The ultimate in a double-branding trend that is sweeping the industry was IHOP's teaming up with Nabisco and cooperatively working out the details over a one-year period for unique Cream of Wheat ingredients that make IHOP's new country griddle cakes extra special. And Morrison's Hospitality Group teamed up with the Idaho Potato Commission in creating and merchandising a Spuddles potato bar concept.

Names certainly sell effectively. Consider the inventive concepts of theme restaurants with costumed characters such as Phoenix-based Bobby McGee's and San Antonio-based Magic Time Machines. Some are named for real people, such as Los Altos, California-based Stuart Anderson restaurants, and others are named after mythical characters, such as California's Charley Brown, New Jersey's Charlie Brown, and the Big Boy character. Still others have legends that have been built up about the named character and the restaurant. Without their legends, these restaurants would have no specific theme and much less interest. Still, food and service are the crucial elements today, not the theme.

Another form of double-branding is naming a restaurant after sports stars, who often are owners too and make a certain number of appearances at the restaurant. If the restaurant succeeds, it is usually because the sports-star owner is smart enough to have an expert run it. Two notable examples are Mickey Mantle's in New York City and Michael Jordan's in Chicago. In addition, one of the biggest sellers in Chicago has been the McJordan's sandwich at McDonald's. Earlier, Mike Ditka's Chicago restaurant closed.

The chain brand can certainly be leveraged for maximum marketing advantage too. Robert Taft, president of Dedham, Massachusetts-based Papa Gino's Italian-pizza restaurants and former chief operating officer of Seattle-based Skipper's seafood shops, is convinced that a widespread chain brand offers maximum media advertising effectiveness for the dollar. "Local marketing is really the key to the chain business," says Tim McCarthy, president of Contract Marketing of Ohio. "It's going back to the roots of this business."

S & A Restaurant Corporation has two distinct brands in Steak and Ale and Bennigan's. Each concept has a definite identity with the public. "This clear identity allows us to use different cost-effective marketing vehicles like television, direct mail, and outdoor advertising without having to explain the concept," said Steven Leipsner when he was chairman-president. He tried to extend the Bennigan's concept and capitalize on existing equity-reducing investment and development costs by planning Bennigan's Cafe America and Bennigan's Sports restaurant. Would that type of strategy blur the original concept in the customer's eyes?

Another type of double-branding occurs when a manufacturer starts its own restaurant chain. New York-based Chock Full o' Nuts, a highly identifiable coffee brand, has launched an upscale coffee-type concept that would go far beyond the old-time Chock Full o' Nuts coffee houses of years ago.

Chains are increasingly searching for alternate brands rather than sticking with just one. Cleveland-based Brown Derby steakhouses is switching some of its restaurants to roadhouses under the appropriate name of The Roadhouse. A mesquite grill and western decor are featured.

Patrick Morris, former Tony Roma's marketing senior vice president, decries the economists' theories that brand loyalty is drastically declining as the consumer seeks individual values. "A brand concept must know exactly what the value of the product is," he asserts. The chain brands that suffer most are those whose prices have become disproportionately high relative to the value offered.

Louisville-based Chi-Chi's has benefited from its chain brand. "Because of our high levels of brand awareness extending over a period of several years," says former president Joseph Micatrotto, "we have developed a reputation for a product that is high quality, enjoyable, and consistent. By virtue of our long-standing reputation, we are a brand that customers trust and hence retain an advantage over independents in this same segment. Our reputation is further enhanced by quality advertising and promotions that provide a strong price-value communication."

Brandability in contract management was sometimes considered a cop-out—a way to get higher prices. Still, Creative Gourmets had not only a strong brand name but also integrity in that name. "We work all our lives to create an image of trust for the values we hold most dear and for the integrity of our brand name," says former Creative Gourmets president Stephen Elmont, "and when we succeed, it is the most gratifying feeling."

ARA uses branded concepts "when and where it makes sense and the client desires," says ARA Global Food Services chairman John Farquharson. "We use those brands recognized nationally such as Dunkin' Donuts in factories or office buildings, and we use our own internal ARA brands, which are growing rapidly. Brand names receive extra recognition in just about every case."

Customers recognize a brand name for its quality. This is achieved through consistent quality and the maintaining of top standards. The chain's unit management in each area is the key to successfully merchandising the chain brand one restaurant at a time, one neighborhood at a time.

The higher a chain is on the economic scale, the more customers will demand. For example, customers want more from a Morton's, with a $53 average per-person price, than from a chain with a $10 average check. "We know they expect more, and we give it to them," asserts parent Quantum Restaurant Group's Allen J. Bernstein. Morton's has launched a mail-order service for its prime steaks. "The same steaks you enjoy at Morton's can be delivered anywhere," is the chain's mail-order slogan as it gains greater brand identity and extra leveraging.

A chain has to be careful about extending a brand name too far, of putting products in the supermarket and competing with its own chain. Bob Evans sausages, which were launched before Bob Evans restaurants, probably enhance the chain's brand name in a supermarket. But salsa in a can at a supermarket could detract from the reputation of fresh salsa in a restaurant.

Brand name alliances are proliferating today. McDonald's is opening at numerous Wal-Mart discount department stores and Home Depot home improvement centers. Meanwhile, Little Caesars is in at least 600 Kmarts, Pizza Hut is in Bradlees, Burger King in Jamesways, Nathan's Famous hot dogs in Caldors, and Chick-Fil-A in a Smitty's Phoenix supermarket. With these alliances, restaurant chains have new audiences to sell to and can merchandise the chain names involved. The restaurant chains profit from the built-in traffic, and the stores gain customers from the restaurant brand's own clout with consumers.

Meanwhile, Home Depot is offering the ultimate in combined leveraging and branding with a new pilot concept in Georgia called Depot Diner, which features products from Blimpie, Burger King, Coca-Cola, Freshens Premium Yogurt, the Hot Dog Construction Co., and Pizza Hut. Morrison's Hospitality Group and/or McDonald's might also be involved in various projected Depot Diners. The Diner is a 1,200-square-foot food court idea that, if successful, will be extended to other Home Depot stores in Atlanta, Los Angeles, New York, and South Florida.

Pizza Hut serves its offerings in some 5,000 high schools, and Taco Bell in some 2,000. Thus, it is not impossible that some school cafeterias will become fast-food franchisees. Taco Bell, the current leader in utilizing nontraditional sites, seems willing to go anywhere in the world to capitalize on its brand appeal; it has positioned kiosks throughout strategic areas of the Moscow subway system.

The Cheesecake Factory, Chi-Chi's, Friendly's, Pizzeria Uno, Taco Bell, TGI Friday's, and White Castle are going one step further and extending brand leveraging by positioning their products in supermarkets. Although some franchisees protest these moves as undercutting the chain itself, evidence suggests that the extra leveraging is a big plus. Consumers generally seem to know and appreciate the supermarket and restaurant brands and to want to try the restaurant brand if they liked the supermarket one, and vice versa. McDonald's and Pizzeria Uno are going even further, offering their best menu items on selected airlines.

Double-branding is also gaining popularity in the hotel field. Duos sharing the same property include Clarion Inn and Comfort Inn in one combination and Days Inn and Comfort Inn in another.

McDonald's, Burger King, KFC, Pizza Hut, Pizzeria Uno, and I Can't Believe It's Yogurt are among chain brands pouring into airport terminals. Buffalo, New York-based Concession Air Corporation (now renamed CA One Services has launched and is managing the operations of hundreds of foodservice chain brands at airports around the country, including some of those mentioned earlier. A most intriguing development is the creation of identifiable chain brand names just for airports or other locations. Marriott Host opened Cheers bars in airports, patterned after the "Cheers" television series.

Duo combinations among chains are also being tried with inherent extra-brand emphasis. Included are Arby's–Green Burrito, Arby's–Mrs. Winner's Chicken, Foster's Freeze–Green Burrito, and Foster's Freeze–El Pollo Loco. General Mills, PepsiCo, and Brinker International are also teaming up their own respective chain concepts at a number of sites.

A chain brand provides a huge advantage. "But you've got to make it clear exactly what your restaurant is selling and then merchandise each chain differently as a separate concept," emphasizes Norman Brinker. The danger is trying to merchandise all the chain brands in a group as one. Each needs a completely separate identity.

COMMUNITY INVOLVEMENT

Perhaps the secret is to be an "unchain chain." The Olive Garden offers varied individual menus at many of its restaurants, but for most chains the menu is fairly standardized and there have to be other ways of establishing an individual image. True, a standardized brand enables a chain to go almost anywhere, but a key goal for a regional or national chain is to try to establish an identity as "the neighborhood restaurant" in each community. One of the best ways to do this is through local marketing and community involvement. With its Ronald McDonald Houses and constant stream of community events, McDonald's is unsurpassed at establishing a community identity, but others are trying.

As quoted by writer Howard Riell of Kingston, Pennsylvania, Ponderosa's field marketing director, Doug Galusha, suggests, "If you're not part of the community, you're an outsider. Customers want to see the kids in the neighborhood working at your restaurant, and they want the restaurant to be involved with the school. You've got to be part of the community to succeed." Ponderosa sponsors community fund-raising programs and has a rebate program whereby groups turn in Ponderosa dining receipts and receive a check for 5 percent of the total. High school baseball teams or scout troops use the rebates to buy uniforms.

For years, independent restaurants have built brand loyalty by emphasizing themselves as neighborhood restaurants and tying in with the local community. Chains that promote their brands through a neighborhood image thereby translate their regional or national brand strength to the local level.

Riell also quotes Seattle restaurant consultant Linda Tobney as observing, "People like to support one of their own. If you can make a national chain personally identify with them, they love to come to your restaurant."

"We're spending more of our time and money in local areas," notes Jeri Galloway, marketing vice president of Universal Restaurants, Grand Rapids, Michigan. "When we give back to the community, it fosters a real feeling of community."

The Olive Garden's strategy is to keep building its national chain "one neighborhood at a time." It has a staff of 15 persons in the field who focus on local events. Each month the chain sponsors an estimated 150 local events that raise money for community projects and another 250 restaurant events contributing food to various groups. Costs of such events range from $20 to help a local charity operate a car wash in a restaurant's parking lot, to $300,000 to sponsor a large sporting event. Projects include fund-raisers for local high schools, day-care services, YMCA programs, and sponsorship of professional baseball, basketball, and football teams. Communities particularly like to see a restaurant bring programs into the school.

To further aid added brand identification, The Olive Garden sometimes has its employees take free samples of the chain's garlic breadsticks to local groups and merchants, thus building more goodwill. The Olive Garden also sponsors the "Discover It" school program to emphasize Renaissance history to elementary school students. Teachers receive full sets of curriculum notes, materials, workbooks, and posters.

Burger King sponsors a "School Nights" program in which principals, teachers, and students host events at a local Burger King and the school keeps 20 percent of the sales. In Tampa, Florida, a number of Burger Kings give free french fries. Pizza Hut offers schools a "Book It" program, whereby local restaurants offer coupon books to teachers, who give the coupons to students when they have read a certain number of books. The program culminates in a pizza party to celebrate the end of the school year. Pizza Hut also gives away half-priced Kids' Pizza Packs on Tuesday evenings.

Garfield's emphasis on mall locations makes its name-brand identity more crucial. "We really are retail," says president Vincent Orza, "and our image and location within malls are crucial to our success." At the same time Garfield's, still largely a regional chain, combines the size and benefits of a national chain with operational advantages associated with local chains. Garfield's features Awards of Excellence programs, recognizing students for academic excellence, and Garfield's Community Chest is a highly visible financial support group for local children's charities and educational foundations.

Community involvement by a small chain can establish an excellent reputation in local neighborhoods—clearly a major advantage. Larger chains have to work much harder to promote their community images. Customer loyalty to a chain restaurant brand often proliferates in direct proportion to that chain's local involvement. This is a double advantage, as the reputation of those chains that do things for the community spreads and becomes a legend in itself, as is the case with McDonald's.

DISTRIBUTION AND BUYING

A chain gains maximum advantage when it can emphasize bulk purchasing, distribution, marketing, technology, and other chain strengths while still presenting an individual image. Those chains that keep their focus on operating restaurants rather than trying to be distributors seem to do better. McDonald's is a prime example, having always eschewed distribution and manufacturing and instead forming alliances with distribution companies (most notably, Golden State Foods Corporation of Pasadena, California, and the Martin-Brower Company of Downers Grove, Illinois) and letting Quaker Oats and other prime suppliers take care of providing the product. McD succeeded by buying from just a few selected distributors, almost from the first, and forming alliances with selected suppliers. Steadfast loyalty on all sides boosted McD and its partners.

Howard Johnson, Burger King, Papa Gino's, Hardee's, Friendly, Marriott, KFC, and Pizza Hut established distribution systems in the 1960s and 1970s. A number of these chains also launched commissaries, manufacturing some of their own products. Some distributed to other chains to help pay for the distribution costs.

Papa Gino's and Hardee's got out of the commissary-production business in the mid-1970s after suffering losses from this endeavor.

Self-distribution diverted the efforts of Howard Johnson's, Sambo's, and other chains and was one cause of their failure. It did give companies "quality control" over their distribution and supply, but it generally was a diverting factor and in some cases even a conflict of interest.

In effect, chains have three choices: (1) no centralized buying, which means no leverage; (2) utilizing centralized buying as much as feasible for maximum leverage and supporting this with specialized system distributors, or a combination of system and local distributors; or (3) self-distribution, a diverting process that we don't recommend.

Some version of choice 2 seems preferable. Yet Burger King, Carl's Jr., Domino's Pizza, Marriott, Pizza Hut, Taco Bell, and White Castle were among those still involved in self-distribution as of early 1994. By then Morrison Restaurants, Inc. had dropped its self-distribution and coffee-roasting operations.

Over the years, chains have wavered back and forth on whether to distribute products on their own, with a distribution center and possibly a commissary processing-supplier center, or to let others do this for them and focus strictly on running the restaurants. Denny's created Proficient Foods as a separate company to sell to other chains as well as to Denny's and, thereby, to at least break even. Through the years, this approach has time and time again proved to be a mistake; the only real justification for self-distribution is to ensure a chain's own quality control and to be certain that a product is always in stock at its restaurants. There is no advantage to a chain's being in the distribution business, and certainly not in selling to other chains or even direct competitors. Distribution is merely another diversion from the core business of a restaurant. The desired purchasing leverage can be achieved in other ways.

Yet a certain fascination remains with self-distribution. Self-distribution chains tend to want direct control of everything. Jack Maier, chairman of Cincinnati-based Frisch's Restaurants, Inc., started running the chain's own distribution center in the 1950s and tried to achieve cost controls over products that way. Hardee's used self-distribution for years until finally giving it up. Denny's Proficient Foods was distributing to the El Pollo Loco chain before

Denny's acquired that chain, based on a tip from Proficient people. In 1993, Proficient was still chalking up a $600 million volume and selling to some 25 other chains, most of them small and medium-sized and not directly competitive with Denny's. Thus, Proficient is a wholly different business activity and at some level diverts Denny's corporate efforts, which should be completely focused on the restaurants. Burger King disengaged from its Distron primary purchasing distribution arm, but the renamed ProSource company still services a significant portion of Burger King.

Chi-Chi's has its own self-distribution setup. It uses two in-house distribution centers to service more than 200 restaurants and thereby realizes substantial savings in freight and truck-load pricing. Key suppliers help Chi-Chi's obtain the best possible price as part of strategic alliances. Chi-Chi's is expanding its use of in-house computers to control food and labor costs.

Sonic is 99 percent organized into purchasing co-ops. They evaluate supplier programs on the basis of those that have integrity and the best interests of franchisees at heart. "We look at quality and consistency first and cost last," chairman Steven Lynn says, "because we know that as we work together and leverage our buying power, costs will fall into line. Using the power of collective purchasing, we have been able to bring food costs down 6.5 percent over the last six years."

Self-distribution still thrives in many small and medium chains. Although larger chains generally have switched to distributors to handle distribution, this group is often more locally focused or in a specific area. Bertucci's, Inc., an emerging chain of Pizzerias, based in Woburn, Massachusetts, utilized its own distribution network to handle its rapid growth (it zoomed from just a few restaurants to more than 40 in seven years) and to fill special product needs. This meant it could control the quality, vendors, menu items, and specifications at a reasonable cost. Outside distributors would not have been happy with the necessary and constant changes in signals, but internally, the system worked well for Bertucci's.

The 52-unit Pietro's Pizza, now based in Bothell, Washington, needed a customized delivery schedule to meet its special needs. Pietro's fresh pizza dough has just a two-day shelf life, and the company found it could be speeded to points throughout the states of Washington and Oregon only with its own distribution trucks and a comprehensive self-distribution system. Pietro's has a 24,000-square-foot warehouse and processing center with eight refrigerated tractor-trailers, which save time and costs.

The Long Beach, California-based University Restaurants Group (URG) feels it can gain access to unique products and beat its competition by using its own distribution system. For example, URG, which includes upscale restaurants such as the Water Grill and Icugini, likes to deal directly with specialized California produce and greens growers, picking up and delivering these delicate items with their own trucks going directly to their restaurants.

East Providence, Rhode Island-based Bugaboo Creek Steakhouse, Inc. (formerly Phelps-Grace Co.) with ten restaurants, distributes half its needs, or at least $3 million worth of products annually, with just one refrigerated truck at a cost of about $60,000 a year—a significant saving because it does not use a warehouse or commissary. Most of all, this gives Bugaboo, now a public company, consistent high-quality seafood products and lower-cost fresh beef.

Other companies need their own central distribution plant. Kittery, Maine-based Weathervane Seafood Restaurants, with 15 units, contracts with local fishermen for 70 percent of its 1.1 million pounds of annual seafood purchases. It has a 320,000-square-foot distribution processing center, three refrigerated trucks, and a staff of 20 (including purchasing people). The annual cost is only $900,000 out of $30 million total sales. This system is well worth the expense, because suppliers can drop off all products to Weathervane at a lower price. Moreover, it can directly test the products for quality at the single center before sending them to the restaurants, via a route on which the farthest distance is 250 miles. Weathervane also distributes steaks, supplies, and materials to its restaurants. Such customization of a chain's own deliveries pays off for small to medium chains. For large chains, however, it has proven to be a questionable investment, as well as a diversion of focus.

If a chain does not have a central distribution center, it must organize its purchasing leverage more carefully than ever.

Purchasing Leverage

A prime challenge is how to coordinate the purchasing power of a chain's volume with the need to distribute products to hundreds or thousands of individual units. Negotiating becomes crucial in coping with this challenge in the distribution process.

One method for limited-menu chains, particularly fast-feeders, is to deal with system specialists—foodservice distributors dedicated to meeting a chain's individual distribution needs. Specialists such as Martin-Brower and Golden State enable strong chains to avoid nonessential services (for example, credit extended to individual units and the need for salespeople to call on the units). McDonald's and other large chains often turn to these specialists for distribution of a high portion of their purchases. But even these chains must often use local distributors for produce, dairy, and other products or for delivery to unit locations that are remote from system specialists.

In the most frequent form of leveraging purchasing clout, a chain's purchasing department receives the necessary local-unit distribution but negotiates for the best deal from a national broad-line distributor offering full lines of food, equipment, and supplies. Chains negotiate with broad-line distributors for central purchasing and for a reasonable fee to deliver to individual units. Sysco, number one with more than $10 billion in annual sales, Kraft Foodservice, and Rykoff-Sexton are among the leading distributor corporations with numerous regional warehouses in the consolidated broad-line business.

A chain must also exercise caution in negotiations to ensure receiving the benefits of any allowances that the distributor receives from the manufacturer. Pennies add up quickly, and to recapture these funds it is necessary to maximize a chain's purchasing leverage. This can be best achieved by a chain's maintaining strategic alliances with its distributors and with the manufacturers that provide products to those distributors. Chains should also seek to audit distributor records when appropriate.

A broad-line distributor, in turn, uses its own leverage by encouraging chains to use the distributor's own "private" label products, rather than always using nationally recognized brands. Because the distributor often negotiates lower prices on its own labels, chains can benefit from these savings. Still, except for truly specialized commodity products, most national chains prefer to deal with major branded food manufacturers for quality and consistency on the most important items.

Sonic prides itself on state-of-the-art programs. "We work off markup, not margin," chairman Steven Lynn emphasizes. "There are no up charges on split cases. We give off-invoice allowances in concert with our marketing calendar promotional combos—which is practically unheard of in the industry. And our hedging programs protect our franchisees against price increases and inventory problems in addition to delivering a quality product."

As a franchisor, Lynn observes, "We certainly could build in some extra dollars over and above the vendor cost. However, our costs to the franchisee are net. We make sure that every available dollar from the vendor goes back to the franchisees."

Chains that franchise face a tougher challenge in leveraging purchases inasmuch as there is a temptation to "mark up" products for franchisees. This practice has resulted in a great deal of litigation, and franchisor executives interviewed for this book discourage the practice of marking-up.

In selecting distributors, some chains opt to negotiate with a series of local or regional distributors rather than the major broad-line nationals. Although it increases the complexity of the negotiating process, this choice often lowers product and distribution costs. Furthermore, it is almost mandatory for certain perishable items.

Ultimately, the goal of leveraged purchasing and distribution is to remove these functions from a chain's individual units and centralize them. One can also anticipate a time, perhaps in this decade, when the distributor, or the chain itself, will totally manage the supply aspects of local units via computers. This would free unit managers to focus more completely on food preparation and customer satisfaction.

Misguided Self-Distribution

Attempting to handle all the distribution and purchasing functions, rather than negotiating with manufacturers and appropriate distributors, often creates difficulties. One past example, Sambo's, illustrates this point. The chain's purchasing and distribution system was saddled with highly inefficient practices through the 1970s. Even when the difficulties were finally straightened out in 1978–79, the new efficiencies proved counterproductive in that they encouraged continued self-distribution and, to some extent, diverted focus from the more than 1,000 struggling Sambo's restaurants that desperately needed full attention.

Sambo's distribution system was a classic story of inefficient leveraging converted to highly efficient leveraging for just a few years, which alone could not save the chain. Karl Willig, a 33-year-old Harvard M.B.A. with commodities trading and meat processing experience, joined M&F Meat Packing in 1977 as vice president in charge to try to straighten out the operation. Willig became president of Sambo's in 1978. He promptly changed the M&F name to Sambo's Foodservice to identify more closely with Sambo's, which provided 80 percent of M&F's sales. Willig brought in Edward Dudley, an executive with distribution and meat processing experience, as foodservice vice president to direct the distribution and commissary operations.

Until 1977, Sambo's executives did not know how to strategically manage distribution and processing. They would send loaded trucks from the Carpinteria, California, center to Oregon and the state of Washington and deliver to restaurants along the route. But the trucks would go all the way back to California virtually empty or, at most, a few would return with some flour. Sambo's did not seem to understand the necessity of backhauling to substantially reduce operating costs.

Dudley and Willig solved the problem by establishing a separate transportation company, SRI Trucking, with Interstate Com-

merce Commission contract authority. Then trucks were able to
return not only with flour but with french fries, frozen vegetables,
and other commodities for Sambo's and other restaurant customers.
The number of return miles with full loads jumped from 40 percent
to 85 percent. In addition, a computerized routing system was used
which—combined with the purchase of larger capacity 45-food
trailers to replace 38-foot trailers—reduced total annual truck mileage from 14 million to 12 million miles.

In Sambo's meat commissary and warehouse operations, processes were reengineered, employees properly trained, yields mea-
sured, and production standards implemented. Meat processing and
warehouse productivity were substantially improved. Vard Ellis,
meat operations director, and Gary Kasprowicz, plant director of
Sambo's Foodservice Kentucky facility, rapidly implemented their
respective upgraded programs. They also improved the Texas cattle
feeding and slaughter operations, providing Sambo's with consistent quality and a low-cost source of beef.

By 1979, Sambo's Foodservice had become a $175 million a
year business and a logistics model of success. "As a business team,
we changed foodservice into a highly efficient distributor," Dudley
says. "Unfortunately, there was not enough time or resources to
regain the momentum that had been lost at the restaurant level. In
retrospect, our shareholders and employees would have been better
served if all our senior management's and Board of Directors' time
and attention had been directed toward rebuilding our sales and operations."

In contrast, when Dudley left in 1981 to join Kentucky Fried
Chicken as procurement, distribution, and manufacturing vice
president, KFC quickly sold its distribution operations. It effectively used third-party distributors such as Sysco, Kraft Foodservice, and selected regional distributors to deliver food and supplies
to KFC restaurants at competitive prices and strong service levels.
Along with establishing a purchasing cooperative, KFC was able to
free assets, improve working capital, and, most important, engage
franchisees as partners in buying the right products at the best
prices from key strategic suppliers.

This international "open book" policy of KFC, coupled with the leadership of leading KFC franchisees like Jim Cornett, Pete Harman, and Bobby Helms, was a decisive factor in KFC's turnaround during the 1980s. Because of KFC's impressive sales and earnings growth, PepsiCo was willing to spend more than $950 million to acquire it in the late 1980s. Dudley went on to become distribution services vice president of Kraft/General Foods.

Given the completely opposite results at Sambo's and KFC—the first, a losing proposition, and the second, a 1980s winner—we wonder whether PepsiCo's decision to utilize its PepsiCo Food Service in-house distribution arm for KFC will pay off. Disappointing KFC operating results from 1990 to 1993, the reported mistrust engendered between the corporation and franchisees over PepsiCo's move away from "open book" purchasing for KFC, and the loss of focus taken away from KFC unit operations bring the entire PFS self-distribution decision into question.

ENTREPRENEURSHIP AND LEVERAGING

Although computers and technology are a necessity, people and entrepreneurship are still the hub of the foodservice business. "Great management makes more money and more success than all the hardware in the world," Eateries' Vincent Orza declares. "We try to give our people the latitude to react, respond, and make their own entrepreneurial decisions."

Papa Gino's Robert Taft sees chain-buying leverage as a major advantage "most of the time" and views a winning technology system as one that helps a chain obtain a maximum return on investment and empowers people in the field. Meanwhile, ARA leverages its bulk buying power with key strategic suppliers to obtain better pricing on its products. These alliances also include research and development and marketing support from suppliers, and in-unit training support and development of proprietary products for ARA's Restaurant Collection Concepts (i.e., its pizza dough mix). ARA's computers are enhanced with an eight-step food production management software system and the ARATRACK product-usage tracking system.

Decentralization once was a prime objective of management in the 1970s. If a chain was not decentralized, it was behind the times. But to be successfully decentralized, a company must originally be strongly centralized. "You need to have the communication channels and systems already in place to allow for systematic decentralizing without a loss of communications, operational controls, and fiscal responsibility," says Patrick Morris, former Tony Roma's senior marketing vice president. "Too many companies tried to decentralize without being very well centralized to begin with. All they did was add more chaos to what was already an unstable system.

Most chains have, in effect, decentralized by adding layers of regional vice presidents and directors and transferring human resource, marketing, site selection, and other responsibilities to regional offices. This is part of the empowerment system necessary for the bigger chains, as they can't exercise full control from one central headquarters. It also allows flexibility in local decision making.

Chains can leverage their pricing too. For example, if full-service chains can offer what customers perceive as 80 percent of the quality of fine dining at 50 percent of the price, they can win. This is a prime reason that fine dining is declining.

As O'Charley's has grown, it has experienced an increase in buying power, as well as supplier respect for the concept. This permits the chain to keep improving margins by lowering costs. "Due to more efficient buying and purchasing," says former president David Wachtel, "we continued with this." Wachtel too believes in keeping people in control of the business and not relegating management to computers. "Like accounting and advertising, computers are a necessary evil, and we must make sure our managers run the computers and not let the computers run them."

Chains must also be on their franchisees' side in purchasing as well as in most everything else. "We pass all rebates along to all our restaurants—company and franchised," says Johnny Rockets' Ronn Teitelbaum. "To maintain a true bulk purchasing advantage, integrity is everything. We'll never agree to take a discount for a payment to a franchisee."

Strong relationships with suppliers pay off in buying power.

"We are utilizing our chain size to advantage," asserts Chevys' Mike Hislop. "We're making longer contracts at lower prices, working on menu planning and development accordingly." These alliances have enabled Chevys to lower its prices at least once a year. Sister chain California Pizza Kitchen designs its own specialized equipment by working in alliance with key suppliers, who help design the equipment just for California Pizza Kitchen.

When a chain has a strong presence in any market, it can sometimes afford to reduce menu prices for customers. A good example is the Greater Phoenix market, where Big 4's Lee Cohn has added restaurants to his group and made some of them larger, partly to build up enough volume to pass on the same lower prices to his smaller restaurants. This principle applies to other regional chains and to national chains, which can capitalize even more on the advantages of bulk purchasing. Unfortunately, too many chains use such opportunities strictly to build their profit margins and not to give customers lower prices and build traffic for the future.

Bulk buying is a major advantage as long as it is not an excuse to put an inferior product on the menu because of pricing. It means balancing the buying power of products with a need for quality in core menu items in which quality can't be sacrificed. Annual buying contracts for meat and other major products not only save costs but can also enhance food quality.

Chains can exercise much tighter controls than independents. Chain restaurant general managers are responsible for producing traffic counts and sales and profit increases at each unit—a leverage that independents don't have. Yet too often there is a feeding-trough mentality. Some chains derive their strength only from size. This alone can be awesome, but true success requires more. Chain operators instead must emphasize a personal approach and the best service. Thus the way to win is by using the individuality of an independent while deploying the full leveraging power of a chain. Jim Peterson, former Whataburger president, is convinced that there must be "no more cookie-cutter restaurants in chains. Unit managers must be given full authority so that they can put individual stamps on restaurants within the context of any chain."

Ron Magruder personalizes The Olive Garden by serving the

most popular products in each market area. For coffee, it's Starbucks in Seattle.

"We believe in consistency but not sameness," says former TGI Friday's president Richard Rivera. "We sell more beverages in the Northeast. People in New England and Florida want something entirely different." And for better or for worse, Burger King is letting some of its units continue to provide table service, and KFC has a neighborhood program whereby local units can adjust their menus and decor to the local environment. These tactics enable a chain to capitalize on its size, as well as to project individuality.

Although technology can perform wonders, it is also often a diversion from focusing on the actual restaurant operation. A computer's greatest value is the time it saves in the back office, allowing a manager to be out front with the guests. The extra information a computer gathers can free the manager for more important things; unfortunately, too many unit managers fail to take advantage of such opportunities.

In 1990, Tony Roma's allowed its servers to do whatever the customers asked. The key for a server or manager was to pretend to be the owner of the restaurant and able to make the decisions. More often than not, this type of empowerment provides the guest with an experience that far exceeds expectations. "At Tony Roma's, it became a religion to adhere to, and encourage use of, this decision grid," recalls Patrick Morris.

The maximum leverage in a delivery system is personified by Takeout Taxi, which delivers food from restaurants to customers and provides computerized mailing lists of millions. Other food delivery services have sprouted in almost every region to capitalize on the advantages that chains already have.

Foodservice chains are also gaining leverage through alliances with convenience stores and supermarkets and in hotels, where chains run some of the restaurants, banquet service, and room service.

For years The Riese Organization tried to keep its identity hidden while utilizing its many franchise chain brand names on major corners and blocks throughout New York City. But Dennis Riese changed that after he became president of this family-owned company in 1992 and merchandised The Riese Organization as a brand, leveraging all its different names for combined marketing. For example, any customer who attended a sporting event at Madison Square Garden merely had to present the ticket stub at a Riese restaurant—no matter what the chain or concept name—to receive a 25 percent discount on a meal.

"It's about time we gained the promotion, advertising, and marketing benefits of our name," declares Riese, whose father and uncle had tried to keep the Riese name a secret when they ran the company from the 1940s to the 1980s. True, no Riese restaurant was actually called "Riese," and perhaps the organization wanted customers to think each restaurant was an individual one and not a chain or part of a large company. In so doing, it sacrificed a great deal of potential leverage. Dennis Riese can still keep changing concepts to other ones within the company every three to five years, if he so desires, but he now has the benefit of the leveraged umbrella.

Chains can also leverage signature menu items to tremendous advantage. "We'll capitalize on our equity in premium-quality pies by launching Bakery Theaters with expanded lines of pies and other fresh-baked items at the front of our restaurants," declared Denver's James Caruso when he moved up to the Bakers Square presidency in late 1993.

The faster a chain can build units, assuming a decent construction quality and a reasonable cost, the more leverage it can exercise. Clearwater, Florida-based Checkers Drive-In Restaurants, Inc. has been able to jump-start its double drive-throughs within weeks of obtaining sites. James Mattei, president, describes a process by which the double drive-throughs are completed within a few days, in prefabricated form, at a central construction facility and immediately shipped to their market—with any required individualized designs—for installation within hours of arrival. That gives Checkers (or any other chain using a similar process) greater flexibility in making its projected units come to fruition almost at will.

"Brandability," purchasing power, marketing clout, construction flexibility, and signature menu items are definite chain strengths. On the other hand, chains generally are slower to move and harder to change. "For goodness sakes, it takes nine months just to change the china," concedes Norman Brinker. He lives by the rule that "it is absolutely crucial for a chain to give special service and care to the customer" and not project a chain image. "You must get it across to the customer that this restaurant is special and personal," he declares.

A chain's real leverage largely depends on its strategic ability to exploit its strongest niches and to match the niche or niches it enters with its own capabilities and strengths. The former philosophy of chains—that there is one way of doing it, one size for all, and a complete sameness throughout—no longer applies. Those chains that can be flexible in downsizing or upsizing, or in capitalizing on local opportunities, will win.

The Life Cycle

*Knowing when and what to change to maximize the
life cycle.*

"A chain can lose individual flair so quickly in this business."
—*Norman Brinker, chairman
Brinker International, Dallas*

HIGHLIGHTS

- A constant struggle
- No absolute maximum
- Saturation limits cycles
- Alternate concepts extend life span
- Unique niche crucial
- Focus on strongest feature
- Persevere through ups and downs
- Hot chains always emerging
- Constant evolution
- Steady excellence

What is the life span of a restaurant chain? When is it time to
change the concept, sell it, or just close the doors? There is no
absolute answer for these frequently asked questions, because it depends so much on the particular chain, its quality, sustainability,
management team, and economic cycles. Theoretically, a chain's
potential life cycle can be almost unlimited, as McDonald's is showing—with nuances added each year and gradual evolution. More
likely, a chain's life cycle tends to be anywhere from three to five

years, for poorly managed or "fad" concepts, to 10 or 20 years for others.

How long can a chain concept sustain itself before it wears out or before customers become bored with it? Is there a built-in obsolescence for each chain? And once it does wear out, can it be given new flair or should it be converted to something else?

These are all legitimate questions in an age when a wide segment of the public, attracted to trendiness, becomes bored with the same idea in any length of time from one month to 10 years. Furthermore, as chain restaurants occupy seemingly every conceivable niche, there is a saturation point at which only the strongest can survive.

Knowing when to change signals is a neat trick, and the multigroup chains have already paved the way in switching to other concepts when their original ones have saturated the market or become untenable. They already have the other concepts ready! Still, it is a tough call whether to diversify and diffuse efforts or to continue with a single concept.

The life cycle dilemma, however, is not unique to chains. Independent restaurants can face the same challenges, but the question becomes more significant in multiunit operations. In this regard, it is worthwhile exploring some of the notable examples that, in effect, became victims of their own success.

Could Victoria Station have thrived beyond its 1969 to 1979 winning years when it grew to 100 restaurants? Probably not. If we had been in the shoes of partners Richard Bradley, Robert Freeman, and Peter Lee in the late 1970s, we well might have reached the same conclusions they or their successors did—that the concept would have to be diversified. But in so doing, the focus was lost. Radical changes seemed crucial because the chain was locked into a railroad boxcar format and it seemed then that red meat and prime rib would no longer be popular in restaurants.

Founded by friends Bradley, Lee, and Freeman before each turned 30, Victoria Station peaked at 100 restaurants—not bad for a chain with such limitations. Victoria Station's two distinguishing characteristics, assets at first, gradually became liabilities. Prime rib, something that could not easily be cooked at home, was an attraction. So were the English-style boxcars. But by the late 1970s, neither was such a novelty any longer, and other prime rib restaurants were emerging.

The single flaw—if there was one—was the lack of flexibility in the railroad boxcars. Although they served the purpose of providing compartmentalized separate rooms, they made it difficult, if not impossible, for the three founders to ever convert the concept. Actually, subsequent management in the 1980s eyed conversions but never really got very far with them. Just a handful of Victoria Stations survive.

The lesson to be learned: Boxcars create an inconsistency, inasmuch as the decor, comfort level, and ambiance do not measure up to the experience of eating in a railroad dining car—at least in the better ones of that day. Besides, who really wants to eat in a boxcar? Furthermore, VS' price-value had eroded as it moved from $10 for an average meal, toward the $15 mark.

Another symbol of Victoria Station's impending decline was a basketball court at its San Francisco headquarters, where executives spent a great amount of time trying to stay in top shape and show their basketball prowess without giving enough time to analyzing the company's vulnerability and what should be done strategically for the future. They were doing so well that they were overconfident and unconcerned about any problems. It is often difficult to anticipate that what one has done so successfully for a decade will no longer magically work, some day—probably sooner than we think in a world that is changing so fast.

Still, Victoria Station's decade at the top is nothing to scoff at in a business where the deck is stacked against any concept making it as a chain at all, and where few even last more than five years.

Sambo's too is a classic example of how large-scale success can eventually lead to failure. Launched in Santa Barbara, California, by Sam Battistone, Sr. as a limited-menu pancake house in 1957, when there were only a handful of pancake houses or family restaurant chains such as Big Boy, Sambo's made the jump from one unit to several, to 100 through the early 1960s, then started to roll toward domination of its market. With Sam, Sr. and his son, Sam D., leading the way, this family-inspired operation branched out through its complex fraction-of-the-action system, whereby it sold 20 percent shares to unit managers. The managers—mostly men in those days—became so committed to Sambo's and their jobs in the 1960s and early 1970s that they set sales and profit—and divorce—records for the restaurant industry.

Could Sambo's have been saved and still be thriving after its 20-year run to become the largest full-service restaurant chain (1,117 units)? The second-guess answer here, is a most definite yes. The coffee shop concept itself was not flawed. The proof is that Denny's, which started at about the same time as Sambo's, is very much in the game as the number-one volume full-service restaurant chain in the United States.

Of course, these conjectures hinge on a series of ifs. If Sambo's had not drastically altered its winning fraction-of-the-action plan under severe pressure from the Securities and Exchange Commission (SEC) in 1977, it could have sustained its strong management team instead of losing virtually every unit general manager within a year. If it had not allowed egos and bureaucracy to prevail (still a common problem for chains), if it had not given up its bottomless cup of coffee price-value image—the ifs go on. The point is that there is no predestined absolute life cycle for any given chain, and it is crucial to focus on the winning tactics that can sustain a chain until such time as it has reached all reasonable limits, which could be 100 years or more—at least enough for three separate generations of customers to have experienced it.

Although Sam, Sr. and his partner, Newell Bohnett, never envisioned more than a regional group of top-flight coffee shops in the West, Sam D. set his sights on bigger goals. He kept his eye on becoming the number-one volume full-service restaurant chain in America. By the mid-1970s, he actually attained this objective with more than 1,000 Sambo's restaurants nationally and a menu vastly expanded from its original seven items that were literally cooked by the Battistone family at the first few units, to at least 150 items and a wide-ranging 24-hour coffee shop concept. Sambo's not only dominated Denny's and Big Boy but outpaced all the full-service restaurant chains of that era.

All this was heady stuff for Sam D., and the chain couldn't do anything wrong. It stood for coffee shop quality in its own niche, as well as for quantity of units and menu items.

Ostensibly, the chain started collapsing from its heights after the SEC—presumably tipped off by a disgruntled employee or employees—investigated the chain's highly publicized fraction-of-the-action program in 1977 and ruled that Sambo's accounting method of counting its sales of 20 percent shares in restaurants to managers and company executives (who had gained shares when they were managers) as revenues and profits was invalid. The SEC gave Sambo's the option of changing the accounting procedure if it so desired, but instead Sambo's—by then perhaps looking for a way out of the vast equity that it had ceded to so many managers—revamped the system, taking the guts out of a plan that had enabled veteran managers to achieve $100,000 annual incomes—heady stuff for the mid-1970s or even for today in the restaurant business. Predictably, virtually every manager quit within a year as morale plummeted and huge work burdens were piled on those employees who remained.

By 1981 Sambo's, facing rapidly declining sales, losses, and cash flow shortages, filed for Chapter 11 bankruptcy protection. It never really recovered, bringing in a series of new managements and new owners and finally trying to convert Sambo's to a slightly upscale but totally confusing concept called Seasons. Sambo's (or the three-month Seasons experiment) faded to the point where this giant, leading chain was sold in bits and pieces to other chains. Virtually nothing was left. Stockholders sued, claiming they had been deceived.

The key factors in Sambo's demise combined most all of the elements that have plagued numerous restaurant chains for years: overexpansion and loss of control, even though Sambo's eschewed the franchising rush of other chains and retained company-owned control through its fraction-of-the-action program; growth of egos and a large bureaucracy that was symbolized by a Taj Mahal-type of headquarters building—a mighty contrast to the chain's early days in which Sam, Sr., Sam D., Bohnett, and other executives didn't even have a real office but operated out of an old garage or at the Sambo's restaurants; menu expansion beyond capacity to maintain quality; a loss of the intense price-value emphasis symbolized by the former 10¢ bottomless cup of coffee being transformed into a 50¢ regular cup; and, finally, the blurring of its blue-collar customer base in the Seasons upgrade.

Sambo's name did not help, either, when it moved into the South and Northeast at the height of civil rights pressures. Most of all, greed—the desire to expand faster and further, to make more and more money, and to look only at the bottom line and the stockholders' demands after the company went public in the late 1960s—eventually destroyed Sambo's. Subsequent valiant efforts under a new management, led by the late Robert Luckey, simply were doomed. The chain had gone too far downhill and didn't have the time to overcome its huge debts or even to transform Sambo's then-terrible image into something viable.

In retrospect, a chain faced with a situation like that has to pull back immediately to a smaller regional area, as Jack in the Box did under Jack Goodall in the late 1970s when he gave up in the East and triumphed in the West. Acapulco ran into trouble in the late 1970s when it relocated across the country, away from its southern California base. It had to pull out of the Midwest and return to its origins, where it regained momentum.

The sad part of cases like Sambo's is that a pioneering entrepreneurial spirit that carries a chain so far initially is destroyed in the rush to "professionalize." How long can the life cycle of a chain extend? Certainly, a century or longer is possible. Columbus, Ohio-based White Castle has already made it through 70 years by sticking to old-time basics of a simple building with a simple menu pegged to the value-priced, tiny, square burger—a perfect fit for a blue-collar-oriented chain. Chattanooga, Tennessee-based Krystal has already lasted 60 years with a version of this same philosophy. Stuckey's fast-food, based in Chevy Chase, Maryland, is nearing its 60th anniversary, and Minneapolis-based Dairy Queen is approaching its 55th.

Too often, the life cycle does not extend nearly that long. All we need do is consider some of the restaurant chain names of the

1970s and their subsequent demise or sharp dropoff: Burger Chef, Farrell's, Hanahans, Howard Johnson's, Lums, and Shakey's Pizza Parlors.

In many ways a life cycle's length is determined by the chief executive who runs the chain and, of course, the management team that has been assembled. "A chain can lose individual flair quickly in this business," observes Norman Brinker. After Brinker left Pillsbury and Steak and Ale in 1984, everything S & A tried seemed to go wrong. It lost direction, diversified its offerings away from its original steak menu, and had no focus. These moves, in effect, cleared a path for a new breed of casual steakhouses, led by Outback, Lone Star, and Longhorn, to supplant Steak and Ale as a leader. Steak and Ale could have gone toward a Ruth's Chris Steak House upscale concept or toward the eventual Outback model, but didn't do either and got trapped in the middle.

Some of Steak and Ale's remaining executives were Brinker's disciples, but without his guidance they were inclined to stray in the wrong direction—again, this is a convenient second from the perspective of a decade later, but illustrative of how a chain's life cycle often hinges on one dominant leader or the lack thereof.

Chili's life cycle has been a constant upward curve for Brinker International. In the decade through 1994, Chili's enjoyed steady unit sales increases each year and kept adapting to its larger base with new prototypes. It was probably utilizing its ninth prototype by 1994. Such flexibility to diversify, or to gain maximum market penetration in a given area, however, is inherent to the Brinker International empire. Besides Chili's, the leader of the casual full-service restaurant chains, the company has added Romano's Macaroni Grill, Grady's American Grill, Spageddie's Italian-themed restaurants, a Mexican-theme concept originally called Nachomama's and renamed Cozy Mel, and On The Border Cafes—an acquision.

Brinker, himself, has been a consistent winner because he never takes anything for granted and is not complacent. He is always exploring new ways of doing things, no matter how successful he is and no matter how many awards he receives. That philosophy has been completely instilled in Brinker International's operations as well.

One of Pillsbury's other descendants, Bay Street restaurants, was still active as of 1994. In its ninth year and under its third ownership, this time led by president Bill Bouffard, the chain shows promise with its seafood emphasis, a menu expansion into more seafood items, an upgraded image, and a classic look while remaining casual. Still, its expansion is crawling along with just 10 restaurants in Texas, New Jersey, and the Chicago area.

There is always a question as to whether a chain like Bay Street can make a breakthrough and move into new market areas that compete with other seafood chains. Finding enough capital to expand is also a problem. Perhaps Bouffard's chain is better off remaining relatively small and concentrating on its own limited regions. "Every couple of years you need some changes or you'll get stagnant," he concedes, "If you don't change, you'll be dead within 10 or 20 years at the most."

McDonald's keeps moving along in the life cycle as a straight feeding station with no pretense. However, McDonald's is the exception. In our fast-moving society and quickly changing foodservice scene, 10 years actually may be a solid life cycle for a chain.

Among the masters of the restaurant life cycle, as noted elsewhere, is The Riese Organization. Originally led by Murray Riese and the late Irving Riese, real-estate experts who owned many prime blocks and corners of New York City's Manhattan, the company fashioned a group of franchise operations from numerous chains to dominate blocks, corners, and sectors of New York City. It deliberately set up life cycles varying from two to eight years at each site, or combined sites of their groupings, so that if one concept lost its novelty to customers, it simply replaced it with another. To the public, it simply meant another new restaurant had opened in town. The Rieses' game was to achieve maximum dollars per square foot for a site, and they did it by utilizing whatever restaurant was appropriate for a given site. Murray's son, Dennis, is president-CEO.

In regard to life cycle, prime sites such as waterfront property are always considered key assets. Chart House, Specialty Restaurants, and the Rusty Pelican thrived with sites like these. However, because the availability of such sites is becoming limited, they should be shepherded and maintained with revitalizations or conversions, rather than sold off. Once a chain obtains these precious sites, part of the game becomes managing real estate for maximum return.

The heart and soul of a winning chain has to be in the restaurants, not in the financial figures, the price of the stock, or the real estate values. A concept must keep evolving, and it is important to note that evolution, rather than revolution, is usually advisable. If customers like things the way they are, then changes should be especially gradual. Consumers are creatures of habit and sometimes don't appreciate rapid changes—unless the concept is already a disaster.

California Pizza Kitchen partners Larry Flax and Rick Rosenfield see it this way: "Our concept is timeless, but we must be flexible and bob and weave with the market. We're way past the stage of saying, 'If it isn't broken, don't fix it.' " They view their restaurants as a stage on which they present a wide variety of Italian, American, Jamaican, and other ethnic ingredients in their pizzas, pastas, and salads and keep appealing to new customers by adding to that mix. "Our challenge is to make sure we're on the cutting edge," they say, "but we're convinced that we'll be around through the next century"—or at least that California Pizza Kitchen will.

Some concepts may be relatively timeless. Chevys' Mike Hislop calls his chain "completely flexible to changing times, from the food to the building. Freshness isn't going to go out of style, and everything in our kitchen is on wheels. We can operate in a lot of different places."

Sometimes it is too late to change a concept once you find it not working. When customer counts, sales, and profits are dropping, that is a sure signal to shake things up. But it is far better to have already gradually evolved with changes. "There is no limit to what Chevys' life cycle can be," Hislop asserts. Yet one limit could be the potential saturation of Chevys, or of Mexican dinnerhouses, in every major market.

Eateries' Vincent Orza has gradually evolved his Garfield's concept. "We have built in an evolving life cycle," he says. "In its

10-year history, Garfield's has and will continue to change to meet the needs and desires of our guests. There is no reason not to change. We must be realistic and realize that guests and competitors may change and want something else. We must try to keep track of the pulse of the industry and of the people who patronize it."

Seattle-based Skipper's Seafood has also gone through a gradual evolution, positioning itself for the future each time with modernized kitchens, broiled entrees, expanded numbers of salads and fresh fruits, a dessert display case, a drive-through window, and a self-service beverage bay. "Our evolution is an ongoing one," former president Robert Taft declared when he was there.

An old-timer that seems likely to emerge as a major national factor is Sonic, which finally has found the winning touch by sticking entirely to its drive-in formula and doing without seating. With some 1,000 units concentrated in the Southwest and Midwest, and capitalizing on an amazingly low investment cost, Sonic is poised for a major move through this decade. The team of CEO Stephen Lynn and president Robert Flack is also well positioned. To this day, Lynn gives thanks for the nonconsummation of a few different chain acquisitions that he pursued through the late 1970s and early 1980s—all of which never quite reached fruition and any of which would have overburdened Sonic with debt and other problems.

Sonic celebrated its 40th anniversary in 1993 as one of a few chains remaining entirely true to its origins. It has updated its physical look periodically and steadily refreshed its marketing and advertising approaches, but it has always retained its basic menu of old-fashioned, made-to-order hamburgers. More now than ever, the drive-in premise—which grew from America's love affair with the automobile—is well suited to America's desire for speed and convenience. The drive-in movie is dead, but the drive-in fast-food place is very much alive in the tradition of Sonic.

Sonic's nostalgic personality, too, is well oriented to keep moving ahead into the next century. Lynn has no plans to change the concept—unless the franchisees lose their belief in it. "It's their faith in the drive-in concept that keeps us focused on success," he asserts. But it was rumblings of discontent about various aspects of the franchisee relationship that caused some 400 franchise units in the Sonic Franchisee Association to join the American Franchisee Association in the fall of 1993 and that ultimately could undermine the foundations of Sonic Corporation, although we don't think that is likely.

A chain's life cycle can be as long as management is capable of making it. "We've constantly changed and evolved," says Outback's Chris Sullivan. He is referring to subtle changes each year that keep driving the life cycle ahead, including perhaps two or three new menu items or slight changes in the uniforms. Houston-based Carrabbas is being launched as an Italian chain version of Outback, which can enable Outback to gain market share at both ends of the life cycle.

Joseph Micatrotto, president of Panda Express and former president of Chi-Chi's, believes the real question is not whether keeping a concept's same menu will cause it to lose its original flair, but rather whether the concept can retain its flair without staying current. The answer has to be no, considering the constantly shifting competitive conditions and ever-changing consumer tastes. "Chi-Chi's is quite adaptable to new times," Micatrotto observes. "Mexican food has solid, underlying strength and has evolved to a point where it is eaten by a broad base of customers with substantial frequency. It is actually becoming a mainstream-type of food. But the key is to build from this solid base by continuously staying tuned to the consumer and the competition and making the necessary adjustments that allow us to offer something valued by consumers and unique in the marketplace."

Actually, by the late 1980s it had seemed that the Mexican full-service chain market was becoming saturated, with Chi-Chi's, El Torito, Garcia's, Carlos Murphy's, and so many other concepts in operation. Obviously, there was and is plenty of room for growth, although Chi-Chi's and El Torito are now consolidated into one company and Carlos Murphy's has acquired much of Garcia's. Independent Mexican restaurants, as well as independents of every type, continue to be competitors in each market.

The Cheesecake Factory's David Overton sees no end to his

chain's life cycle. "In 10 years we may roll out a new concept in addition to this," he says, "but we envision The Cheesecake Factory continuing indefinitely."

In 1991 the board of Robert Giaimo's Silver Diner chain met to decide whether the diner segment will continue as a strong one into the next decade. "We unanimously concluded that our particular segment is timeless," declares the always optimistic Giaimo. Many disagree with this assessment, and he has his own struggle to obtain the necessary financing to expand beyond Maryland. (The company raised expansion capital by early 1994.) "We need a wide menu to capture a broad enough base of customers," he asserts. "and we've had to limit ourselves to 200 items. But others are selling the same food items all the time. We will emerge as a leader."

Ronn Teitelbaum of Johnny Rockets believes it is better to be slow to react to change. "I don't like to change," he says, "and any changes in the life cycle should be gradual."

Steak and Ale and Bennigan's were mature concepts by the early 1990s, if not before, and needed revitalization. While Steven Leipsner was president, he charted a course whereby Bennigan's could grow for the next decade with some modifications and a partial evolution to Bennigan's Cafe America. Steak and Ale seemed to have less potential but could be a low-growth piece of the portfolio and be converted to casual offshoots such as its Side Street Grill.

Another way of extending life cycles is to view a chain's properties as a portfolio. Thus, Leipsner viewed Steak and Ale as the equivalent of a slow-growth treasury bond, Bennigan's as a blue chip, and some new concepts he was trying to unveil as potential growth stocks or even speculative assets. Each part of the portfolio would have a purpose. After ousting Leipsner in the fall of 1993, parent Metromedia Company seized direct management of the chains, having been dissatisfied with the flat sales during Leipsner's one year of charting a revitalization course. Leipsner's new concepts were shelved.

ARA's John Farquharson sees the company's restaurant and contract-feeding concepts as flexible and easily adaptable to local menu variations and contemporary promotional themes. "We only discontinue a concept on a location-by-location basis if it is not successful," he says. A prime example is ARA's closing of the Ninety-Fifth restaurant atop Chicago's John Hancock Center after 23 years of ups and downs in operating it. As is inherent in many top-of-building restaurants, the view was often more spectacular than the food.

"The concepts must be kept current," Farquharson declares. "The more flexibility, the better. It's much easier for the local ARA operator/manager to adjust for local variations." This was the case with the Ninety-Fifth, whose ownership was finally taken over by managers who had been running it for ARA.

The toughest thing for Big 4's Lee Cohn was to keep pace with the rapid changes in consumer dining-out behavior. "I actually found that making constant revisions in a successful concept dramatically lengthens the life span of that concept," he asserts. "The wrong thing to do is to wait until the concept is on its way down to start changing it."

The stronger a restaurant's theme, the sooner it may need to be changed. As long as the restaurant switches with customers' indicated tastes and demands, it can endure for many years (i.e., 5 to 50 years, anyway). TGI Friday's is an example of this durability, as it keeps evolving as a slightly different type of theme restaurant every few years.

Pizza Hut keeps evolving gradually under PepsiCo. Its 1990s look features a brighter decor and an adjusted menu with a few new items such as Grand Pan pizza. It also is pushing more heavily all the time into the convenience market of home delivery and is wielding a knockout punch to Domino's once-dominant home-delivery business. This shows how needs can change over an entire life cycle. Domino's also became vulnerable in the late 1980s when it started competing on price rather than quality and was hit hard in the price wars. Misfired strategy can cost a chain niche-leadership and shift the whole thrust of the life cycle battle.

As some chains mature, they may be satisfied with minimum sales growth as long as their profits keep climbing—even if slowly. International Dairy Queen (IDQ), with more than $2 billion annual systemwide sales, was in a slow-growth phase with few new products until a 1993 introduction of Royal Fudge N Cake, chicken strips, and a barbecue beef sandwich in its Dairy Queen units finally broadened its image. Until then, IDQ obtained sales growth only from new units.

In a bid to increase its traffic, Dairy Queen also tied in with Tom & Jerry movies and included over 12 million related premiums with its Children's Treatmeals as it finally became more aggressive. Dairy Queen has been around for more than 50 years and very likely will be for at least another 50 years, owing to its sheer size and penetration of the soft-serve ice cream market, the dedication of its mom-and-pop franchisees, and its clout in small to medium communities. Yet considering all the competition, there is no absolute point of distinction anymore. Although IDQ will continue to emphasize Dairy Queen, it also has Orange Julius shops, Karmelkorn treat shops, and Golden Skillet franchise chicken units in its stable of chain brands.

Another life cycle master, discussed earlier, is Chicago's Richard Melman, who wants to be known as an independent rather than a chain operator. He hates to replicate anything, always striving for a new format. To Melman, success means never having to repeat oneself, although his LEYE company does have two Shaw's Crab Houses and has cloned its Tucci Benucch, Maggiano's, and the Corner Bakery at least once each. Still, his idea of life cycle is based on a number of highly individualized concepts. Most of his restaurants last longer than might be expected, although he has, inevitably, had a few failures at difficult locations.

Other such multiconcept innovators include San Francisco's Laurence Mindel, founder of the Spectrum Foods restaurant group and molder of the Il Fornaio restaurant group; Michael Weinstein of New York's Ark Restaurants Corporation; Lee Cohn of Big 4 Restaurants; and Ray Lindstrom of Seattle's Restaurants Unlimited, Inc.

Another important aspect in considering why life cycles are getting shorter is the copycat phenomenon. So many restaurants are so much alike in the chain world that consumers, in effect, choose just the one or two that they prefer in each segment, often based on convenience or a desire for variety. The classic example is the casual restaurants segment in which TGI Friday's, Houlihan's, Bennigan's, Houston's, Applebee's, Ruby Tuesday, and so many others are vying for supremacy.

"Be true to thyself" is a key to a long life cycle. This can be accomplished through signature menu items and by carving out a distinct and noteworthy niche, rather than trying to be all things to all people. Perhaps the exceptions are the rule. Le Peep was a popular Denver-based breakfast chain in the early 1980s that emphasized a special, tasty breakfast menu headed by eggs and pancakes. It seemed to have the potential to succeed as it expanded across the United States—until new management took control and decided that the answer to Le Peep's financial problems was to switch to a full-service coffee shop-type menu and keep it open for longer hours than the 6:00 A.M. to 2:00 P.M., one-shift, distinctive operation. The result has been a me-too concept that seems to be going nowhere—if it somehow manages even to survive.

Defying the odds against a conglomerate's succeeding in the restaurant business, General Mills has fashioned its own restaurant group in what some see as "permanent" life cycles within popular segments of the family restaurant business. It bought a few Red Lobster restaurants in Florida in 1970 and molded this venture into by far the number one seafood chain in America. Then, starting in the early 1980s, it grew The Olive Garden into the foremost Italian restaurant chain. In addition, by early 1994 it had launched the China Coast Chinese restaurant chain, after one final test in the Indianapolis area.

Although General Mills has endured its share of failures (some of which it controlled by pulling back from only semisuccessful pilot chains), it has managed to be number one over a long period in two key niches, probably by delegating responsibilities to superior restaurant executives who care: Joe Lee, who developed and guided Red Lobster; Ron Magruder, who has led The Olive Garden's growth; and special concepts director Blaine Sweatt, who has been in on the ground floor of developing both The Olive Garden and China Coast. There is nothing fancy about Red Lobster and The Olive Garden, just basic price-value with wide family appeal.

As mentioned earlier, McDonald's has survived the classic life cycle. Although cynics have maintained throughout its four decades that McD is slumping, is dependent on real estate rather than restaurants for profits, and can't sustain the momentum, and although someday it may falter and drop from the top, it has maintained a steady upward movement to the point where there are very few places in the world, much less in America, in which McD is not represented.

McDonald's has built a rock-stable executive core—in complete contrast to the musical-chairs instability of Burger King and other fast-food chains. It has remained focused on one objective only, and that is McD. It has refined its menu and added chicken, fish, salads, and now pizza, to its core burger items. And it has responded to consumer activist pressures by trying more healthful items, such as the McLean Burger and salads, and reducing or eliminating cholesterol in cooking processes. McDonald's has remained true to its original goal of being a fast-food chain. The one exception occurred in the late 1960s and early 1970s when McD, like so many other chains, tested other concepts. Fortunately, the tests—led by founder Ray Kroc—failed, and McDonald's was able to focus its time and energy on just McDonald's.

McDonald's has also retained its entrepreneurial spirit by evading acquisition and remaining an independent company. Despite persistent rumblings that PepsiCo would like to add McD to its restaurant empire of number one chains in various segments, the reality is that with a $25 billion worldwide volume and immense marketing and financial power, McD could acquire nearly any entity it wanted. However, McD has astutely stayed away from the acquisition trap of debt accumulation and diversion of efforts.

Howard Johnson's provides a classic life cycle lesson. It was entrenched as the number one restaurant chain in the 1950s, well before McD developed any clout. Howard Johnson's owned foodservice on America's toll roads and highways. But it sat there complacently and never really grew. The founder, Howard D. Johnson, made it work, but his son, Howard B. Johnson, could not emulate that success and was more interested in protecting the real estate as an investment, rather than developing the chain. He also became enamored with the hotel business. Moreover, the company's adherence to commissary-supplied foodservice contributed to a perception that it was not in the quality food business. So Howard Johnson's remained static while McDonald's and others overtook and vastly outdistanced it.

Marriott Corporation's life cycle is a somewhat different story. Actually, J. Willard Marriott, Jr., was more aggressive than his father. The son added hotels to the restaurant network his father had launched. Eventually Marriott Corporation decided to focus its attention on hotels and foodservice management-contract feeding and sold off its dinnerhouses, Big Boy and Roy Rogers, while keeping a few cafeterias, perhaps for sentimental reasons. Marriott, Jr. was convinced that the company's expertise and profit potential were on the hotel side, but the company had to trim down its various segments and for a while faced a very real threat. It finally seems solid after restructuring into two companies. Meanwhile, its restaurant cycle has already ended after a run of several decades.

Just as the retail industry has developed a pattern of newer companies emerging and overtaking established ones, the same may be true in the restaurant industry. Sears was once undisputed number one among retail chains. Then Kmart challenged, and Wal-Mart proceeded to overtake them both. Sears faltered with a vast ego-ridden program of acquiring financial, insurance, and other companies. Now Sears is trying to pull back to its basic roots.

Among those foodservice chains bidding to emerge as stars of the industry, and with blossoming life cycles, are Applebee's, Hooter's, and Ruby Tuesday casual restaurants; Cracker Barrel Old Country Store family restaurants; Checkers double drive-throughs; and a bevy of casual steakhouses led by Outback, Lone Star, Longhorn, and Santa Fe Steakhouses of Florida. How many of these, and other emerging chains, will be here for the long run remains to be seen. Chances are a few will make it big in the long-term, a few will do OK, and a few will not last beyond this decade—the business is that tough.

Interestingly, while the public talks constantly about healthful foods, it currently is the steakhouse segment that is gaining faster as customers in reality favor taste over healthfulness. Two main healthful food chains of a decade ago—Atlanta-based D'Lites and Tennessee-based Fresher Cooker (unrelated to the Columbus, Ohio-based blossoming Cooker chain)—are no longer operating.

Can chains be reincarnated after falling? Perhaps yes. Sizzler family steakhouses and Long John Silver's fast-food seafood shops are examples of chains that have undergone up-and-down cycles over the years because of variances in consumer demand for steak and seafood, respectively, and because of economic cycles. In 1993 they were trying to fight their way upward again, partially dependent on an economic upswing.

Wendy's was faltering badly in the late 1980s. A new team led by chief executive James Near, who did a remarkable job of refocusing management on the basics, and the return of founder David Thomas as a winning advertising personality helped it rebound remarkably in the fast-food burger wars.

IHOP, founded in 1958 as the International House of Pancakes, finally hit its stride in the late 1980s as it broke away from its traditional and narrow pancake bill of fare, offered a wide-ranging menu, and got its franchising under control nationally.

Chains have also been able to fight their way out of bankruptcy at times. Some seem to think that Chapter 11 reorganization is a solution, rather than a last resort. Hence there was a surge of Chapter 11 filings in the early 1990s. REGI, the diversified group that owned Coco's, El Torito, and Casa Gallardo restaurants among others, deliberately filed a Chapter 11 reorganization plan in November 1993. This was a financial maneuver to pave the way for an infusion of investment group capital and conversion to a restructured corporation, Family Restaurants, Inc., and included the acquisition of Foodmaker's Chi-Chi's chain.

GE Capital Corporation, a major lender, found itself in control of at least two operations as principal creditor when the Stamford, Connecticut-based Service America diversified foodservice management company and the Costa Mesa, California, Del Taco, Inc. chain filed for Chapter 11 reorganization.

Columbus, Ohio-based Rax—originally a roast beef fast-food chain—could never find a steady image and in late 1992 filed for

Chapter 11. It was a prime candidate to go out of business or to be absorbed in bits and pieces by other chains, but it did emerge from Chapter 11 a year later. Meanwhile, the jury is still out on whether the Popeyes and Church's chains, can recover after going into heavy debt, filing Chapter 11, and emerging from it under new ownership and fresh management as America's Favorite Chicken. Popeyes' adventurous founder, Al Copeland, was doing all right until 1990, when ego may have got the better of him and he acquired problem-ridden Church's, which dragged him and the company into a sea of debt and operational problems.

Chains can build their life cycles through acquisitions of other chains, which then generally disappear. Hardee's, based in Rocky Mount, North Carolina, merged with a Western chain called Sandy's in the early 1970s and converted Sandy's into Hardee's. A decade later, former Sandy's president Jack Laughery, who quickly became Hardee's chief executive, astutely acquired Burger Chef, which had never come anywhere near its potential under General Foods. Finally, in 1989 Hardee's acquired Roy Rogers from Marriott—a deal that Laughery had been trying to put together for years but which was consummated under new management.

New executives at Hardee's determined that Roy Rogers should be absorbed into Hardee's, just as were Sandy's and Burger Chef. However, Roy Rogers had a popular image in several markets—particularly in the Middle Atlantic states—and customers rebelled against the transformation to Hardee's. The whole mess convinced some observers that Hardee's should have changed its own units to Roy Rogers, but that would have been too extreme. Instead, the conversions to Hardee's were reversed in 1992 and 1993 as Hardee's tried to move back to a winning position with Roy Rogers now a major wing.

The challenge in achieving a full life cycle is how to adapt past strengths to future needs of the marketplace. A chain's life cycle is dependent on the ability of leaders and strategic planners to mold a concept to the needs of a changing marketplace without eroding the product differentiation that gave it a uniqueness in the first place. Concepts may change, but the points of differentiation shouldn't.

UNIQUE NICHE

To extend its life cycle or sometimes even just to survive, it is crucial for a chain to carve out a special niche in today's crowded marketplace, to define something it stands for, rather that trying to be all things to all people. Yet too often a chain tries to be something that it simply isn't.

This problem has afflicted more than a few fast-food chains striving to widen their menus too far from their origins. Burger King, which has veered back and forth year after year under a variety of managements, introduced dinner service in October 1992 to try to capture a decent share of the 4:00 P.M. to 8:00 P.M. market. Admittedly, the beleaguered chain needed help in trying to generate more dinner business. Fast-feeders traditionally have been strong at lunch but often falter at dinner—a meal for which they don't have the image to attract enough customers. Yet an attempt to provide some sort of full service or to raise prices often defeats its own purpose.

Some observers—and apparently more than a few consumers—felt that the idea of hosts and hostesses bringing meals to the table that customers had ordered at the counter detracted from Burger King's fast-food focus. Burger King finally halted the experiment, allowing franchisees to keep the special dinner service only if they so desired.

On the other hand, McDonald's has succeeded with candlelight dinners because this is done as a novelty in certain locations where customers appreciate it.

A wiser approach to the dinner challenge is that of Hardee's, which introduced fried chicken on the bone and chicken sandwiches in 1992 and heavily promoted these items. At the same time Hardee's introduced the Frisco burger, providing a potent one-two punch. Although the Frisco and other burgers substantially outsold chicken at lunch, chicken prevailed at dinner.

Some menu extensions are natural ones that don't necessarily blur an image. For example, in 1992 the 4,700-unit Little Caesars pizza takeout chain began experimenting with spaghetti, ravioli, and lasagna and was planning to extend them even though pastas previously did not seem to travel well. Domino's Pizza has shied away from pasta, while Sbarro and Pizza Hut began to offer this item. Here, in a sense, by remaining true to its origins and not changing, Domino's became vulnerable.

TURNAROUNDS

Although it is easy to fall quickly in the restaurant industry, chains can also turn around—and have done so in many cases—by making necessary adjustments. But sometimes fine-tuning is not enough, and a chain has to do something drastic, such as changing its name or perhaps filing for Chapter 11 reorganization as many have done over the years.

General Mills got into a classic life cycle problem with its Red Lobster chain in the early 1990s and tried to fight its way out. Red Lobster, which for more than two decades had grown under the General Mills umbrella, seemed to falter a bit as it reached maturity and, to some, became a tired concept with a dull familiarity and sameness. This was at the same time that The Olive Garden was prospering and China Coast was emerging.

By 1992 Red Lobster was on the high side of casual restaurant chains with a $14 per-person average dinner ticket, as compared with $9 for The Olive Garden. Red Lobster's same-store average sales were off by as much as 5 percent or more, although the chain's average per-unit volume was still hovering at slightly under $3 million.

Jeffrey O'Hara, Red Lobster president, moved for a turnaround in late 1992 by dropping the price of some 20 entree items, comprising at least half the menu, to less than $10. He also tried promotions such as 30-shrimp dinners for $9.99 along with a $1.99 children's shrimp dinner. This alternating cyclical strategy of Red Lobster has been used over the years to extend its market base. It has essentially been dependent on the blue-collar market, which was hardest hit by the recession. O'Hara's strategy apparently paid off, and Red Lobster enjoyed a pronounced rebound in 1993.

Among the changes initiated by O'Hara were an upgrade in employee services; encouragement of managers and other employees to spend more time with customers; a sharpening of plate presentations, giving the appearance of more on the plate; and an effort to sell more appetizers and desserts. Among new products being tried to enliven the dining experience were an Island Grill shrimp dish, oven-roasted marinated chicken, and nachos. The chain also downsized its smaller markets with lower investments and volumes but still realized over $2.5 million average annual sales per unit.

Red Lobster is the only national full-service seafood chain. Its closest chain competitors are far behind—Morrison's L & N Seafood, with 40 restaurants, and Sea Galley restaurants, with 30 in the Pacific Northwest. Still, the real seafood competition for Red Lobster is the local independent who knows how to price the market and woo the customer. (This is true in other aspects of the chain industry as well.)

Two different leadership styles are evident in the more formal, strategic-thinking O'Hara and the relatively casual Magruder, who loves talking to people and is very much in the public limelight, having won almost every restaurant operator and chain award. There is a place for each, and each can achieve success in his own way.

Another major turnaround effort is under way by Carvel, with Steven Fellingham succeeding the late Tom Carvel, who personally was Carvel's lead pitchman. Fellingham is trying to broaden the chain's base from its soft ice cream orientation with a bevy of new products—a tricky maneuver.

Craig Miller, president of Uno Corporation, has tremendous insight on turnarounds, having been a Red Lobster executive for 11 years before joining Pizzeria Uno's parent in 1983. "Red Lobster was 100 percent fried food almost 20 years ago," he says. "No broiled seafood. They had ebbs and flows but flourished on low prices. Then they slumped again. There are just so many choices and so much competition."

Miller's thinking about positioning his chain crystallized in early 1993 after Morrison Restaurants, Inc. withdrew a takeover bid for Pizzeria Uno. Morrison felt that the $100 million price was too high. "We thrived in the 1980s," Miller recalls. "It was a booming economy. So the pizza competition poured in—like Bertucci's with full-service pizza. Still, you shouldn't let competitors lead you anywhere. Only customers should or can."

Pizzeria Uno tried to concentrate on quality for non-pizza products. It was known for its unsurpassed signature deep-dish pizza, but had lost the focus on this unique niche by branching into other products. Miller is trying to bring it back to its deep-dish origins and adding "only true quality products" to the mix. "A mediocre burger drags down your image when you're trying to get good products besides your core," he declares. "We want our burger to be better than Chili's, and we want to reposition ourselves as a casual-dining leader." Miller is dedicated to the precept that "nobody can emulate our deep-dish pizza."

His turnaround efforts are geared to a handful of company-owned restaurants that need substantial improvement and whose franchise system needs better direction. "We'll spend hours with the marketing managers talking about each restaurant," he says. "The president has to be out in the field personally seeing everything. You can't sit in an office. We have executive and board meetings, but it's the casual meetings with people that are important. If employees feel you are listening to them, they will gladly work for you."

Pizzeria Uno's manager turnover is almost zero. "We're keeping our emphasis at the unit general manager level," he says. "Our big weakness may be middle management, and our regional vice presidents may need more training."

How do you fight back from a disastrous year? John Creed, chairman-CEO of Chart House, Inc., not so fondly recalls 1992–93 as a non-year. "Riots in Los Angeles wiped out our entire summer in southern California," he says. "Also we faced Hurricane Andrew in Florida, a 7.5 Richter-scale earthquake, Hurricane Iniki in Hawaii, and—as a natural disaster closing act—the storm of the century in New England." (At least Creed has a good sense of humor and a positive outlook—crucial attributes for a winning executive.) Furthermore, he says, "Coupled with a huge dislocation of defense-oriented businesses and an obdurate recession, we were kept

off balance the entire year." It all culminated in a $4 million re-
structuring charge and a resultant minimal 4¢-a-share profit. "Not
the kind of year that builds confidence with shareholders, directors,
or management," Creed observes.

In tackling the resultant turnaround challenge, Creed first ana-
lyzed the problems. "We had enjoyed unparalleled success over our
32-year history," he says. "We didn't have market share; we were
the market. This success over a sustained period was, and remained,
one of our greatest strengths, but also our Achilles heel. The dic-
tum that success breeds failure is a hole into which many have
fallen. Our company finds itself stubbornly locked into old habits,
complacent ways of thinking, and thus locked out of progress and
an ability to sustain its growth."

As chains mature, it is not unusual for them to find themselves
in this position as they move from one development stage to another. "It's what you do about it that counts," Creed emphasizes.
He and his staff investigated and found the internal problem was
that prices had escalated out of the reach of Chart House's customer
base. He also hired an outside firm, which found that the real problem was execution, that "the quality of food and service had become
inconsistent."

Still, the chain refused to face up to the dilemma and instead
made an abortive move to take the pressure off Chart House "while
the company recovered, hoping that something would stick and
eliminate the need to deal with the real problem." They launched
three new concepts: Beaches, Mangos, and Islands. Only the latter
showed any potential.

Finally, another outside firm was brought in for a full look and
discovered that the underlying problem was a lack of operational
consistency. "Our customers' expectations had risen," Creed says,
"but we had allowed ourselves to accept a prior, lower standard.
And we had no voice to our market, having shunned advertising for
30 years, almost as a badge of our own self-reliance. We were very
good at apologizing—not the hallmark of a superior service-
oriented company."

This time, Creed and his staff listened. Noting that "a willingness is often the precursor to change," they raised their standards

on all products, launched a wait-persons' evaluation program focusing on their ability to sell, and switched to a new menu format. They also hired an outside firm to "restage" the restaurants' table settings, lighting, uniforms, music, plate presentation, and a host of other aspects.

Chart House's greatest challenge is in its home area of southern California, where it has 16 restaurants. "This is our oldest market, and it's where we will concentrate most of our attention," Creed says. "The life cycle theory merits consideration. But I think our locations are so strong that a commitment to evolve into a customer-focused company with a clear, consistent voice to the public will help us regain our share of the market very quickly."

The chain's research showed that the Chart House brand is well recognized nationally and evokes good memories, but the public "by and large forgot about us, particularly in southern California." Once a chain like Chart House is no longer a "new hot concept," the fickle public tends to move on to the next one. The challenge always is to build enough customer loyalty over the years to counteract this tendency.

In the summer of 1993, Chart House embarked on an aggressive marketing communications program to make the public more aware of the chain, through local unit marketing on a regional basis in southern California and, finally, nationwide. Then, too, in late 1993, Creed was still trying to complete the final payoff of the debt stemming from his group's 1985 leveraged buy-out of the chain.

It seems to be a fact of life that chains—like most businesses—shift gears and drive ahead only when faced with adversity and crisis, not when they are rolling along as if nothing will ever stop them.

HOT CHAINS

As we move through the 1990s, what are some of the hottest restaurant chains in the cycle for now and the future? They are chains that have carved out specific, unique niches and are building from these focal points.

A shining example is The Cheesecake Factory, which was averaging a stunning $8 million average sales per unit on six restaurants in 1993. Customers like it not only for its 38 different types of cheesecake but also for its more than 200 items of every type for breakfast, lunch, and dinner. With an average check of $14 per person, it looks like one of the fastest growers, even considering that each unit is a big investment. This chain defies the conventional wisdom that favors keeping the menu relatively simple and limited to a set of key items. Each item is thoughtfully selected, and the quality is undeniable. The Cheesecake Factory went public in 1992 and racked up a $4.2 million net income on $52 million in sales that year.

Based on 1992 annual sales per square foot and sales per seat, as reported by San Francisco-based Montgomery Securities, the productivity of leading chains was as follows: The Cheesecake Factory, at $627 and $19,700 respectively; Outback, $450 and $13,846; Chili's, $399 and $11,019; Applebee's, $357 and $9,942; Cracker Barrel, $340 and $18,750; Bertucci's, $309 and $10,625; and Spaghetti Warehouse, $174 and $6,000.

Other prospective fast movers, some of which most likely will emerge as leaders and others of which may falter, are Claim Jumper, Boston Chicken, Inc., Pudgie's Famous Chicken, Au Bon Pain, Rally's, Checkers, Sonic America's Drive-Ins, Taco Cabana restaurants, Chevys, Nathan's Famous, O'Charley's, Old Country Buffet, The Olive Garden, China Coast, Fresh Choice, La Salsa, Subway, Little Caesars, Red Robin, Black-eyed Pea, Longhorn, and Lone Star. It is important to note that this list consists primarily of casual-type full-service chains and fast-food chains. Morton's and Ruth's Chris Steak House are the two primary upscale, high-check-average chains.

The casual restaurants segment, is indeed, the most crowded and the most competitive. It's where everyone wants to be. Among major chains in this segment are Chili's, Applebee's, TGI Friday's, Houlihan's, Hooter's, Ruby Tuesday, Spaghetti Warehouse, and Outback.

Mexican chains seemed to have peaked by the late 1980s, but

they experienced a new surge in the early 1990s, and this could be expected to continue through the decade—particularly in the midpriced range where there is room for growth. Technomic, Inc. estimates $4 billion in 1993 sales for Mexican quick-service chains (with Taco Bell taking more than 75 percent of that) and about $2 billion for midpriced Mexican full-service chains, while upscale Mexican restaurants account for almost $2 billion. The main trend is toward the midpriced Mexican full-service segment as consumers trade up from fast-food and down from fine dining.

By early 1994, Family Restaurants, Inc. and PepsiCo were vying for dominance of the Mexican full-service market. Family Restaurants, which owns the some 165-unit El Torito and Casa Gallardo Mexican restaurants, acquired the major portion of the largest Mexican full-service chain, Chi-Chi's with some 240 restaurants, to create a national powerhouse without much site overlapping.

Chi-Chi's, at the same time, moved to spiff up its menu and remodel its restaurants as it prepared for battle. The chain sought to boost its some $500 million in annual sales with both expansion and higher traffic while maintaining a less than $10 value-priced average check. Meanwhile, $350-million-volume sister El Torito was freshening its image with six rotating special entrees, including combinations sparked by a red-corn tortilla, shrimp salad, and fresh swordfish.

PepsiCo, not content with status quo, acquired the 37-unit Chevy's Mexican Restaurants in 1993. Taco Bell then-president John Martin designated Michael Hislop to continue as Chevys president and retain full direct authority over that chain as it expands. Hislop is eyeing acquisitions of existing smaller Mexican chains for conversion to Chevys as part of a major national expansion, with an ambitious goal of 300 Chevys by 1996.

Chevy's seems well-positioned in the casual Mexican derby. Besides having Taco Bell's muscle behind it, it has heavily promoted a Tex-Mex menu in television ads. It makes salsa and guacamole once an hour, cooks tortilla chips continuously, and makes flour tortillas in special ovens that the customer can see. As noted earlier, to promote its image of freshness, no cans are ever used; Hislop even makes a point of asserting that it is impossible for anyone to ever even find a can on Chevys' premises.

Other big players in the Mexican casual restaurants derby are Dallas-based El Chico Restaurants, Inc., under president Michael Jenkins, and Scottsdale, Arizonia-based Carlos Murphy's, under William Lewis, which acquired the remains of Phoenix-based Famous Restaurants (Garcia's). Then there are a series of regional Mexican chains that may emerge, including San Antonio-based Taco Cabana, Dallas-based On the Border, Bedford, Texas-based DF & R's Don Pablo's, Seattle-based Azteca, Louisville-based Tumbleweed Mexican Food & Mesquite Grill, and Columbus, Ohio-based Cantina del Rio, owned by Bob Evans Farms, Inc.

Of course, Taco Bell dominates the Mexican fast-food market with a greater than 80 percent market share that can only grow as John Martin eyes more than 200,000 points of access (carts, kiosks, snack bars, and vending machines) in addition to his Taco Bell empire, which had more than 4,500 units by mid-1994.

There apparently is always room for funkiness, as evidenced by the relative success of Peter Morton's Los Angeles-based Hard Rock Cafes and Robert Earl's Planet Hollywood. Morton filed suit against Earl, asserting that Earl—who had rights to Hard Rock Cafes outside the United States—had basically copied Morton's Hard Rock Cafes in designing New York-based Planet Hollywood. We will not attempt to predict how long Planet Hollywood will be around, but by early 1994 it had opened and drawn initial huge crowds in New York City, London, Costa Mesa (California), and Chicago and was planning to open in Phoenix, Minneapolis, New Orleans, and Maui, Hawaii. Meanwhile, the Harley Davidson Cafe, Dave and Buster's, and Medieval Times are other funky restaurants that have entered the fray.

Foodservice has had an uneven history in convenience stores but seems to be taking hold strongly in gas-station settings. Among others, British Petroleum Oil transplanted the idea of its successful BP Food Plus convenience stores to U.S. cities, with gourmet coffees, fresh-baked breads, muffins and cookies, burgers, deli-type subs, and breakfast biscuits.

Boston Chicken, Inc., one of a number of rotisserie chicken chains (Kenny Rogers Roasters is another prominent one) is moving nationally into major contention. By early 1994 it was in some 40 states and was being positioned for a push to establish 450 units by former Blockbuster Video executives, whose philosophy was to launch chicken units in somewhat the same way they had launched video stores. The former Blockbuster executives running Boston Chicken, Inc. include Jeff Shearer, president, who earlier was chief operating officer of Bennigan's, Saad Nadhir, vice chairman, and a number of others in key roles.

Even with all the talk about trendiness and exciting new chains, some of the old standbys are still hot. Although Checkers, Rally's and Taco Bell's Hot 'n Now may lead the way in double drive-throughs, old-time In-N-Out Burger may be the best around, although content to stay in California rather than expand into other areas. This focus may be why In-N-Out shines in its own regions. Also not to be overlooked are old-timers White Castle, Krystal, and Sonic Drive-Ins.

As of mid-1993 the leading growth chains, as listed in *Restaurants & Institutions* in terms of percentage sales increases, were Au Bon Pain, Bertucci's Brick Oven Pizza, Boston Chicken, Inc., The Cheesecake Factory, Chuck E. Cheese, Grady's American Grill, Morton's, Old Country Buffet, Sonic Drive-Ins, and Taco Cabana.

In the Italian restaurants sphere—also one of the hottest segments—The Olive Garden is dominant. Other chains are challenging, including Sfuzzi under Robert Colombo and San Francisco-based Milano's under Charles Patel. Pino Luongo has made a bid for prominence with Coco Pazzo and other concepts, whereas Biche seems to have fallen back.

Among the top chains in average per-unit volume are The Cheesecake Factory, $8.5 million; Claim Jumper, $5 million; Cracker Barrel, $3.5 million (including the gift shop); Outback, $3.0 million; Spaghetti Warehouse, $2.5 million; Chili's, $2.3 million; Applebee's, $2.1 million; and Bertucci's, $1.8 million.

Chains may take new forms as part of a cycle emerging for the middle and late 1990s. Specialization is winning in popular niches more than ever, with upscale coffee bars, noodle shops, and take-out places emerging in strength in urban areas.

EVOLUTIONARY CYCLE

Many of the strategic decisions that chains or groups of chains face are related to their position and phase in life cycle development. A life cycle includes a chain's complete evolution, and problems can occur anywhere along the curve. Winning executives find a way to manage the necessary transitions.

The initial phase should involve careful growth, refinement of concept, and tests for expansion potential. Decisions must be made on franchising, financing, and geographic areas for expansion. Examples of chains in this phase are The Cheesecake Factory, Chevys, Fresh Choice, and Hot 'n Now.

Once the potential is proven with a viable return on investment, a chain can be launched across the country in a second phase. Prime examples currently are Applebee's, The Olive Garden, and Outback. A key to economic success is to achieve a positive ratio between the annual sales and the initial investment cost. If the land, building, and equipment package cost $1 million, the unit must achieve at least $1 million in annual sales to satisfy the ratio. Many chain restaurants are doomed to failure from the first because they go for too many frills and, thus, show a negative ratio. Warner LeRoy put a huge investment into his gigantic Potomac restaurant in Washington, D.C., and was unable to make it with $10 million in sales the first year. To show real success and growth potential, a chain should be averaging in annual sales at least 1.5 times the initial investment cost. This is especially important in today's environment of steadily rising food, labor, and occupancy costs.

In the third phase, a chain is growing toward maturity, and same-store sales typically begin to stall or show little growth. Copycats have proliferated, and it is time to refine the concept and the menu. Chains such as Chili's, Ruby Tuesday, and TGI Friday's are in this phase, and one of the solutions to saturation is to move into worldwide markets.

In the fourth and final phase, a chain is at full maturity and often faces serious challenges. The result could be Chapter 11 or a vast turnaround-repositioning effort. Like each of the preceding three phases, the fourth is a tricky one and must be handled adroitly.

Management sometimes uses "life cycle"—as though it predetermines the life of a restaurant—as an excuse for closing restaurants that could be successful if they were properly managed. In many cases the length of a life cycle depends on chain executives' ability to predict the future and determine a course of action, adjusting the concept to fit the needs of a new marketplace. A concept doesn't suddenly become unfeasible overnight. If it has not evolved over a period, time simply catches up with it.

There is no one overriding formula for a long, successful life cycle, and in certain situations 10 years might be considered fine. But chains wanting to gear up for a long run—if not a "permanent" endless one—are well advised to build a noncomplacent stable of top management and engage highly motivated unit managers and employees who are psychologically as well as financially committed to the chain. More than that, it requires an entrepreneurial approach that doesn't let professionalism take away the excitement and challenge of the business, a chain committed to a basic nonfrills specific niche and not to being "all things to all people."

These are the ingredients required not only for a championship season but for a series of such seasons in today's fiercely competitive, ever-evolving world of restaurant chains.

Leader of the Pack: The Big Mac

"The fact that we were selling just 10 items, had a small facility, and used a limited number of suppliers created an ideal environment for really digging in on everything."
   —Fred Turner, senior chairman and former
    chief executive, McDonald's Corporation,
    Oak Brook, Illinois,
    on the chain's early days

McDONALD'S AT A GLANCE

- Executive stability and teamwork
- Loyalty on all sides
- Will to win
- Franchisee inspiration
- Individuality
- Leveraging edge
- Ultra-branding
- Community-minded
- Sales oriented, savings conscious
- Unstinting dedication
- Customer driven
- Marketing wizards
- Global dominance

LEADERSHIP STATUS

One chain stands out so far above others in leadership and innovation that it merits a special chapter for itself. As the embodiment of our eight winning links, McDonald's, perhaps believing it has all the answers, has stayed away from most all industry associations and conferences, insisting that it is an organization unto itself. Few would dispute that, although they would like McD to be a more active part of the industry and participate in industrywide activities. And while McD has been trying to participate to some extent, particularly in the National Council of Chain Restaurants' government affairs group, we still see their total focus on McD, 24 hours a day, seven days a week, to be a plus.

Although some are jealous, McD provides a great example of a chain implementing our eight links, and thus is a superb role model to emulate: the absolute focus on one concept, unclouded by diversification efforts or attempts at manufacturing or distribution, and McD's determination to plow straight ahead on its own mission—to stretch its lead and market share as the absolutely dominant chain in the world.

Nothing deters McDonald's from its mission, and the winning operating principles in this chapter stem from this premise. It has molded a formidable three-way machine—the company, the franchisees, and the suppliers working together as a team. This system encourages more creative menu ideas from franchisees than from anyone else.

McD deserves to be a status symbol. Those who say the chain is "just fast-food junk food" are guilty of snobbery and don't see the reality of McD as a responsible corporate citizen helping the community and meeting the public's needs. Because McD is constantly in the limelight, it is subject to criticism above and beyond most companies. "I wouldn't be caught dead working at McD" is a view held by some Americans who perhaps recall their teenage years slaving away at fast-food places. McD, the globe's number one volume foodservice chain by a gigantic margin, indeed is the generic term for fast-food in the United States and in the world.

If it falls short of being a status symbol in the United States, McDonald's is admired throughout most of the world as a symbol of quality food and power. That inevitably breeds resentment too. Still, a Big Mac or a Quarter Pounder is arguably the best food available at any Moscow restaurant (with the theoretical exception of much-touted "private" luxury restaurants, none of which we have ever been able to find).

CONTINUITY

McD has achieved remarkable stability in its executive ranks. Its top four executives have a combined total of 85 years of McD experience, and its top 30 executives, 700 years. This represents an average of at least 21 years experience each, remarkable in an industry notable for its constant turnover. McD has layers of top-management strength, including a number of executive vice presidents, senior vice presidents, and a phenomenally strong cadre below that level. A major league baseball team that had this first-string, second-string, and third-string strength would almost be guaranteed of winning the pennant and, probably, the World Series every year. McD would assert, however, with considerable merit, that everyone is on the first team.

McD is a bureaucracy in an age when a chain's headquarters staff is supposed to be lean and mean. But the system works for this organization. McD puts a huge emphasis on a decentralized field through regional directors in each area. If there is one criticism of McD company-owned field operations, it is that unit managers too often are strictly implementers, carrying out exact formulas and specifications. That is something McD is trying to change by training managers for increased interaction with customers.

McD's strength and stability could also be construed as a weakness, inasmuch as there is limited room for top executives to advance and any such progress is slow—unlike the situation in McD's earlier days when there was an executive vacuum, allowing top people to advance.

In the some 40 years of McDonald's corporate existence, the

chief executive baton has been passed from Ray Kroc to Fred Turner to Michael Quinlan, who appears set for this decade. Next in a theoretical line of succession would be vice chairman Jack Greenberg, U.S.A. president Edward Rensi, and international president James Cantalupo. However, Quinlan sees the three as being equal, and it is not clear if and when the logjam for McD executive succession will be broken, or that it even should be broken. Rensi and Quinlan like to joke that they are the young guys at ages 48 and 49, respectively, while Cantalupo and Greenberg are the old guys at 49 and 50.

The four seem to thrive on their challenges and on their constant efforts to move McD one step ahead of the latest hot competitor. In an industry that typically burns out many of its executives by age 50 or 55, if not before, these four are the exception, energized by adversity as well as success. The one sure thing is that they keep moving relentlessly ahead in a straight line without worrying too much about the questioning and criticism of their policies that may arise.

Quinlan and Rensi came up through the ranks at McD. Quinlan started in 1963 as a part-time mailroom employee after earning B.S. and M.B.A. degrees from Loyola University in Chicago. Rensi started as a McD grill man in 1966 in Columbus, Ohio. Cantalupo and Greenberg both made the transition from Arthur Young & Co. Cantalupo came aboard in 1974 as comptroller, and Greenberg, former Arthur Young tax services director, came to McD as executive vice president and chief financial officer in 1982. The four mesh well, coordinating their varied skills, and look like a team in place at least through the year 2000.

When Greenberg was promoted to vice chairman in 1992 after having spent 18 months learning operations as a crewperson, counter server, and regional manager, industry observers speculated that this marked the emergence of financial "bean counters" over operations (or Greenberg over Rensi) as the preeminent force and the potential future corporate CEO. However, McD got where it is by melding the financial and operations aspects. Operations and Rensi remain strong, as does the highly respected Cantalupo. Furthermore, Greenberg is hardly just a bean counter and has a keen appreciation of the operations side of the business.

Fred Turner, Kroc's direct disciple who turned 61 in 1994, remains active in long-term planning and policy making as senior chairman. He joined McD in 1956 as one of Kroc's first managers, actually an assistant unit manager. He became chairman-CEO in 1977 when Kroc moved up to be senior chairman.

Other chains are constantly trying to lure away McD top executives, particularly the senior vice presidents and vice presidents who might be more available. Rarely does one leave the mother ship, which offers security and a compensation scale, including stock options and benefits, above anyone else's. Besides, one doesn't leave a tightly knit family. An exception was Don N. Smith, who on January 2, 1977, became Burger King president, shortly after having been named McD executive vice president and chief operations officer and having been put on a fast track toward the top.

Most all McD executives have an intense loyalty to their chain. After all, many of them grew up with McD as their second home. In an age when loyalty does not seem to matter and executives disappear from chains at the drop of a hat, McD does show a fierce loyalty to its executives and employees.

The charge that keeps cropping up—that there is an "old boy" network—has more to do with the camaraderie and spirit at top levels than with any deliberate discrimination. If anything, Quinlan and Rensi, in particular, are constantly seeking ways to increase McD's diversity at every level.

As a corporation, McD succeeds because it does not operate like a corporation but remains true to entrepreneurial principles, letting franchisees and managers do everything they can to serve the customer. It is interesting to speculate that if McD, during its financially rocky early days in the late 1950s, had been acquired by a large corporation, it could have been ruined as was Burger Chef after being acquired by General Foods. As it happens, McD could acquire just about anyone today but wants to remain its own company, totally focused on stretching its worldwide lead.

This dedication to the task goes right down the hierarchical line at McD. We once asked McDonald's of Canada president George Cohon why he was spending so much time (12 years) on what appeared to be a futile pursuit to open a McD in Moscow. "I'm focused on this task, and we're definitely going to overcome all the bureaucratic obstacles and succeed." And he did—in spades.

Contrary to their image of being a conformist, noncaring set of corporate individuals, McD executives have a wide array of personalities. Cohon and some of the other more successful executives— including Rensi—tend to be mavericks who, while loving the company, love the customer even more, and "do it their way." The synergism of McD is effected by a plan of action emerging from contrasting viewpoints, operational versus financial considerations, and other such discussions.

There is a legend that McD had a war room, and the legend is true. It was a simple conference room, circular, so that no executive dominated in the seating arrangement and executives could exchange ideas and mold strategies on an equal basis. To McD, the burger battles are a war, and the struggle to be the best or to keep widening any lead or advantage over the competition is an endless, never-ending quest—now conducted in regular conference rooms when meetings are held.

Executive staff members take themselves very seriously at McD. This is a war, not a game. Yet they also know how to enjoy themselves and have fun. They realize that as serious as a situation may be, McD will overcome it, just as it has overcome all the nasty, unfounded rumors of worms in McD burgers and other innuendos over the years.

LEVERAGING ADVANTAGES

McD does a phenomenal job of leveraging its brand name worldwide, with more than 6 percent of annual sales spent in marketing. McD is a brand known to probably 99 percent of Americans (the only ones oblivious to it are babies and those who have been complete shut-ins for the last few decades). McD also does a remarkable job of leveraging its purchasing power and its sites (they own 60 percent of the sites and have 20-year leases on most of the others) and on steadily reducing their construction costs.

From the first, McD eschewed distribution and manufacturing. Instead, it formed alliances with foodservice distribution companies (most notably, Golden State and Martin-Brower) and let the Quaker Oats Company and other prime suppliers take care of providing the products. Kroc's handshake and mutual trust were good enough for these relationships to thrive in the early days, and that trust still exists. McD not only boosted its own interests by favoring select distributors and manufacturers, but gave those companies a tremendous boost too—and that has not been forgotten over the years. McD still enjoys fierce loyalty from those companies.

These relationships have enabled McD to keep its eye strictly on its burger units and to avoid self-distribution and manufacturing. But the big difference in the 1990s is that McD is leveraging itself to the hilt as a burger, chicken, and breakfast chain, focusing carefully on each of these segments. McD may already be the world's highest-volume chicken chain—possibly ahead of even KFC in this regard—as well as, of course, being the undisputed burger leader.

THE KROC LEGACY

From the first McD that he opened in Des Plaines, Illinois, April 15, 1955, at the ripe young age of 53, Ray Kroc stuck to a Keep It Simple Stupid (KISS) slogan, which in many ways remains the watchword of McD. It was Kroc who melded the three key groups—franchisees, managers, and suppliers—into one cohesive force. Each group was an entrepreneurial-minded one, and this was no easy task.

Yet Kroc had the personality to do it. By the mid-1970s, when a mini-bureaucracy had grown up at McD's Oak Brook headquarters, we had occasion to go through the building and inquired if there were any possible way to talk to the venerable Ray Kroc. "He's busy, it's impossible," we were told. But Kroc believed in an open-space office arrangement, with no doors and no locks, and just then he suddenly popped up in a nearby space and said hello. He proceeded to charm us, never once talking about the business of McD or revealing any inside information but rather casually chatting about baseball, fishing, and anything of general interest.

The point is that while he loved the business, he exuded an interest in customers, and in people in general, and he presented an overwhelmingly convincing case for his own convictions. He listened carefully to what anyone had to say, then usually went with his own original plan, although he would reverse direction at the drop of a hat if he saw real merit in another person's ideas. Kroc had to be a benevolent dictator in McD's early days or it never could have become the chain it is. In fact, it well might not have even survived without his spark and determination during some tough times in the late 1950s.

In the early 1950s, Richard and Maurice McDonald started flashing a neon sign at their San Bernardino, California, McD burger drive-in, declaring: "Over 1 million sold." By 1995 the signs on each McD will read: "Over 100 billion sold."

The McDonald brothers launched the first McD. But Kroc, a salesman for the Multimixers from which the brothers fashioned their milkshakes, had the dream, the vision, and the fortitude to build a chain from this foundation. He had spent 25 years selling equipment to the foodservice industry but had never worked in a restaurant. He thus brought an objectivity to the business.

When Kroc would go to Bill Veeck, the Chicago Cubs operations manager in the early 1950s, with ideas for increasing attendance and thus promoting snack sales at Wrigley Field, Veeck would tell Kroc to "stick to selling paper cups." Veeck and Kroc eventually became stars in their respective fields. Veeck went on to become owner of the Cleveland Indians and a baseball promotional genius while Kroc, with unparalleled flair, became owner of McDonald's and also bought the San Diego Padres baseball team. It is fortunate that Kroc did not take Veeck's advice.

Kroc obtained the franchising rights to McD restaurants from the McDonald brothers in the mid-1950s, overcoming a series of roadblocks posed by the McDonalds. Certain other chains with potential faltered because they treated franchisees as second-class citizens, but Kroc succeeded because he respected the franchisees and treated them as equals. Kroc experimented with franchisees in California and signed up 18. But by 1957 it was obvious that McD's new system in California—far from Kroc's Chicago headquarters— was in absolute chaos with little uniformity among the far-flung franchisees.

Subsequently, Kroc was careful to sign franchisees closer to his own headquarters. McD's early mom-and-pop franchisees became the bulwark of the chain. Unlike other chains, McD did not permit franchisees to sign up with anyone else and thus steered them toward total dedication to the McD system. This approach was mutually beneficial, with loyalty to McD generally paying off handsomely.

Kroc was a fanatic about pricing and about sticking to the McDonald brothers' 10 basic menu items to ensure control and simplicity. He became irate when a Reseda, California, franchisee, Bob Dondanville, added roast beef to the menu and raised the price of a burger from 15¢ to 18¢. Dondanville ignored Kroc's demands that he get rid of the roast beef, roll back the burger price to 15¢, and shave off his beard. Kroc finally ousted Dondanville from the McD system when he opened a Hamburger King unit competing with McD in violation of the contract.

Yet Kroc delighted in hiring diverse people and mavericks who could think differently than he did. Late one afternoon, when Kroc was leaving McD's home office, he spotted advertising manager and Ronald McDonald creator Barry Klein in the company parking lot with long hair flying in the wind. Kroc told his public relations consultant, Al Golin, "That fellow better be darn good if he expects to stay in the company." Deep inside, Kroc was tolerant of a person's idiosyncrasies—as long as the individual performed well for McD. Kroc hired Fred Turner as a McD unit assistant manager because he liked Turner's spunk and verve; Turner eventually became the chief executive. In turn, it was the managers' intense loyalty to Kroc that kept McD going during its initially tough financial times.

Kroc's own experiment with a Hula Burger (a toasted piece of pineapple with a slice of cheese on a bun) was a colossal failure, as were his efforts with Ramon's pie shops. Later, McD flopped in a 1980s regional test of Hot Dog McNuggets. But McD succeeds because it keeps trying and is willing to fail along the way—as long as it wins in the long run.

OVERWHELMING DOMINANCE

McDonald's is by far the world's number one chain in volume ($15 billion in the United States and $10 billion outside the country), prestige, and influence. It is already the number one volume chain in Japan and will be number one, or close to it, in more than a few of the some 70 countries that have Golden Arches. In this decade, that total is likely to stretch to 100 countries. In fact, if the moon or Mars is ever colonized, it's a good bet that McD will be there.

In the United States, an estimated 97 percent of American consumers eat at one of McD's units in a given year. More than half live within a five-minute drive of a McD, a convenience that the chain is trying to extend by building more and more units closer to where people live and work.

More than 1 billion pounds of hamburger meat (called 100 percent U.S. beef by McD) are eaten annually at its U.S. restaurants, making McD the nation's largest beef purchaser. It also buys 10 percent of the entire U.S. potato crop to serve its renowned french fries. McD has thus changed the entire landscape of the food-processing industry.

Egg McMuffins, introduced as breakfast items in the early 1970s, and Chicken McNuggets, launched in the early 1980s, also had a huge impact on food processing. The one limitation on McD's introducing any product chainwide often has been the question of whether there would be enough guaranteed supply of that product nationally. (Now McD's projections include the term "worldwide" instead of "nationally," and conceivably someday McD will talk in terms of dominating the entire universe—or at least a dense segment of it.)

Of all U.S. Coca-Cola sales, McD accounts for well over 5 percent and almost single-handedly has given Coca-Cola a foodservice sales lead over Pepsi-Cola—a situation that McD relishes because PepsiCo's restaurant chains are direct fast-food competitors.

McD has created more millionaires than any other chain in the world. By conservative estimates, well over 100 of its franchisees are millionaires and more continue to join the ranks all the time.

McD requires some measure of conformity throughout the chain. Yet as John Love observes in his 1986 book, *McDonald's: Behind the Arches,* "The fundamental secret to McD's success is the way it achieves uniformity and allegiance to an operating regimen without sacrificing the strengths of American individualism and diversity. McD manages to mix conformity and creativity." Contrary to the public's image of McD as a tight corporation, it does not operate by organizational chart but rather with considerable flexibility.

McD has had a tremendous impact on America's restaurants. It launched ultraefficient cooking equipment and influenced the meat, potatoes, and dairy industries by creating a huge demand. It revolutionized food packaging and distribution, as well as food processing. McD changed everything "by showering the lowly hamburger, french fry, and milkshake with more attention, more study, and more research than anyone had dreamed of doing," Love notes. "Just as manufacturers had streamlined assembly plants, McD streamlined foodservice."

The way Fred Turner sees it, McD attained its efficiencies through specialization. "It wasn't because we were smarter," he declares. "The fact that we were selling just 10 items, had a small facility, and used a limited number of suppliers, created an ideal environment for really digging in on everything."

McDonald's pioneers succeeded because most of them had never worked in restaurants, had not attended the prestigious hotel-restaurant management schools, and had no preconceived notions. They were willing to experiment and try new things, testing different formulas and products until they found what looked like a winner.

Marketing Wizards

"Experimentation is always important," says McD marketing senior vice president David Green. "But customers always come back to tell us what they're comfortable with and what they feel is the McD image. They cast their votes at the cash register."

McD does not rest on its laurels. "More than any other brand in the world," Green says, "we have established a personality, an image, an enduring reputation with our customers. You could even say we've become a cultural icon." McD has to satisfy multiple target groups in its marketing. "We have a constant personality," he notes, "and then we customize our approach within that personality to reach each demographic segment."

McD has achieved the ultimate segmentation in its marketing. It promotes a relevant message to each market it targets: for children and families, Ronald McDonald, Happy Meals, special promotions, and Playlands at 2,500 McDs; for teens (or tweens, as Green calls them), specific ads with a cast of characters doing things that teens enjoy doing; for young adults between 18 and 34, "We understand your life-style and your need to get a meal quickly and efficiently"; for minority groups (African American and Hispanic), special features for each group; and for seniors, the price-value of meals. (Presumably, the age group from 35 to 59 fits into a "family category," or McD uncharacteristically is missing a major market segment.)

Starting in 1993, McD stepped up its appeal to seniors with a program by which customers 60 years old and older could buy coffee or a soft drink for 25¢ without any additional purchases.

Local marketing and a local image are emphasized, as well as national network advertising. Besides using television, radio, and newspaper ads, McD highlights tray liners with products or promotions, point-of-purchase and menu board displays, and calendars of upcoming special events. Franchisees are encouraged to get involved in local community activities and generate goodwill.

Ideas at McD traditionally have emanated from the franchisees. Philadelphia area franchisees launched Ronald McDonald House, a St. Louis marketing manager started the Happy Meals program, and Pittsburgh franchisee Jim Delligatti launched the Big Mac in 1968. A Santa Barbara, California, franchisee, Herb Peterson, created the Egg McMuffin and the breakfast program in 1971. McD, in effect, created a whole new eating-out period and showed that breakfast certainly could, and often should, be eaten away from home.

Throughout its marketing efforts, the McD personality, reflecting a wholesome, economical family restaurant, has remained constant. Basic family values are always at the root of McD marketing and advertising. Other chains are often overwhelmed by McD's awesome advertising clout, and many confess to being virtually helpless in the face of this power.

Good Citizens

McDonald's strongly believes in community education and is emphasizing an apprentice program for high school students. "Training is a way of life for McD," Edward Rensi declares. "It's time to base our education system in an industrial society instead of an agrarian society," he says. "The challenge of educating our youth belongs to all of us." Rensi emphasizes how McD completely changed the outlook of its 1,100 employees in Moscow. "We taught them how to smile, and now they are happy there." McD also sponsors nutrition education and reading programs for elementary school children.

McD's Hamburger University, based in Illinois, also has campuses in Germany, England, and Japan and annually trains 3,000 crew people, managers, and prospective managers, using 20 different languages.

McD is dedicated to recruiting, training, and developing physically and mentally challenged individuals as crew members through its McJobs program, and persons over age 55 through its McMasters program. The company also sponsors Ronald McDonald Children's Charities and the Ronald McDonald Houses, which have some 160 locations in 10 countries to house 2,300 families a night so they can be near seriously ill children receiving treatment at nearby hospitals.

McD also emphasizes its role as a corporate good citizen in regard to the environment. "We have an ongoing commitment to manage solid waste, conserve and protect natural resources, and promote sound environmental efforts," McD declares. In 1989,

McD launched a McRecycle USA program, purchasing $500 million worth of recycled products in three years. It is a founding member of the Buy Recycled Business Alliance, a group dedicated to developing and expanding the market for recycled products.

Because stockholders over the years had raised questions about this issue, McD emphasized its policy of using "locally produced and processed beef, if available, in every country where we do business. In all cases, McD does not, has not, and will not permit the destruction of tropical rain forests for our beef supply. This policy is strictly enforced and closely monitored."

Cliff Raber has been McD government relations chief for 20 years and is one of the restaurant industry's strongest voices on Capitol Hill. He has worked hard to unite the industry for franchising cooperation. But McD wants its own voice heard in Washington and in state legislatures, and that voice is not always in harmony with the voices of other chains. Still, Raber and McD speak their minds on their concerns.

Fantastic Figures

It is difficult to keep an up-to-date scorecard on McD because its figures keep moving upward so fast. It is on the very high side of restaurant public companies, with a 20 percent return on average common stock equity and 18 percent return on average assets, which it has maintained fairly consistently over the years. It's no wonder that at the annual McD stockholder meeting on the campus of Hamburger University each May, for each stockholder who asks a tough question about the rain forests or challenges the chain's nutritional values, hundreds are more than happy with what their company and its stock are doing.

McD calls itself a three-legged stool made up of the company, the franchisees, and the suppliers. It actually has added a fourth leg to that stool—customers, and it is going extra miles to please customers and to consistently gain extra market share. "We want to make McD by far the easiest quick-service restaurant choice," declares Greenberg. "We'll open more and more sites as near the customer as possible."

McD has a vision of as many as 1,200 new units (roughly two-thirds of them outside the United States) annually, in every conceivable type of location. This means an average of at least three McD units opening somewhere in the world every 24 hours. In addition, McD will open satellite units as carts, kiosks, mobile and catering units, in-store and service station units. A key to the stepped-up expansion pace is that McD is giving franchisees, who have always been the backbone of the system, a chance to expand and develop satellite locations.

There was a point at which McD was testing so many products that this effort could have become a diversion to its main menu focus. Now Edward Rensi acknowledges that when it comes to pizza, "customers don't think of McD first." Pizza was in just 500 McD units at the end of 1993 and will be used more in connection with sites at tollways, office buildings, and universities. Still, dinner sales jumped 10 percent thanks to big-sandwich meal combos—Big Macs, double Quarter-Pounders, $1.99 Happy Meals, and other extra-value meals.

Although sales of McD healthful food items such as the McLean burger are not exactly soaring and the bulk of McD customers come for the big sandwiches, Rensi still sees a place for the McLean burger, apple-bran muffins, and the McGrilled chicken sandwich. "These satisfy the needs of a certain segment of customers," he says.

LEVERAGING POWER

Rensi is eyeing an eventual potential $3 billion annual volume from satellite locations. An initial 125 units had opened by the end of 1993, at least 70 of them in Wal-Mart discount department stores. When McD took over some of Wal-Mart's snack bars, sales immediately tripled because of McD brand identification. McD also tested units at selected Amoco, Mobil, and Texaco service stations and in a Jewel supermarket near Chicago. It conducted McDelivery tests in 80 units of Virginia's Tidewater area, focusing on large orders of McNuggets, Mighty Wings, and french fries.

McD leaves no stone unturned in exploring new opportunities.

It thus departed, at least partially, from its focus on only foodservice through a rapidly expanding "test" of Leaps & Bounds, indoor educational playgrounds. Through 1993 it had opened 31 and was set to launch 60 more in 1994. The significant fact is that Leaps & Bounds was a new, diversified brand and did not have the McD name. "Actually, we're leveraging our expertise obtained in the 2,500 Playlands at McD units by going well beyond that into a larger educational indoor-play format," a McD spokesperson said. (McD signed a deal in mid-1994 to sell Leaps and Bounds.)

Rensi emphasizes the chain's leveraging power domestically with a combination of its brand-name visibility, purchasing power, and ability to cut costs. But he also sees McD value pricing of combination meals, at $1.49, $1.99, $2.99, and so forth, as "a proprietary brand of McD in the eyes of the customer"—an assertion that Taco Bell's John Martin might contest.

James Cantalupo, too, notes the power of the McD brand worldwide, with 4,700 units in 70 countries outside the United States in mid-1994. He views Germany, England, France, Canada, Japan, and Australia as McD's six core global markets. McD even serves its offerings on Swiss and German railway dining cars and on a huge cruise ferry sailing between Helsinki and Stockholm. Local fare can be found on the McD menu in countries such as Norway, where McLak salmon sandwiches are on the board next to a Big Mac. And in Montreal, McD seasonally features lobster sandwiches.

Four-fifths of all units, nationwide and abroad, were franchised or affiliated, and 60 percent of the land and buildings were owned by McD. Systemwide, McD topped $23 billion sales for the year, had $12 billion in assets, and generated $1.5 billion in cash from operations.

Two-thirds of its restaurants are franchised to more than 3,600 owner/operators around the world, including 2,600 in the United States. Initial franchisee investments in new units range from $430,000 to $560,000, of which up to 60 percent can be financed.

It's the pennies that count, and they add up immensely in the McD system. McD grinds out savings and efficiencies in a great many ways. For example, it is saving $2 million a year and enhancing quality by consolidating worldwide sesame seed purchases under two suppliers in Mexico. It also realized $7 million in annual savings on the bulk buying of Happy Meal boxes. McD's combined global purchasing efforts enable it to save $50 million a year. It has also instituted another economy measure: changing to a deep-frying, oil-filtering powder saves each restaurant $2,000 annually by extending the shortening's life.

McD also saves money by sometimes using lower-cost materials; for example, glass-front restaurants provide lower energy costs and a brighter environment for customers. With real estate costs higher overseas than in the United States, McD is serving more people in less space through more efficient design.

During the halcyon days of the 1980s, McD didn't have to worry much about costs and savings. But now it is every bit as dedicated to more efficient operations and resultant savings as it is to generating more and more sales. If McD percentage growth slows on a unit-for-unit basis, that is understandable because of the already high averages giving less room for growth. But with health care and all other costs sharply rising, McD is looking for ways to save money to pay for these benefits.

Although McDonald's does everything it can to follow through on service to the diversity of its customers by employing a large proportion of minorities and disabled persons, and although minority groups are well represented at the unit levels, McD had only one woman and one African American on its mostly all-white board as of late 1993. McD flatly denies that it has perpetuated an "old boy" network, and it presumably is just a matter of time before it does something to remedy the imbalance on its board. McD is a leader in voluntary affirmative action and has 19 minority men and women as company officers at headquarters. Half of middle management is female or minority, at company-operated restaurants 70 percent of restaurant management is female or minority, and almost two-thirds of franchisees in training are female or minority.

McD has engineered flexibility and more efficiency into its building designs and has cut the initial cost of a new unit from $1.6 million to $1.2 million between 1990 and 1993. The cost should drop to $1 million by 1995. One way McD reduces the construction cost is through a computer that in 2½ hours puts together the whole construction package that formerly took 2½ weeks. Now that McD can open a restaurant for $1 million, it can afford to go to small towns.

Moreover, McD can build quickly. In 1971 it set an apparent world record by building a restaurant inside Tokyo's Ginza department store in just 36 hours. McD has buildings of all types, the oldest one dating back to 1220 in Shrewsbury, England.

INNOVATIVE MENU ITEMS

Franchisees led the way in McD product introductions. First McD Cincinnati franchisee Lou Groen introduced a fish sandwich at his Cincinnati McD in the mid-1960s. Then Pittsburgh franchisee Jim Delligatti launched the Big Mac at Uniontown, Pennsylvania, in 1967. This soon became the backbone of the McD's menu. It featured lettuce, cheese, pickles, onions, and a "secret sauce" in what many felt was a delicious combo.

"Some local drive-ins and chains were serving double-deck burgers," Delligatti recalls. "To broaden our customer base, I decided to create one of my own and I wanted it to be big." But his original Big Mac needed refinement, and instead of continuing with McD standard-size buns, Delligatti tested a new, thicker, double-cut sesame seed bun that would give the Big Mac stability. It made the sandwich easier to handle as a triple-decker and easier to hold when eating. The Big Mac is now known around the world for its two all-beef patties, special sauce, lettuce, cheese, pickles, and onions on a sesame seed bun. (The legend goes that anyone who can say all that in one breath gets a special award.)

Delligatti devised the special sauce by mixing various ingredients together. The chain soon adopted this magical sauce for the Big Mac, and it quickly became a symbol of McD's restaurants, which henceforth would be known as the Golden Arches or the Big Mac. Customers also refer to McD restaurants as a Big Mac attack.

Perhaps the two most sought-after "secret" formulas in the world are McD's special sauce and KFC's fried chicken recipe, devised by Colonel Harland Sanders. It seems hard to believe, but nobody is known to have broken these secret codes. Even if someone did, would the person who "steals" the secret recipe know how to make the product with the fine-tuned expertise that makes it great?

Without breakfast, McDonald's might not be the dominant power it has become. But the challenge in the early days was to find a unique distinguishing factor that would make a McD breakfast unique among all others. Herb Peterson, a franchisee in Santa Barbara, California, got a brainstorm and started tinkering with an Eggs Benedict sandwich that Jack in the Box had launched. After working for months, he finally devised a special slice of cheese that could be melted on a hot egg for the exact consistency desired. To make the egg appear like a poached egg, he developed a cluster of Teflon-coated rings that, when placed on the grill, gave the eggs the shape of an English muffin. He then added grilled Canadian bacon, and suddenly there was a potential breakfast sandwich for McD—and a revolution in the food world.

This incident exemplifies McD ingeniousness at every level. Kroc, who lived near the Santa Barbara restaurant, tried the new product one day and instantly fell in love with it, eagerly consuming two of the egg-bacon-muffin sandwiches even though he had eaten a full lunch an hour earlier. Peterson thought he had sold the idea to Kroc based on an extensive flip-chart presentation of its potential profitability, but Kroc had fallen for it only because he loved the taste. As would happen so often, McD won because of excitement, not just economics.

When the Krocs and Turners were having dinner one evening shortly after Kroc's discovery, they discussed possible names for the new sandwich. "Why not call it the Egg McMuffin?" Patty Turner suggested. Why not indeed? And so a new sandwich and a new name were born.

However, before the new breakfast could be introduced nationally, other items had to be perfected to go with the Egg McMuffin centerpiece. Sure enough, Pittsburgh franchisee Delligatti perfected his own hotcakes and sausage, and—when scrambled eggs were added—McD was ready to roll as by far the leading breakfast chain. By the mid-1970s, McD had been completely transformed,

under president Fred Turner, from a drive-in, counter-service operation to a sit-down, full-menu national power.

From then on, McD always faced the challenge of balancing the
need for new menu items to broaden its appeal with the need to
maintain a manageable production system that could provide the
speed of service desired. It would try to remove slower movers from
the menu as it added new items, but the menu still jumped from
10 items in the early days to a total of some 50 items, and service
was affected at times. McD has struggled to avoid the pitfalls of a
production orientation, whereby its own needs dictate its actions,
and instead to concentrate on a customer orientation, whereby it
develops the entire system solely to serve the customer's needs.

McD has devised "an enhanced production system" that greatly
increases its ability to serve food hot and fast. Virtually all U.S.
McD restaurants are using the system for breakfast and by late 1994
will have adapted it for lunch and dinner too.

Rensi likes to call McD a quick-service restaurant rather than a
fast-food restaurant. The former sounds more dignified and implies
better quality. Rensi and the other top executives have intense pride
in McD and consider it part of their own families. Any attack on
McD is an attack on the family.

"Our business has the same sizzle as our food," Rensi declares.
He notes that McD has changed from being an operations-driven
company to a customer-driven one. "We want to make the hamburgers juicier, the french fries crispier, and the salads fresher for
the customer," he asserts. Most of all, he wants the McD massive
training system extended to put ever-more emphasis on face-to-face
and eye-to-eye personal service and interaction with the customer.
He delights in calling McDonald's newer line of drive-throughs, of
which there were 700 by late 1993, face-to-face drive-throughs and
wants more of those opened. McD seeks to make its drive-throughs,
the one area in which errors in orders periodically occur, almost
error-free and continues to work on systems and interaction with
customers toward this end.

Jack Greenberg sees McD's prime leveraging strengths as its
supply and distribution systems,—allowing it to purchase food and
paper from independent suppliers, and a restaurant manager to

make just one phone call for a complete delivery—thereby saving $50 million a year with these efficiencies; the totality of the whole McD experience; the brand name as the world's second-best known next to Coca-Cola; and site development ("We can design and construct faster than anyone else").

As the most visible fast-food chain, McD was criticized for serving "junk food loaded with cholesterol." But the chain tried to improve that image in the early 1990s with the introduction of the 91 percent fat-free McLean Deluxe burger, cutting fat by 45 percent and eliminating cholesterol in its french fries through a switch to 100 percent vegetable oil, moving to 99.5 percent fat-free milkshakes, and offering low-fat frozen yogurt.

McD also offers fresh tossed salads rather than the difficult-to-manage salad bars of other chains, reduced calorie dressings, and whole-grain cereals with 1 percent low-fat milk. It wisely decided not to take the McLean burger off the menu as of mid-1994 even when that item did not measure up to projected sales, because McD's image as a restaurant offering a choice is crucial. The reality is that customers talk about the need for lighter and healthier foods, but then eat Big Macs and other heavier foods that they consider tastier. The one sure way to cause a sales decline in any product is to put a heart symbol next to it, leading customers to conclude that "it must not taste good."

Pizza and pasta were tried in order to boost dinner sales. Baked apple pies were successfully tested and have replaced fried apple pies. If McD had a weakness, it was that products were endlessly tested and retested without necessarily being introduced. Now the decision-making time is likely to be faster, and new items will more quickly be included or abandoned.

Michael Quinlan, in particular, may never be completely satisfied, always seeking more for McD. "We're the largest in the world, but we serve only one-half of 1 percent of the world's population," he declares, "and only 1 percent of the total population of other countries. We have an enormous potential to increase our global market share." Still, on any given day 20 million Americans and 6 million others around the world eat at McD. Quinlan describes McD's ever-changing challenges as serving customers in the 1970s, satisfying them in the 1980s, and exceeding their expectations in the 1990s.

McDonald's keeps touting the fact that it is the world's number two brand after Coca-Cola. Yet one reason that Coca-Cola is first is that it's in the McD units all over the globe. Given the insatiable desire of McD top executives to win at all costs, we believe that one of their unpublicized goals is to somehow overtake Coca-Cola in brand name recognition. For those who scoff at such an idea, we must remember that to McD nothing is impossible and it doesn't settle for second place anywhere—not when its four top executives and so many others all the way down the line have such complete dedication.

The Thin Line: Success Versus Failure

"For all of the increased competition and the ever-present specter of saturation that confront managements, the restaurant business is one where companies still can control their own destinies and where the opportunities for growth still can be most exciting."
> —*Robert L. Emerson, financial analyst, in his 1979 book, Fast Food: The Endless Shakeout, Chain Store Publishing Corporation*

HIGHLIGHTS

- Rough seas
- Causes of failure
- Overcoming obstacles
- "Sustainable competitive advantage"
- Surviving the endless shakeouts

Restaurant chains encounter a multitude of dangers as they navigate uncharted waters between success and failure, survival and extinction, prosperity and poverty. The warning signals often are nuances that some leaders read and others don't.

Interestingly enough, principles uncovered in an extensive study of 13 fast-growing chains with annual mid-1970s revenues between $15 million and $60 million, documented in the winter

1977 issue of *The Cornell Hotel Restaurant Administration School Quarterly* by Earl Sasser and Ivor Morgan of the Harvard Business School, hold just as true in the 1990s as they did then. Among the challenges that abound in the restaurant industry, they pinpointed competition for labor, sites, and ultimately for customer dollars as growing more intense. From interviews with the chief executives or chief operating officers, they exposed nine obstacles to maneuvering safely through the chain foodservice Bermuda Triangle. Any one of them could sink the ship or at least cause extensive damage:

1. Management's failure to realize that there are four basic but different functions to manage—new unit development, concept development, operations, and marketing. "In the early years of a chain's life," they observed, "the emphasis is on new unit development and operations. By performing those functions well, the chain thrives. But as it expands into other geographic areas, it faces strong competitors, and the functions that differentiate the successful chains from the mediocre ones are marketing and concept development."

2. Failure to delegate responsibility. "The managerial style and competence of the chief executive sets the tone for the entire company, which ultimately affects the ability of the firm to attract or develop good managers." Sasser and Morgan noted that the inability of one founder to delegate responsibility to his subordinates led a subordinate to declare after the founder's death: "Thank God, he died. He was ruining the company." (Actually, it would have been better had the founder named a successor as chief executive, retired, and lived happily ever after.)

3. Failure of the management team to develop the skills necessary to manage a larger chain. "The management team must grow as the firm grows. . . . An existing management team may be capable but not receptive to changing established patterns of behavior."

4. Lapse of management motivation. During the course of growth of a successful chain, the management team often tends to lose its enthusiasm and to become complacent. "Unfortunately, they scatter their attention in a variety of directions."

5. Haphazard growth. Expansion for the wrong reasons means growth that the chain cannot handle and that endangers its health. "The offender is often a public company which, in order to maintain a very high growth rate for the benefit of the financial community, adds a number of units to its system. In many cases, the new operations turn out to be unprofitable for a host of reasons."

6. Failure to change a mature concept. "Many chains attempt to grow with an out-of-date concept. Management often does not recognize that a concept is dead. . . . New management and capital are often necessary to renovate the company, both in its direction and facilities."

7. Diversifying too quickly. "Sometimes the source of a chain's problems is just the opposite of sticking with an outdated concept. . . . Too often the entrepreneur is obsessed with finding new horizons to conquer after the company's initial direction has been set and many functional departments are well advanced in their development."

8. Breakdown of communication. "The establishment of clear functional areas produces communication gaps that must be bridged."

9. Poor franchisor-franchisee relations. "If the franchisor-franchisee relationship is not well maintained, the consequences can be painful for both sides. Only the lawyers who represent them in court will profit."

All nine of these expansion-failure factors are even more relevant in today's ultracompetitive markets than they were almost two decades ago. Sasser and Morgan—and perhaps also the executives they interviewed—deserve a prize for their prescience. Turn each of these nine failings inside out and we have prescriptions for success.

Sasser and Morgan also gave specific ideas for succeeding in expansion, and many of these ideas still hold true today. Among their suggestions are:

Avoiding competition with larger chains as "the clout of the larger ones almost ensures them victory in open confrontations"

Choosing market areas that are not saturated with competing concepts

Clustering units in selected market areas for supervision, purchasing, transportation, construction, and advertising economies

Consistently outperforming competitors by delivering superior service

Maintaining the flexibility to react to market changes.

But the most intriguing suggestion—and one taken very seriously today—is to develop an "unchain" image by knowing the local markets better that anyone else, gearing promotions to the local community, and providing managers with a local orientation.

An unchain chain can indeed win against larger competitors by being a neighborhood restaurant that behind the scenes also achieves the economies of scale. But if it wants to gain the necessary marketing and advertising clout, it must admit to being a chain and act like a chain—unless it depends strictly on word-of-mouth (which well may be the best form of advertising anyway).

Sasser and Morgan's insights could help chains weather the rough voyage ahead. But, as they noted in peering into the future, "The restaurant industry will continue to be affected by events beyond its control" (i.e., downward economic cycles, endless government regulation, and huge costs in health care and other mandated benefits).

COMPETITIVE FACTORS

Adapting the framework of Michael Porter's 1985 book, *Competitive Advantage,* to the chain restaurant industry, three knowledgeable observers assert that a chain's success or failure hinges primarily on a set of strategic factors. In an article in the 1993 *Journal of Food Products Marketing,* Rajan Chandran and Michael F. Smith of Temple University's Business School and Arvind Parkhe of Indiana University's Business School deal with Porter's contention that any company's profitability depends mainly on the industry's attractiveness and the company's relative position in that industry. They analyze five competitive forces relating to foodservice chains: the threat of entry of new competitors; the bargaining power of buyers; the threat of substitute products or services; rivalries among existing chains; and the bargaining power of suppliers.

Within the foodservice industry, the three professors write, the prime barriers to competitive entry are high initial capital requirements, economies of scale, and the strong brand identity associated with McDonald's, KFC, Pizza Hut, and other major chains. "Buying power is high, due to a well-informed public and high substitutability among products and restaurants," they observe. They portray rivalries among foodservice chains for the away-from-home dollars as intense. "The bargaining power of suppliers to this industry, however, is limited due to the competitiveness of the input markets and the competitiveness of most inputs. Thus of the five major competitive forces, only supplier power is favorable in the context of foodservice. The other four forces point to a harsh competitive environment which serves to limit the industry's overall attractiveness."

A company's profitability, they note, also depends on its relative position within its industry. "A firm that can position itself well may earn high rates of return even though the industry structure is unfavorable and the average profitability is therefore modest," they add. As an example, they cite McDonald's (a role model for much of the industry, although most chains don't like to admit it) 21.2 percent average return on equity and 27.4 percent annual earnings growth from 1965, when it went public, through the late 1980s "despite foodservice chains continuing to have traditionally higher mortality rates than other retail businesses."

The basis for relative superior performance in the long run is a sustainable competitive advantage either "in the form of low cost or in the form of differentiation" (uniqueness), they say. Cost leadership can be obtained "by exploiting all possible scale or absolute cost advantages to achieve low costs while maintaining near parity with competition in terms of differentiation and price." Chains can achieve differentiation, they suggest, "by such methods as refashioning their physical facilities to reflect changing consumer tastes and menus, starting home delivery, or selecting and training employees to provide superior service." However, the practice of differentiation "must lead to a price premium greater than its cost."

Although low cost and differentiation are the basic generic strategies for success in any industry, implementation and success in the foodservice industry are related to concept, personnel, adaptation, growth, and location, according to these authors' interpretation of Porter's framework.

As successful examples, they cite Taco Bell which, having developed a unique concept with market appeal, communicated that concept to a broad target audience and carefully monitored the execution; General Mills Restaurants, Pizza Hut, and Shoney's, placing extra importance on employee training; Sizzler, Wendy's, and Red Lobster adapting their menus to changing consumer tastes; McDonald's controlled growth "to realize economies in purchasing, advertising, real estate, personnel training and operations" and steadily increasing sales per unit "through round-the-clock use of existing facilities"; as well as "judicious choices" of high-traffic, low-rental locations" by various chains. They add the significant caveat that "successful growth is constrained by financial and human resources, competition, and consumer acceptance."

Explaining some of the causes of chain failure, they point to Sambo's, Arthur Treacher's Fish & Chips, and Burger Chef as "giving little attention to executing operational details" and having financial and human-resource constraints. They emphasize the example of Burger Chef, which in early 1968 had 850 units and was closing the gap on McDonald's 950 by opening 300 units annually, as compared with McDonald's 100 annually. Burger Chef had enlarged its field staff and opened new territories. Yet it did not have the financing to handle rapid growth and thus was acquired by General Foods.

General Foods initially pumped massive resources into Burger

Chef but dropped the 54-person field staff that scouted new properties and supervised new-unit development. General Foods, in all its wisdom, decided to save time and money by engaging independent real estate brokers who knew little about fast-food and tended to grab locations anywhere. Chaos ensued, and by 1971 General Foods halted the pell-mell expansion program and took a $75 million writeoff on Burger Chef. From then on, Burger Chef plummeted steadily downward while McDonald's kept soaring. One strategic fork in the road can make all the difference, and once a major mistake has been made, it cannot be redeemed very easily.

The three authors also depict Shakey's, IHOP, and Ponderosa as faltering in the late 1970s by being "unwilling to change or to recognize market changes." Poor execution of each concept, as well as food perceived as bland, mediocre service and atmosphere, and "uninspiring advertising" sped their paths downward. IHOP has recovered to excel in a tough segment, and Ponderosa keeps fighting its way back under Metromedia's leadership in the 1990s.

Successful chains excel in all these basics, but unsuccessful ones and failures can hardly define their concepts in a relevant manner, lack a unique niche, are poor implementers, and are slow to respond to consumer and environmental changes.

As far back as 1979, Robert L. Emerson projected ongoing chain saturation and a constantly shifting chain restaurants scene in his book, *Fast Food: The Endless Shakeout,* published by the Chain Store Publishing Corporation. "An inspection of the results of large hamburger chains shows that a shakeout is by no means a new phenomenon," he observed. "Rather, it is an ongoing process." He emphasized that "for all of the increased competition and the ever-present specter of saturation that confront managements, the restaurant business is one where companies still can control their own destinies and where the opportunities for growth still can be most exciting."

History has a habit of repeating itself. That has been the case in the 1980s and early 1990s shakeouts. Prospects are that shakeouts and consolidations will be even more a fact of life through the rest of this decade as well-run companies survive and prosper while others flounder.

Conclusion: Forging the Links

"Motivate them, train them, care about them and make winners out of them. . . . If we treat our employees correctly, they'll treat the customers right. And if customers are treated right, they'll come back."

—*J. Willard Marriott, Jr., chairman,*
Marriott Corporation

Putting all the links of the chain together, what does it really take to win? Some of it is intangible—positive thinking, spirit, the elusive chemistry of an executive team and how they relate to the field people. Surely the greatest test comes in a no-growth situation during a flat economy. That is when excuses proliferate, citing the economy and government regulation, making it almost impossible to succeed. Yet the great executives know how to spur growth and win even under such circumstances.

As the chain industry reaches maturity, one might expect a calming down and a period of stability rather than constant shakeups and changes. Yet as the industry experiences second and even third-generation leadership, there is bound to be turmoil. Some of the winners undoubtedly will be the newer chains that are beginning their life cycles and don't have to "change" much because they are relatively new. They, however, are entering their own life cycles.

A key point made throughout this book is that winners know how to manage the factors behind the numbers, rather than just the numbers themselves. After all, numbers are in effect the measure of operational and marketing efforts. When numbers prevail in a chain's strategic thinking, that is often the first step in a march to failure.

A winning chain needs a special niche, a well-positioned concept. The overall odds, however, remain best for those positioned as fast-feeders or those in a mid-priced casual dining niche. Top-flight service and a completely customer-oriented approach are musts. But it also takes a strong, stable management team, fine-tuned expansion, and tight cost controls that don't sacrifice the spirit of the operation.

We believe it will also be critical for restaurant chains to reengineer their organizational approaches. Chains must identify and exploit profitable niches that match their own capabilities, keep an eye on consumers' perception of value (quality and other factors, as well as price) in all planning; and tighten focuses to narrower niches rather than wider segments.

Also essential are intangible leadership qualities, as emphasized by veteran National Restaurant Association (NRA) executive vice president and staff chief Bill Fisher. Among his nuggets of wisdom are these: As the song goes, "If you don't have a dream, you'll never have a dream come true"; "Success comes not from everything going smoothly and occurring perfectly, but rather from surmounting adversity"; "Creativity does not arrive as a finished product. It comes in parts, and you have to assemble it"; "The guaranteed way to never stumble is to never step forward."

Think of the chain executives who would agree with and follow this philosophy; these are the winning executives of the winning chains. Among them certainly would be Norman Brinker, Joe Lee, and John Martin. Any one of them may stumble at times, but they get up and keep plugging away.

Let's look at the factors indicative of a losing chain team:

- A concept that can be incorporated into anyone's menu and thus is neither unique nor economically feasible
- An inflexible concept that does not allow the addition of fresh ideas and so loses its competitive edge
- Poor execution: dirty units, unconcerned management, high personnel turnover, low morale
- Overexpansion and poor controls

- Too many frills and too high an initial investment ratio that requires unattainable sales goals

- Constant executive turnover, which inevitably leads to constant unit manager turnover

- Weak management, focused only on numbers bought by rapid expansion rather than by steadily increasing customer traffic

- Failure to spend time in the field or to care about the business

- Believing only in gut feel and not doing any research, or vice versa.

- Being a complete individualist and not a team player

Turn each of those factors around to its opposite, and you likely have a winner. What is needed is a solid concept or concepts, based on a clear reason for existence, with an excellent perceived price-value and no real geographic limitations; strong focus on the individual restaurants with incentives and motivation, consistent cleanliness and sensitivity to customers; and a management carefully balanced between financial monitoring and controls, and innovative operations and marketing-advertising.

A winning concept must be sound in menu, decor, pricing, economics, systems, and customer acceptability. Furthermore, customers and servers should be considered equal priorities. And the chief executive should be a visionary who knows how and when to refine or modify the concept and who retains an absolute commitment to the company's culture.

A number of different management styles and programs can lead to success. Here are the eight key strategic links that emerge as the winning principles for chains of all types and styles:

1. An extroverted leader who communicates a vision, values, and a bottom-up organizational philosophy

2. A culture that provides both motivational and monetary rewards

3. An absolute dedication to doing everything for the customer's benefit, not for the short-term benefit of executives or stockholders

4. Adhering to an operational focus that is not diverted by anything

5. Utilizing marketing and merchandising to achieve an individualized "unchain" chain image

6. Solving challenges within the parameters of the restaurant chain industry's economic realities

7. Leveraging the natural advantages of a chain without over-centralizing

8. Knowing when and what to change to maximize the life cycle

A final thought occurs as we reflect on what we have written: No business is more people-oriented than the restaurant business. Interaction between customers and chain staffs is maximized as nowhere else because of the frequency of relatively low-ticket transactions and the large number of employees involved. The complexity of a production "factory" in a restaurant makes the challenge greater here than in any other form of retailing.

Yet we are convinced that few, if any, other industries offer a product as basic as food and an experience as pleasurable as the enjoyment of it. Perhaps that is why it ultimately takes a leader with emotion, courage, spirit, and a passion for pleasing others to forge a winning restaurant chain from the eight links.

Index